THE RURAL SETTING THESAURUS:

A Writer's Guide to Personal and Natural Places

ANGELA ACKERMAN
BECCA PUGLISI

DEDICATIONS

To every writer who ever dreamed, and then had the courage to follow that dream wherever it led.

And especially to Lee, for not using the ants.

First print edition, June 2016
ISBN-13: 978-0-9897725-5-6
ISBN-10: 0-9897725-5-1

Edited by: C. S. Lakin (www.livewritethrive.com) and Michael Dunne (www.michael-dunne.com/)

Book cover and interior design by: Scarlett Rugers Design 2016
www.scarlettrugers.com

EBook formatting by: Polgarus Studio
www.polgarusstudio.com

MORE WRITERS HELPING WRITERS® BOOKS

TABLE OF CONTENTS

CRAFTING SETTINGS THAT CREATE
EMOTIONAL CONNECTIONS

The recipe for good fiction includes a number of key ingredients such as compelling characters, high stakes, an emotional connection between readers and the story's cast, and engaging conflict. But there's another important piece that is often overlooked, to the detriment of many potentially great books: the setting. Every scene in every story has one, whether it's part of a sprawling kingdom (Middle Earth), a room onboard a cluttered spaceship (*Alien*'s *Nostromo*), or locales found within a sleepy little town (Maycomb County, Alabama). Big or small, familiar or foreign, the setting in each scene should be unique and memorable. It's the responsibility of the author to elevate a story's locations so they take on a life of their own and imprint themselves upon readers in an unforgettable way.

Readers the world over know what it's like to fall in love with the settings from a favorite book. Whether the locations were real or fictional, they felt as if they'd *been there*, or they wished they could go. As authors, we want to create this sense of nostalgia at the end of a book; we want readers to wish they could go back. But how does this happen? What makes a setting tangible and as interesting as the characters themselves?

For one thing, the locations for a given story need to be more than simple stage dressing. Vibrant settings are thoughtfully chosen. They're places that hold meaning for the character and evoke emotion. They provide opportunities for conflict and personal tragedy and growth. As such, birthplaces, bedrooms, schools, workplaces, hangouts, and vacation spots play a pivotal role in shaping who a character is and who he will become. There is an inherent emotional connection between a setting and the characters who frequent it.

Written effectively, this emotional connection reaches out to include the reader too. Hogwarts, The Overlook Hotel, Tara—settings like these create an emotional response in readers because the author wrote them in a way that evoked feelings. Through the use of symbolism and multisensory descriptions, by using the setting as a vehicle for establishing mood or introducing conflict, the author pulled readers in, allowing them to experience life along with the characters in their worlds.

This is what readers want: to get lost in a book—to be so completely immersed in the story that there's an unsettling jolt when they're returned to real life. It's the author's job to make this happen for readers, and one of the most effective ways to do it is by bringing the setting to life— making it dynamic, even epic.

Fortunately, it's not as hard as you might think.

THE SETTING AS A VEHICLE FOR CONFLICT

One of the beautiful things about setting is that it can be used as a vehicle for many other important story elements. Take conflict, for example—definitely a necessary component. **Story conflict** can be simply defined as a struggle or difficulty that impedes a character from achieving his goal. It might be a physical roadblock, a confrontation with a friend, or an internal struggle (such as addiction or self-doubt) that makes it difficult for him to overcome his Achilles' heel and move forward.

When it's written well, conflict begets **tension**. In real life, tension is that tight, stretched sensation in the belly that makes a person feel jittery. For readers, it's essentially the same thing; it stirs their emotions. To keep readers engaged, there should be tension in every scene, whether it's triggered by a fistfight in a bar or a character opening the fridge to discover that *someone* has eaten the last piece of pie. Small or large, loud or quiet, conflict and its resulting tension are important for maintaining the reader's interest.

To be effective, conflict needs to be recurring and frequent while varying in intensity. Introducing it in an organic fashion sounds tricky, but the truth is that many of these difficulties can naturally be found in the setting.

PHYSICAL ROADBLOCKS

While conflict can be subtle and understated, as in the case of an internal struggle, it is most obvious in the form of an actual obstacle that keeps the character from his goal. The setting can provide these roadblocks in a way that makes sense for the story. J.R.R. Tolkien was a master at this and often utilized Middle Earth to generate conflict for his characters. In *The Fellowship of The Ring*, Frodo and company needed to cross the mountain Caradhras in order to reach Mount Doom. Conflict arrived in the form of a supernatural blizzard that tumbled boulders down around them and buried the treacherous path in snow, forcing them to turn back. Caradhras not only impeded their goal of destroying the ring, it also caused internal friction within the company as they disagreed on which way to go next.

It's important to remember that not all conflict is life-threatening. If every chapter contained life-or-death, catastrophic events, not only would the story begin to read as melodramatic, the reader would soon grow accustomed to the constant tension, and it would lose its punch. Small-scale conflict can be very useful for creating minor difficulties that cause the hero to doubt his mission, his partners, or even himself.

Continuing with Tolkien as an example, in *The Hobbit*, Bilbo and his companions are already frustrated by the difficulties they've experienced while trying to reach the Lonely Mountain when they find their path blocked by an enchanted river. While trying to cross, the corpulent Bomber falls in and slips into an unnatural sleep, and the company is forced to carry him around for weeks. Already discouraged, this added inconvenience ramps up the tension in the group, causing them to doubt their purpose and the likelihood of achieving their goal.

Rural landscapes like mountains and rivers often create the most organic hurdles, but physical obstacles can be found in urban settings too. A traffic jam on the way home from work, a locked door, police tape roping off a crime scene that the hero desperately needs to see—every setting has its physical obstructions that can be used to create problems and increase tension. Using the roadblocks that naturally occur within your setting is a good way to create authentic conflict that reads seamlessly.

MIRRORS TO A PAINFUL PAST

In real life, everyone has baggage—past experiences that cause quirks, sensitivities, phobias, and flaws to develop. The same should be true for our characters. Simply put, they have issues, and many of these issues can be traced back to a specific setting, such as academic failures in the classroom, a brutal attack in a dark alley, or abuse in one's home. Conflict can be introduced through revisiting an old, painful setting because it will bring to mind bad memories and stir up unwanted emotions for your character, reminding him of when he was most weak and vulnerable.

But sometimes this isn't all that happens when a painful site from the past is revisited. Occasionally, the memories are so dreadful, the events so traumatic, that reminders of these haunting grounds trigger a visceral response that catapults the hero into further conflict.

In the movie *First Blood*, John Rambo is a war veteran and former POW trying to find his footing in post-war America while battling his demons. After an unfortunate encounter with a closed-minded sheriff, Rambo is arrested. During the booking process, he is verbally abused by the officers and forcibly held while being shaved with a straight razor—the very item used by his Vietnam captors to torture him during his captivity. The similarities between his current setting and his traumatic past act as a trigger. Rambo assaults his captors, breaks out of the police station, and sets in motion a series of events that makes it virtually impossible for him to reenter society in the way he had hoped.

While this is a dramatic response to a past event, it's legitimate, considering Rambo's circumstances and past abuse. Different characters might respond in ways that are more subdued but will still cause problems that must be overcome. They may lash out at those around them, damaging important relationships. They might run away from a difficult memory, postponing the healing that needs to take place for their goals to be achieved. They could shut down completely, rewrite the past in their own minds, regress into fantasy, or lie in order to cover up the past—the possibilities for conflict are virtually endless when a character is reintroduced to a painful setting.

This is where knowing your character well is vital to understanding what will set him off and how he will respond. To shape a setting where plot complications can develop, it's imperative that we have a thorough understanding of our characters' backstories and the events that have molded them into the people they are in the current story.

PERIPHERAL TROUBLEMAKERS

So much of story conflict is relational—which makes sense, considering our characters inhabit flawed worlds filled with flawed people. As a result, while the setting itself can create problems for characters, it's often the people within that setting that cause the most trouble. Conflict can be found literally anywhere, in every possible setting: in an upscale boutique with a snooty salesperson making snide comments to a scantily clad customer (*Pretty Woman*), on an isolated fishing boat where old tensions cause stretched-thin tempers to flare (*The Perfect Storm*), or on an island with tiny but fierce natives (*Gulliver's Travels*).

When you're writing a scene that needs a pinch of conflict, think about the people who would naturally inhabit that place. Which ones would be likely to cause trouble for your hero? How hard would these peripheral characters have to push? A little planning can help immensely when you're looking for a setting with potential complications for your character.

A word of caution, though: beware of clichés when it comes to settings and their rabble-rousers. Bars are common hangouts for drunks, but trouble can also be found in the form of underage customers trying to score drinks, short-tempered barmaids who don't appreciate being hit on, or bored bouncers looking for action. Sometimes a little brainstorming is all that's needed to find the ideal supporting cast members to make life difficult for your hero; to this end, each entry in this book contains a list of people that can typically be found in that location. Use this list to think about who might come and go in your setting and how their goals might clash with your main character's.

FAMILY DYSFUNCTION

It's true that conflict is likely to occur when people get together, and the chances for conflict greatly increase when emotions run high. Given this, it should come as no surprise that some of the most fertile breeding grounds for conflict are settings involving family.

No family is perfect; each one has some level of dysfunction, and this dysfunction (and the conflict that results) should be evident in the places where families exist and interact. For this reason, when you're writing a tense family scene, consider choosing a spot where the family equilibrium is most unstable. The local church, a neighborhood pizza parlor, the backyard, or the attic can all provide conflict in the form of family drama or negative memories and feelings associated with past events.

The setting is also a great vehicle through which important family information can be shared, along with any defects or flaws you wish to reveal.

Brianna pushed the door closed as quietly as she could and paused. No fire in the hearth, no voices echoing through the house. With a sigh, she stamped the snow from her boots—carefully, so it hit the mat and not the spotless floor—and set her suitcase beside the couch. Dad would be seriously annoyed when he found out she'd come home unannounced, but everything was such an event with him. For once, she could walk into the house without having to navigate a party or welcoming committee. And it would buy her some time to figure out how to break the news.

She took a slow turn around the room but nothing had changed in the last three months. Her ski trophies still stood on the mantel like Marines, spaced precise inches apart. To the left, her brother Bryce's wall of fame held a geometric arrangement of music awards, pictures of him performing at competitions, and his acceptance letter to Juilliard. Brianna's wall held images that profiled her own rise to success: being appointed captain of the ski team, crushing the state slalom record, blurring across the finish line at the Olympic qualifiers.

She stepped back and scanned the entire wall. No camping trips, no birthday parties, no family vacations. She chewed her lip, one thumb drumming her thigh, nose wrinkling against the cold-ash smell from the fireplace. Crystal statuettes, leather furniture, surfaces smooth and empty and free of dust . . . This room looked like a magazine cover and had about as much warmth.

The garage door rumbled, giving her a start. She smoothed her shirt and took a deep breath.

Let's get this over with.

Readers can glean a lot about the family dynamic from the details delivered in this scene. The living room is cold—from the spotless floors to the crystal knickknacks to the frames displayed in stark geometric patterns. The only images in the room are ones that celebrate accomplishment. The people who occupy this space aren't loving or warm; they're mostly interested in appearances and success.

All this is conveyed through the setting description. By focusing on details that are important to the main character, the author is able to paint a clear picture of both the physical scene and the conflict that exists beneath the surface, ready to erupt with the slightest nudge.

Family dysfunction runs the gamut from pesky annoyances to intentional digs to destructive actions and attitudes that take a lifetime to overcome. Personal settings are ideal for reminding characters of old, hurtful memories that bring emotions to the surface, increasing vulnerability. They're also useful for bringing family together and igniting the fireworks fuse. When you're looking for some meaningful conflict in your story, examine the character's history and consider using a family setting to up the tension and create complications.

THE SETTING AS A VEHICLE FOR ESTABLISHING MOOD

It's easy to think of a setting as a fixed element. London is London; it doesn't move or change, right? While the location itself may be fixed, the city can look vastly different when certain variables are altered. The time of day, the weather, the season, even a change in narrator can make a setting look very different than it did just the day before. And no factor has more influence over the setting than mood.

Mood can be defined as the emotional atmosphere that a piece of writing creates—the feelings it evokes in the reader. It's an important device because the mood of a scene prepares the reader for the events that will follow.

As an example, the audience's very first view of the Bates Motel is unsettling. It stands alone on a scrubby hill, towering over the sparse trees. The exterior is dark and subdued. The windows are opaque—repelling the light and revealing nothing. This first glimpse elicits a feeling of unease from the audience; they instinctively know that something bad is going to happen here. This is the mood that Hitchcock created simply by introducing his movie's setting.

In both films and books, settings are often established early on, since a clear picture of the time and place is needed to ground readers in the scene. As such, it's a handy vehicle through which mood can be conveyed. Before writing a scene, be sure to identify which mood you're going for. Then you just need to choose and employ the right techniques to create the perfect atmosphere.

WEATHER AND SEASONS AS EMOTION GENERATORS

Weather can easily convey a desired mood because we automatically associate specific feelings with certain kinds of weather. Rainy days are gloomy. Sunshine makes us feel happy and buoyant. Fog is oppressive. Because weather phenomena often produce predictable feelings, writing them into a scene is a good way to generate the desired mood.

> The tumbled walls of the ancient ruins stretched upward, basking in the sun's glow. Indeed, they were warm to the touch, their stone surfaces worn smooth from centuries of wind and rain. Overgrown grasses hugged the stones' knees while snapdragons and cornflowers nodded in the gentle breeze.

Via carefully chosen weather clues, this paragraph depicts a peaceful, serene setting. The gentle breeze, the sunlight, and the warm stones work together to give readers a sensation of comfort—and without any characters to add their two cents. The weather itself is enough to create a strong mood that will impact readers, but it's often easier to do this when characters are present. Their emotional responses to the weather come across loud and clear to readers, triggering their own feelings and allowing them to experience the exact mood intended by the author.

> Distant thunder rumbled as Mark took his first step into the ruins. Sweat stuck the dry raincoat to his skin and he hoped for a cooling breeze, but the air was as still and heavy as the stones that hemmed him in.
> Ancient markings crisscrossed their surfaces, gouged so deep that their edges looked sharp enough to cut. Almost against his will, Mark reached to touch the nearest one. Thunder cracked overhead, making him jerk back. Breathing deeply, he tucked his hands into his pockets and slowly continued on, placing his feet carefully and avoiding the ominous stones.

In this setting, the encroaching thunder and oppressive air show that a storm is coming. That alone might be enough to give the scene an atmosphere of approaching danger. But Mark's response to the weather is our biggest clue as to what we should be feeling. He's uneasy and seems hesitant, almost reluctant to enter this place. The reader picks up on his disquiet, and the mood is set.

Closely aligned with the weather are the seasons of the year. They vary in intensity depending on location, but each season has clearly recognized characteristics, from the changing colors of fall to the long hot days of summer. This universality means that seasons naturally lend themselves to symbolism that can set the mood for a scene or an entire story. Take this passage from Washington Irving's *The Legend of Sleepy Hollow*:

> As Ichabod jogged slowly on his way, his eye, ever open to every symptom of culinary abundance, ranged with delight over the treasures of jolly autumn. On all sides he beheld vast stores of apples; some hanging in oppressive opulence on the trees; some gathered into baskets and barrels for the market; others heaped up in rich piles for the cider-press. Farther on he beheld great fields of Indian corn, with its golden ears peeping from their leafy covers and holding out the promise of cakes and hasty-pudding; and the yellow pumpkins lying beneath them, turning up their fair round bellies to the sun and giving ample prospects of the most luxurious of pies.

Autumn is the perfect backdrop for Irving's story because it gives the reader a false sense of security. Fall brings to mind the cozy remembrances of cooling weather, soothing foods, and comfort found indoors by the fire. What we tend to forget about fall is that it's a sign that the year is dying. In a short time, winter will come with its frigid temperatures and blizzards that smother the world, just as the headless horseman will soon fall upon Sleepy Hollow and the unsuspecting Ichabod Crane.

When considering the time of year to set your story, think about any recurring themes and which seasons might best reinforce those ideas and feelings. Winter is often symbolic of death, endings, barrenness, and despair. Alternatively, springtime, with its newness and rebirth, is a strong backdrop for new beginnings and second chances. Youth, innocence, and coming-of-age stories are often set in summer, while autumn can represent preparedness, a focus that turns inward, or a coming change.

Each season can stand for many different things. When thoughtfully employed, they can be powerful tools, just as carefully chosen weather elements can reinforce a desired mood and prepare readers for what's to come. But there are some drawbacks that should be carefully considered when you're writing about seasons and the weather.

As with any element of a story, these can be overwritten and overdescribed. This results in a form of melodrama that can be off-putting to readers. As is true with many descriptive techniques, less is usually more. If your scene occurs in the burning-hot summer, it's not necessary to describe the drooping plants, the heat waves, the panting dogs, the sweat beading from every pore. Choose a few well-chosen details to describe the heat, then let it go. Your audience will appreciate your restraint.

Another potential problem that comes with weather and seasonal descriptions is the ease with which they drift into cliché: the air that feels as if it came from an oven, humidity that hits you like a wet towel, a winter wonderland of snow. These familiar expressions come quickly to mind when we're in the drafting trenches, but that's the problem with clichés of any kind: they're the easy way out, the sign of a writer who's either unwilling or unable to come up with new phrasings.

The most surefire way of keeping your descriptions fresh is to always consider your point-of-view character's personality, experiences, and frame of mind. Describe the weather through his lens, and you'll be sure to write something unique that fits him and his story. For example, sunlight is typically associated with happy feelings and positivity. But it could bring on negative emotions if your hero is part of an underground society living in a post-apocalyptic world. A rainy day, which can elicit sadness or depression for many, might be uplifting for an introverted character looking for some solitude. Because every character is different, you can often turn a stereotype or cliché on its ear by adapting weather choices so they make sense for your hero.

There's one last thing to keep in mind when writing the weather into a scene. As writers, we tend to fall back on the same weather references: heat, cold, sun, rain, and wind. But there are so many options that can be used to set the scene, from simple features like dew and frost to major events such as dust storms and blizzards. Many times, the familiar references do make the most sense. But to be sure you've chosen the best weather element for your scene, explore all the possibilities. For a thorough list of options, check out the "Weather and Earthly Phenomenon Thesaurus," which can be found in full at One Stop for Writers, our online description library.

SETTING THE STAGE WITH LIGHT AND SHADOW

What's one of the first things a person does to set the mood at home for a romantic evening? She turns down the lights. This simple adjustment is a big step toward creating a calm, receptive atmosphere. Just as the amount and quality of lighting will influence the way people feel in real life, we can adjust the mood for both characters and readers in our stories by playing with light and shadow.

Most everyone has familiar places that they've visited in daylight. But enter that same place at night and it becomes unfamiliar, with a totally different feel. By changing the amount and quality of light in a given place, you can shift the mood without changing the setting. For example, consider L. M. Montgomery's description of Birch Path, a recurring location in her *Anne of Green Gables* series:

> It was a little narrow, twisting path, winding down over a long hill straight through Mr. Bell's woods, where the light came down sifted through so many emerald screens that it was as flawless as the heart of a diamond.

One can easily envision this scene under the trees. The green-tinged sunlight gives the scene a lighthearted, cheerful feel, and though the season isn't mentioned, late spring or summer is inferred, simply by referencing the light.

But the same path traveled later in the day by a character in another frame of mind can look and feel vastly different. Here is Birch Path again, traveled by a more mature Anne in the third book of the series:

> Anne felt lonelier than ever as she walked home, going by way of the Birch Path and Willowmere. She had not walked that way for many moons. It was a darkly-purple bloomy night. The air was heavy with blossom fragrance—almost too heavy.

The darkly-purple light, combined with Anne's loneliness and the cloying odors, give the scene a heavy, melancholy feel that wasn't there before.

People respond to light in a feral way: well-lit areas are deemed safer, putting us at ease, while darker spots have more weight and feel heavier both on the body and the spirit. When setting the mood for a scene, carefully consider the lighting. How much light is there? Where does it come from? Is it hard or soft, comforting or blinding? Is it constant and totally revealing, or does it allow for shadows and hidden places? Questions like these will serve as a guide for how to light a scene in order to set the desired mood.

CHOOSING THE RIGHT NARRATOR

While lighting is an important piece of the mood-setting puzzle, its effect will depend largely upon the viewpoint narrator. As an example, let's return to Bilbo Baggins in *The Hobbit*. One of the difficulties he encounters on his journey is being knocked unconscious far below the Misty Mountains. When he comes to, his surroundings are described as being so dark that once he opens his eyes, he can't be sure that he actually has awakened. The effect on Bilbo is so overwhelming that he sits down in misery and is forced to take some time to pull himself together.

It makes perfect sense that such a setting would have this effect on Bilbo, a creature who values comfortable surroundings, rich meals, and cozy hobbit rooms with delightful views. Because of Tolkien's character building earlier in the story, the reader knows Bilbo and expects this emotional response when he's thrust into this dank tunnel. And just like that, the mood is set.

What's curious about setting and mood, though, is that they are entirely dependent upon the character, as we learn when we see this same setting from Gollum's viewpoint. We know from his lamp-like eyes and his ability to watch Bilbo from afar that Gollum has inhabited the tunnels for many years. The darkness and stillness, rather than bringing on despair, merely give him a sense of normalcy. They create a different mood for him, one of confidence and security, knowing that he is the master of this particular domain.

One setting, two different points of view. This example not only illustrates the effect a narrator or viewpoint character will have on a scene's mood but also shows how descriptions can provide contrast. In stories, the author's point is often illustrated by showing the stark difference between two characters, objects, organizations, places, etc. The *Hunger Games'* District 12 wouldn't have been so desperate and dim if it wasn't seen alongside the shining extravagance of the Capitol. Hogwarts was happiness personified when compared to Privet Drive. As authors, we're almost always trying to say something. To get your point across loud and clear, consider using a bit of contrast in your setting descriptions.

STYLE MATTERS

The author's style is yet another way to convey mood. As an example, let's examine the following passage, taking note of specific word choices.

> Sunlight filtered through the clouds, sparkling on the gravestones and warming the field that housed them. Paula smoothly maneuvered the humped-up ground, the grass underfoot absorbing the sound of her footsteps. A lavender-scented breeze whispered among the stones and caressed her skin. She drew in a deep breath and smiled.

The mood in this graveyard setting is an unusual one of peacefulness, and it's established through words carefully chosen to be calming: sunlight warming the stones, the grass absorbing her footsteps, the breeze whispering among the markers, the aroma of lavender—a scent known to have a relaxing effect. Words like these convey the character's state of mind and infuse the graveyard with tranquility.

Sentence length and fluency also reinforce this mood. This passage flows with long and smooth sentences, giving the setting a languid, meandering feel, which is precisely the author's intent. Lengthy sentences like these lend themselves to emotions that are lower-energy, such as contentment, nostalgia, or wonder. Short sentences, on the other hand, often best express high-energy emotions: fear, anxiety, anger, impatience, excitement, etc.

To show the effect that style can have on the mood of a setting, let's use the same scene above but change the style.

> Breaths heaving, Paula tore through the rocky graveyard. She tripped over a broken marker, its jagged edge cutting her shin. Sunlight stabbed at her eyes. She squinted, wiping away stinging sweat, and glanced behind. No one yet. But they hadn't given up. They'd never give up. A gust of smoky wind buffeted her. She choked on its burning reek and stumbled on.

Our sunny graveyard's mood has changed drastically with some new word choices. Instead of Paula stepping peacefully through the graveyard, she's tearing through it. The sunlight is harsh, stabbing at her, and the gentle breeze has become a violent, reeking wind. The sentences are also no longer fluid; their choppy structure gives the passage a brusque, hurried feel that lends itself to Paula's dire situation.

As seen here, writing style can be instrumental in building a specific mood. Experiment with word choice, sentence length, fluency, and even paragraph length to find the combination that conveys the emotion you want readers to experience.

FORESHADOWING: THE BREAD CRUMBS OF A STORY

It doesn't take a lot of description to clue readers in to what they should be feeling. And that mood doesn't always rely on what's currently happening in a scene; sometimes, it's more about what's *going* to happen.

Foreshadowing is a literary technique whereby the author hints at things to come. This technique can be most effective when it's linked with emotions such as fear, excitement, unease, or gratitude; because of this, foreshadowing and mood often go hand in hand. Since emotions are easily associated with certain locations, the setting is the perfect way to lay the foundation for what's coming while also establishing the mood.

Because of their visual nature, movies are great for using the setting to foreshadow future events. The final scene of the original *Terminator* ends with ominous clouds taking over the sky. It hints at the coming nuclear storm and cements the final mood in the movie as one of grim acceptance as Sarah Connor embraces her fate as the mother of the future.

A good literary example can be found in *Pride and Prejudice*, when Elizabeth first sees Mr. Darcy's Pemberley House.

> It was a large, handsome, stone building, standing well on rising ground and backed by a ridge of high woody hills . . . Elizabeth was delighted. She had never seen a place for which nature had done more, or where natural beauty had been so little counteracted by an awkward taste. They were all of them warm in their admiration; and at that moment she felt that to be mistress of Pemberley might be something!

With this passage, the author gives us a glimpse of Elizabeth's future. It's true that she's already turned down a marriage proposal from Mr. Darcy, but recently she has learned new things about him that cast him in a more positive light. Now a visit to his home provides the perfect opportunity for Austen to hint at events to come. That final line foreshadows a brighter future for Elizabeth; she's pleasantly surprised, even delighted, with Pemberley. Her response to the house is a reflection of her changing feelings toward Mr. Darcy himself. The resulting mood is one of hope—both in her future and in the personal growth that is enabling her to move past her former pride and prejudice.

THE SETTING AS A VEHICLE FOR STEERING THE STORY

When writing, *story* should always be at the forefront of our minds. We should be asking ourselves questions like, "Is what I've just written steering the story?" and "Is this scene, interaction, passage, or subplot driving my character toward his goal?" The momentum of both the character and the plot is what keeps events on track and maintains an appropriate pace. *Story* should be the litmus test against which our writing is continually measured.

Some elements are more intuitively related to determining where the story is headed: the character arc, conflict, overall structure, etc. But the setting can also be useful for moving the story forward because it provides factors that naturally affect the plot and characters. When manipulated, the setting can be used to push a story in the direction it needs to go.

BASIC NEEDS: WHAT'S MISSING FOR YOUR CHARACTER?

One constant in every story is that the main character has a goal to work toward, such as finding love, protecting her family, or winning accolades and fame. Each of these goals is rooted in a human need, something that characters and people in the real world share.

These needs, called **basic human needs** by psychologist Abraham Maslow, are primal and drive people (and therefore characters) to do what they do. They focus on five primary areas: physiological needs, safety and security, love and belonging, esteem and recognition, and self-actualization. True happiness and fulfillment come when all five needs are being met. But if one need is missing or taken away, a character will be driven to try and to get it back. Because of this, basic human needs can be very powerful tools in steering the story.

For example, look at former superhero Bob Parr in *The Incredibles*. At the beginning of the story, he's living in suburbia, hiding out as a regular guy, and he's absolutely hating it. Living well beneath his full potential, his need for self-actualization is missing. As a result, when he receives an invitation to put his superpowers to work again, he jumps at the chance. This decision not only generates ample conflict in his work and family life, it also precipitates his introduction to the villain of the story—an introduction that never would have taken place had he been fully actualized and living contentedly in his suburban world.

This is the beauty of using settings to manipulate a character's needs. When things are going well, most characters, like their human counterparts, are perfectly happy to stay right where they are, enjoying the status quo. Left to themselves, they probably would go nowhere. So we have to prod them—adjust their circumstances to get them where we need them to be.

When you're choosing a setting for a story or scene, take into account your character's needs. Which one is missing? Is there a certain location that can accentuate that lack and force him into motion? If nothing is missing, which settings might remove a need and upset his equilibrium, pushing him in a new direction? Dropping your character into a place that affects his needs is one way to get him headed where you want him to go.

TESTS: WILL YOUR CHARACTER PASS OR FAIL?

The hero's journey is gradual. Through story events and his interactions with others, he learns about himself—his motivations, desires, strengths, and weaknesses. With each new revelation, his confidence and abilities increase, inching him closer to his goal. But with newfound knowledge naturally comes doubt and insecurities.

Tests are an established part of any hero's journey; they force him to question who he is, what he really wants, and why. In addition, tests also keep the reader invested because they contain the possibility of failure. They tap into readers' emotions by making them doubt the hero. Will he achieve his goal or give up when the opposition becomes too great? Will he make the right choice or choose one that will set him back? For our stories to escape predictability, our characters need to be given opportunities to fail. Tests are a great way to provide those opportunities, and settings are a great way to provide the tests.

In *An Officer and a Gentleman*, Zach Mayo and his fellow recruits are made to run an obstacle course. It's an easy exercise for him; in fact, he's made up his mind to beat the record for completing it. But Zach's biggest weakness is self-reliance taken to an unhealthy extreme, making him apathetic, uncooperative, and self-serving. This is the weakness he must overcome if he wants to belong (which would meet the unfulfilled need that he's always lacked). And while he's given many opportunities to change his ways and embrace interdependence, he doesn't succeed until the end of the story. Zach is running the course, on pace to beat the record, when one of his platoon mates falls behind at the wall that has always stymied her. This time, he gives up his chances of breaking the record to help her get over the wall so they can cross the finish line together. The obstacle course setting was used to test his character, and while he often failed, eventually he came through with flying colors.

But remember that it's not always the setting itself that provides the test; it can also be the people, objects, and circumstances within the setting that give the hero an opportunity to prove himself. Is your character a struggling alcoholic trying to overcome his addiction? Put him in a setting where alcohol is abundant or available—a bar, a wedding reception, or a sporting event. Does a certain person bring out the very faults he's trying to overcome? Choose a setting where it's likely for that person to make an appearance.

OPPORTUNITIES FOR REFLECTION

While tests are necessary for our characters, they're tense in nature. They're stressful, not only to the characters experiencing them but also to the readers who are sharing in the story. While tension is great in terms of maintaining the reader's attention, it can become tiring without a break. High tension needs to be interrupted by occasional downtimes so readers and characters alike can catch their breath.

These downtimes also give characters a chance to reflect on what they've just been through. If a test has been passed, the heroine is able to bask in her success, gaining confidence to move on and face even bigger tests on her path to fulfillment. Failed tests give characters the chance to see where they went wrong, where they need to grow, and what they should do differently next time. A time of reflection in this scenario can also segue into another immediate test: does this failure cause the heroine to give up or soldier on?

The settings you choose for these pensive moments will depend largely upon the main character and the type of book you've written. Reflection scenes are typically quiet, providing a simple backdrop—a bedroom, a campfire, a drive through the country—so the character can concentrate on what she needs to learn before facing the next test. But these peaceful settings won't work for every character. What if you have an extroverted protagonist who gains energy from being with others? Her most productive reflection times may come during a noisy party or while walking down a crowded street. Does she work through problems by talking them out or bouncing ideas off a friend? This scene might be best set at a neighbor's apartment or over coffee in a restaurant.

It's also good to remember that in times of personal scrutiny, characters will often seek out safe places. Just as wounding events can create negative associations with certain settings, positive feelings can be linked to locations that provide safety and security. To make these reflective moments especially poignant, set them in a place that has emotional significance. Where did her happiest memories play out, and which places made her feel safe? Is there a location tied to a past achievement that she might revisit? Answers to questions like these can provide a list of possible settings for your character's reflective moments. Personalizing these spaces will not only add emotion to the scene, it will also make your story unique and create a sense of realism for readers.

FIGURATIVE LANGUAGE:
THE KEY TO ENHANCING YOUR SETTING

We've shown the setting as a versatile story element that is more than just a static time and place. It not only can help to steer the story, it also provides conflict and establishes the proper mood—both of which work together to create an emotional response in readers. But this only happens when the setting is described well.

When drafting, we're often tempted to convey the setting in its simplest terms:

> It was a cold and foggy afternoon.

But this setting can be so much more evocative, as we see in the following sample from Charles Dickens' *A Christmas Carol*:

> Old Scrooge sat busy in his counting house. It was cold, bleak, biting weather, foggy withal, and he could hear the people in the court outside go wheezing up and down, beating their hands upon their breasts and stamping their feet upon the pavement stones to warm them. The city clocks had only just gone three, but it was quite dark already—it had not been light all day—and candles were flaring in the windows of the neighboring offices, like ruddy smears upon the palpable brown air. The fog came pouring in at every chink and keyhole, and was so dense without, that, although the court was of the narrowest, the houses opposite were mere phantoms.

Extra work has gone into describing this setting, and while the writing in most classics is more heavy-handed than is typically found in modern stories, the figurative language that worked for the masters still applies today. Along with the sensory details, Dickens' use of simile and metaphor turn a simple urban courtyard into one with depth, texture, and feeling. This is the beauty of these techniques; they create a crystal-clear image that grounds readers firmly in the scene and allows them to picture exactly what's happening as they read. They also enable the author to highlight important objects or symbols in a scene, as well as sometimes providing a much-needed dose of humor.

Because of the benefit they can add, let's take a look at some examples of figurative language and how they can be used to enhance a setting description.

SIMILE AND METAPHOR

Figurative language is best described as words that say one thing but mean another; it's language that isn't literal. One of the most common examples of figurative language is the use of comparisons, and the most popular comparisons are the **simile** and **metaphor**. The only difference between the two is that the simile uses the words *like* or *as*, whereas a metaphor doesn't, instead stating definitively that one thing *is* the other. For example:

> The water was as black as ink. (Simile)
> Without the moon's light to brighten it, the water turned to ink. (Metaphor)

And:

> The flock of birds sounded like an angry mob. (Simile)
> The flock of birds was an angry mob working itself into a frenzy. (Metaphor)

Both similes and metaphors are very helpful when you want to paint a mental picture of your setting, creating vivid imagery while also promoting word economy. In addition, the choice of metaphor can help to establish the mood for a given scene, as the following two examples show.

> The math wing hallway stretched on for miles. It was like a parade route, and I was the clown, smiling my way through bruising elbows and hard shoves, acting like it was all so funny when really I just wanted to hide in the bathroom and cry.

Now take a look at the same setting described with different imagery.

> I made my way smoothly down the math wing hallway—a moving point on a perpendicular line that intersected the science hall. I nodded at the other points, called out a casual, "Hey!" as we traveled the lines that would take us where we needed to go.

Both these examples establish the time and place: it's a school day on the math wing. But so much more is conveyed with the comparisons that are used. The first example uses a simile to express the character's feelings about the setting. It's not a happy place for her. By contrast, the character in the second example is perfectly at ease. The metaphors comparing the math hallway to a perpendicular line and identifying the students as points tell the reader that the viewpoint character is into math, and this is a comfortable place for her.

The benefits of using metaphors and similes to describe the setting are vast. Not only do these comparisons create a mental image for the reader, they also provide important information about the setting and the characters who inhabit it.

USING SYMBOLS TO EMPHASIZE THEME

While similes and metaphors draw comparisons between two different objects, symbolism gives meaning to a word, phrase, or object that goes beyond the literal. This allows writers to convey important themes or reinforce feelings, ideas, and beliefs through either universal or personalized symbolism.

Universal symbolism is the most common, taking widely held perceptions and beliefs from the real world and applying them to fiction. This can range from people viewing a teacher as a trustworthy advocate for children to equating the color white with purity. Utilizing universal symbolism is one way a writer can do more with a description, implying a commonly held meaning, emotion, or mood with the fewest words possible.

Personalized symbolism may include commonly held beliefs but is typically tied to the point-of-view character's own associations. The smell of oatmeal might represent poverty to a character who was forced to eat it each day during a lean winter. A gift of a dandelion might represent forgiveness to a hero who once offered one as an apology for a childhood wrong. Personalized symbolism is not only powerful—when done well, it is gratifying to readers because they understand the special meaning behind the symbol and are privy to the character's emotions as they are exposed to them.

Keep in mind that a symbol is subtler than a simile or metaphor in that the symbol's meaning is never overtly defined. It is written into the story in such a way that readers intuitively recognize the everyday object for what it is meant to represent. Upon finishing Stephen King's *The Stand,* readers might not think to themselves, *Oh, I see. Mother Abagail is a symbol for Moses.* But if they're familiar with the biblical story, their subconscious will very likely make the connection and they'll feel a sense of rightness—a mental *Aha!* that connects the reader to something deeper within the story.

MOTIFS: SYMBOLISM ON A LARGER SCALE

Connecting readers with our stories is what we all hope to achieve as authors. This is why, the vast majority of the time, the stories we write contain a central message or idea—a **theme**—that is being conveyed through its telling. Sometimes the theme is deliberately included during the drafting stage; other times, it organically emerges during the writing process. However it occurs, the theme is often supported by certain recurring symbols that help to develop the overall message or idea throughout the course of a story. These repeated symbols are called **motifs**.

For example, consider the *Harry Potter* series. One of the motifs undergirding the theme of good vs. evil is the snake. It's the sign for the house of Slytherin, from which so many bad wizards have emerged. Voldemort's pet, Nagini, is a giant snake. Those who can speak Parseltongue (the language of serpents) are considered to be dark wizards. By repeatedly using this creature as a symbol for evil, Rowling creates an image that readers automatically associate with the dark side of Potter's world.

Because motifs are pivotal in revealing your theme to readers, it's important to find the right ones. The setting is a natural place for these motifs to occur because it contains so many possibilities. It might be something from nature, like the ailanthus tree in *A Tree Grows in Brooklyn* or Huck Finn's Mississippi River. Your motif could be a simple object within the setting, like the seemingly random feather in *Forrest Gump* that represents destiny. It could be a season, an article of clothing, an animal, a weather phenomenon—it could be anything, as long as it recurs throughout the story and reinforces the overall theme.

As was mentioned earlier, themes can either be planned or accidental. If you know beforehand what your theme will be, think of a location that could reinforce that idea—either through the setting itself or with objects within that place—and make sure those choices are prominently displayed throughout the story.

If your theme emerges on its own, you can always bolster it by adding motifs after the fact, using the same selection process. For ideas on possible motifs and how they can be used to emphasize the theme of your story, please reference the "Symbolism and Motifs Thesaurus" at One Stop for Writers.

HYPERBOLE

Much of what we do as writers is to fulfill a given purpose: to entertain, inform, persuade, or reveal, among other things. If the point of a given passage or scene is to make a statement, hyperbole is a good way to do it. This technique can be defined as exaggeration used for the sake of emphasis, as can be seen in the following setting description example.

> Marcy's dorm room offered a scary look into the aftermath of the apocalypse—beds were buried in lumps of clothing and shoes, granola bar wrappers and crumbs peppered the floor, and a sour smell hung in the air, likely a product of the bacterial experiment disguised as a dirty stack of dishes in the sink.

The author uses a few exaggerations here that can't possibly be true. Marcy's room isn't the site of an apocalyptic event, and the contents of the sink are more likely yesterday's dishes than a scientific experiment gone wrong. Readers know that the writing isn't literal, yet the author's message (Marcy is a slob) comes through loud and clear. Through the use of hyperbole, the heroine has been characterized clearly and humorously, and the purpose of this description has been accomplished.

While this literary device is often used to amusing effect, it can also be employed with serious subject matter.

> As the sun slid behind the western peak, the shadow patches under the trees coalesced into a dusky void that sucked up every sound: the suddenly still wind, a hawk's cut-off shriek, the cessation of small animal noises in the leaves. A shudder worked its way up my back. I dropped my load of sticks and started on the fire.

In this passage, the shadows haven't created an actual void and they aren't vacuuming up all the sounds in the forest. But by over-exaggerating the darkness and connecting it with the sudden silence, the author emphasizes that something isn't quite right here, which creates tension and a feeling of unease for the reader. Once again, the author's point has been made.

If you'd like to make a certain statement with a given setting description, consider over-emphasizing some of the elements. A note of caution, though: as with most figurative language, if this technique is used too often, the narrative will start to read as melodramatic and your point may be missed. With hyperbole, remember that a little goes a long way.

BRINGING THE INANIMATE TO LIFE THROUGH PERSONIFICATION

When it comes to enhancing the setting, one of the most effective figurative language techniques is that of **personification**: adding human characteristics to an inanimate object. Done well, this can add a sense of movement and emotion to an otherwise sterile scene. To see how this works, let's start with a setting that contains a simple house on a cliff:

> At the edge of the bluff stood an old house with chipped paint and crooked shutters.

This description does the job of establishing the house and its location. But it's static. To add a sense of motion, let's apply some human movement to the house.

> The house squatted at the bluff's edge, its lines crooked from so many years spent leaning into the wind.

Aha! The house is gaining a little character now. We get a clearer picture of it as we imagine it squatting at the edge of the cliff and pushing against the wind. But we can do more:

> The house squatted at the bluff's edge, its lines crooked from so many years spent leaning into the wind. Sand had scoured its skin so it showed more board now than paint. The open door sagged to one side like a slack jaw.

By adding skin and a jaw to the house, we've given it human details that not only enhance the visual image but also add an element of emotion. Readers know what it's like to have one's skin scraped by sand. They associate certain things with slack jaws, like illness and old age. With these details, this setting evokes a sense of sadness or even pity. By personifying the house this way, we've established the emotion we'd like readers to feel when they envision it.

The beauty of personification is that it can be used to elicit any feeling, to create whatever image the author desires. With just a few changes, the sad little house can be transformed into a completely different structure.

> The house stood at the highest point of the bluff, perfectly erect, lording over the pathetic trees. Its newly painted skin glistened. Its windows gleamed, staring unblinkingly at the cloudless sky.

Here, we have a very different house, one that's shining and well cared for and stands perfectly upright. But with its unblinking eyes and its "lording," we get the sense that it's looking down on everyone and everything. This house doesn't elicit warm feelings; it feels rather the opposite of inviting and friendly.

As these examples show, personification is highly effective for infusing life into otherwise bland settings. By adding human characteristics to inhumane things, they become familiar and relatable. Through this technique, authors are able to instill feeling into their settings, starting readers on an emotional experience that will continue throughout the scene.

COMMON SETTING SNAGS

So far, we've mentioned many ways in which the setting can be a useful tool to enhance your writing. But as with any story element, it does have its difficulties. Here are a few sticky spots that can develop when you're writing descriptions, along with methods for avoiding them.

RAMBLING DESCRIPTIONS

This is one of the main reasons that settings get a bad rap—because writers overdo it with the descriptions. It's also a huge culprit behind why young readers don't like the classics. Long-winded, overwrought passages of description used to be the norm, but this is no longer the case. When we reread some of our public domain favorites, it's easy to wonder how many of them would have been published today.

Authors don't like to think of themselves as salespeople pushing a product, but that's part of what we do. We write books that we hope people will read. To be successful at this, we have to understand our audience. The world has changed since the time of Jane Austen and Charles Dickens. Readers today are used to things happening very quickly; most of them are big fans of Getting To The Point. If we want to engage and hold on to these readers, writing long passages of setting description is not the way to do it.

So how do we keep our descriptions from going on and on? The solution is both simple and complicated: pare each descriptive passage down to just the details that are truly necessary. To do this, you have to know what you want to accomplish with your setting. Are you using it to establish the mood, evoke certain emotions, foreshadow, set up future events, or characterize? Decide what you're hoping to achieve with a given description, then choose the details that will fulfill those purposes. Make sure you've included enough description to ground readers, then move on.

TIME CONFUSION

It's easy to think of the setting as strictly *where* a story is taking place, but the *when* is a big part of it too. Since most stories play out over time, in and out of days, months, and even years, it isn't difficult for readers to become confused about how much time has gone by. Expressing this passage of time is easy if you've written a certain kind of story—one in which dated diary entries or newspaper headlines play a part, or one that contains a countdown of some kind. But in most cases, letting readers know *when* in the story they are requires more subtlety. Luckily, this can be accomplished with a few setting tricks.

For stories that cover long periods of time, chapter or section breaks can be used to jump from one time to another. In this way, seasons, months of the year, common holidays, or the weather can be used to show readers how much time has passed and "when" it is now. For instance, chapter 27 of *Anne of Green Gables* occurs in winter. But chapter 28 opens with this:

> Marilla, walking home one late April evening from an Aid meeting, realized that the winter was over and gone with the thrill of delight that spring never fails to bring to the oldest and saddest as well as to the youngest and merriest.

Here, the author states both the month and the season but avoids clunkiness by not declaring either outright ("It was April now."). Instead, she infuses emotion into the temporal reference through a common occurrence that is nearly universal: the excitement that comes with winter turning into spring. In this way, the temporal reference is disguised, making it less obvious. This example shows how a chapter break combined with a setting reference can effectively express the passage of time to readers.

While a chapter break is a good way to cut out large chunks of time, it doesn't work so well when the jump is of shorter duration. When only a day or an hour has passed, you obviously can't reference the seasons. Here, you have to think of what in the setting might change in a relatively short period of time—say, while a character waits for important news.

> Chandra had paced the floor until her feet ached, crossing in and out of the warm shaft of light that fell through the waiting room window. But no one came with news. No one even checked in. Soon, even her one bit of warmth disappeared as the clouds steadily built up and blocked it out. So she sat, inwardly wound as tight as a yo-yo. Outwardly, her only movement was the thrum of her fingers on the wooden chair arm.

Here, we are shown that time is passing through references to the weather. It's gradually shifting, indicating a slow change—possibly an hour or two, or an afternoon or morning going by. In this way, weather can be a handy tool for showing that time has passed without ever mentioning the clock.

Another way to show this is through the change of light. Is your scene set in early morning? Then show the sun's changing position as it moves from just over the horizon to midpoint in the sky. The same can be done with the moon and its position throughout the night. Are events happening as the afternoon progresses? The quality and brightness of the light as well as the movement of shadows can indicate that time is passing.

In addition to these techniques, try to find common routines that indicate time shifts. Children heading off to school and returning home, morning and evening rush-hour traffic, or even the pattern of showering, eating breakfast, and heading off for the day are all familiar routines that can be used to show readers that time is flowing forward.

FLASHBACKS AND DREAMS DONE RIGHT

Few plot devices have been reviled as fervently as flashbacks and dream sequences—and for a variety of reasons. When you come right down to it, these devices are essentially interruptions that pull readers out of the current story; whenever that happens, we run the risk of losing the reader. To avoid this, it's important to keep flashbacks and dreams as short as possible so we can get readers back to the story they're most interested in.

Unfortunately, it's often the setting that plays a part in these passages going on for too long. When a flashback or dream is introduced, the setting usually changes, and it has to be described adequately so readers can get their bearings. As a result, authors can overdo the description, which adds to the lengthiness and overall bloated feeling of the flashback or dream.

To solve this, we want to do more with less, keeping setting descriptions short and sweet. Figure out the bare minimum of what needs to be shared so the reader won't be confused. Focus on setting details that are necessary for what you're trying to accomplish, and make sure they do double duty to elicit desired emotions, since many times this is an intended result of the dream or flashback. In short, zero in on the important details, convey them quickly and succinctly, and get back to the real story.

Another difficulty with flashbacks in particular is the confusion that can result when readers are pulled back and forth between the present and the past. The last thing you want is for your readers to be disoriented and perplexed by what's happening. One way to clarify things is to make the flashback's setting distinctly different from the one in the regular story. Choosing a completely different location for the flashback can be effective, since this will let readers know that there's been a change. If this doesn't work for your story, look for something else in the flashback scene that can be altered, such as the weather, season, or time of day.

If the flashback takes place far in the past, be sure to reinforce this with pertinent details of the time, such as a major difference in the character's appearance, relevant fashion trends, or a shift in pop culture. But don't waste word currency on sideline details; make each description choice meaningful to the flashback event and the characters involved.

When it comes to writing dreams—especially recurring dream sequences—clarity often comes by deciding beforehand how those passages should look. Will they be realistic and crisp or hazy and unfocused? Dreams can go either way. Decide how to write them, then overemphasize that look: make them overly stark and bright or very clouded and blurry. When this technique is utilized, readers will recognize that they're entering a dream sequence because it will look and feel different than the rest of the story.

SCENE DESCRIPTION: SHOULD I TELL OR SHOULD I SHOW?

You don't have to write for very long before you start hearing how showing is preferred to telling. And it's true that showing is usually better; it draws readers in through the use of sensory details, it elicits emotion, and it shares information through the context of the current story rather than interrupting the story to do so. But telling also has its place—particularly when you need to express something quickly without bogging the story down in details or slowing the pace. Both showing and telling have their benefits when it comes to describing the setting. So how do you know if you should show or tell?

WHEN TO SHOW

To Create Mood or Emotion

The purpose of creating mood or emotion with your setting is to draw readers in—to make them feel whatever it is you want them to feel. Simply telling what the setting looks like (*the nursery was empty*) doesn't accomplish this. But showing does.

The walls were pink—she knew they were, despite the drawn blinds that dimmed everything to an overcast gray: the rocker, the diaper supplies on the changing table, the silent mobile. Even the pacifier laying facedown in the center of the rug—as far from the crib as a just-sitting-up baby could fling it. Sarah stood in the doorway, unblinking eyes burning, staring at that damned pacifier. She'd been too embarrassed to ask someone to pick it up. Now everyone was gone, and it was too late.

As you can see, if you want to evoke a certain feeling or set the mood, showing can be very effective.

To Describe Unusual or Unfamiliar Settings

We never want readers to be confused about where the story is taking place; we don't want them having to backtrack and reread in an effort to regain their footing in the story. To avoid this, many writers—particularly in the fantasy and science fiction genres—go overboard when describing their unusual settings, causing reader interest to flag.

Similar to familiar settings, unusual ones should be shown just enough to give readers a clear visual image. One way to accomplish this is to start big, with the overall setting, and end small by focusing on one facet within it. When describing a space outpost, for example, it's not necessary to go into detail about its distance from Earth, the quality of the atmosphere, and the alien species that coexist there with humans. Give a general overall impression, yes, but then zero in on smaller details that show what you're trying to get across. Its age, for instance, could be revealed by focusing on the dilapidated structures or the ghost-town quality of its walkways. Another way to describe a particularly difficult element of a foreign setting is by using a comparison, which can create the right imagery with only a few words.

To Reveal Backstory

Backstory is another device that gets a bad rap—mostly when it's revealed in huge info dumps that bore readers and slow the story's pace. But some of this information must be shared for readers to understand the characters and their motivation. In almost every situation, backstory is much more effective when it is shown rather than told, and the setting is a great vehicle through which to reveal important information from a character's past.

To Describe a Setting That Will Undergo Significant Change

If a setting is going to be altered in some way, it's important for readers to be able to clearly see the before and after images. The destruction of District 12 in book two of *The Hunger Games* wouldn't have been nearly as devastating to readers if Suzanne Collins hadn't shown the setting so clearly early on. Evolving settings need to be shown, both initially and after the makeover occurs, for readers to get the full effect of what has happened.

To Lay the Foundation for an Important Setting

For each character, certain settings will have more significance than others. One may be the site of an emotional experience from the past. Another might be the place where essential supporting characters live, which means the hero will be spending a lot of time there. Because readers should be introduced carefully and thoughtfully to places like these, it's better to show them than explain through telling. If the setting is one that the character will frequent throughout the story, that first visit will be particularly important and should be described accordingly. After that, unless the setting undergoes a significant change, a simple summary line is all that will be needed to let readers know where the character is.

To Foreshadow

The setting is often a natural place in which to include clues about what will happen later in the story. The weather, light and dark, symbolism, and props in each location can be used to hint at important events to come. Because we don't want readers to miss these clues, it's necessary to firmly establish them, and telling isn't the best way to accomplish this. On the other hand, showing enables authors to infuse emotion and mood into the description, thereby making it meaningful and memorable to readers.

WHEN TO TELL

During High-Action Scenes

Fights, chases, climax scenes: when things are happening quickly, we don't want to slow the pace with intricate setting descriptions. In cases like these, keep the focus on the important events by describing just the basics of the setting. After that, minimal descriptions can be shown or told in conjunction with the action, whichever makes sense for the scene.

When the Viewpoint Character's Personality Calls for It

Remember that everything should be filtered through your narrator's point of view. If he's a pensive, rambling sort, then taking some time to show the setting makes sense. But if he's practical and efficient with no interest in his surroundings, he's not going to care much about the setting; in this case, mentioning it in passing might fit better with his personality. Just be sure to lay this foundation early on so readers will understand his starkness in regard to the setting details.

For Effect

Telling can often be used to make a point or express something in a way that's both catchy and memorable: *It was the best of times, it was the worst of times*. This same technique can be used when describing a setting. To be fair, these telling bits are usually followed with a bit of showing to flesh out the description, but imagine a book, chapter, or scene that opens (or closes) with one of these telling lines:

The house was clearly haunted.
It was the lamest birthday party ever.
I woke up in the chicken coop.

Lines like these are more about style than description. While they set the scene in the most basic of ways, they also say something about the characters, the narrator, or the author. Telling in this way can be effective, but for it to really work, it needs to be done purposefully.

As you can see from this breakdown, showing is almost always the better option when it comes to writing settings. It creates multidimensional and realistic environments, builds emotional connections, and pulls readers deeper into the story. And yet there are times when telling works too. As always, know what part the setting has to play in a scene, and you'll have a better idea of how much to show and when to tell.

RURAL SETTING CONSIDERATIONS

While much of the information in this volume can be applied when writing any setting description, the entries themselves are focused on home, school, and rural sights. Urban and natural environments are inherently different, each having their own challenges. To address those, let's look at rural settings in particular and how to describe them more effectively in fiction.

RESEARCH NATURAL SETTINGS CAREFULLY

It's easy to get lazy when we're writing about a familiar outdoor setting. Mountains, forests, lakes, hiking trails—we've all seen these, have possibly even grown up or spent large quantities of time in these areas. As authors we might feel like we have a firm grasp on, say, the mountain setting. But what kind of mountains are you writing? If you grew up in the Appalachian region of the eastern United States and your story is set there, you're probably good to go. But write those mountains into a story set in the Canadian Rockies or the Swiss Alps and you're going to be in big trouble.

Natural landforms vary widely depending on where you find them—not only in the way they look but in the flora that grows there, the animals that frequent the area, the length of day and night, variations in temperature, seasonal considerations, and many other things. For instance, there are at least ten different types of waterfalls; is yours the cascade, punchbowl, or segmented kind? Likewise, while alligators might be a common sight on the banks of a Florida waterway, you won't find them anywhere near a Canadian river.

If you're writing a natural setting that occurs in a real place somewhere in the world, research that area carefully so you can write it realistically and consistently. The last thing you want to do is alienate your perfect audience—the readers who live in the place where you've set your story—because the details aren't spot-on.

ADD ORGANIC ACTION

One reason readers oppose long paragraphs of description is that the passages are usually passive. There's nothing happening for lines and lines while the author goes on about the architecture or indigenous shrubbery. Passive paragraphs slow the pace and read as boring, which is something we definitely want to avoid.

To sidestep this landmine, give your static descriptions a sense of motion via the character's actions. For indoor scenes, you can easily describe the environment while the character whips up a pan of brownies, opens the mail, feeds the dog, or puts away groceries. Of course, these mundane activities should add to the scene rather than overpower it, or you run the risk of boring the reader. But small motions—ripping open a bag of dog food or cracking an egg into a bowl—can be interspersed with the descriptions to break up narrative stretches and add action.

This can be even easier in outdoor settings, where action organically occurs through natural phenomena. Here, you can utilize the wind and its effects, running water, cloud movements, shifting shadows, or nearby animals and insects to add action to the scene. Short references like these can lend a sense of movement to even an inactive passage like this one:

> By the time I got home, full dark had fallen. The bullying wind came in
> gusts, parting my hair and running its fingertip touch along my scalp, but I
> stood in the cold, staring at my house. Light flickered at the windows, and I
> caught a scent of chimney smoke that I swore smelled like stew cooking. From
> here, it made a soft and homey picture. Inviting.

Nothing is really happening here—the main character is standing still in the yard, staring at her house. But there are small actions: the gusting wind parting her hair, flickering lights—even the chimney smoke isn't doing anything, but the reader gets a sense of it drifting, filtering into the sky. All these small details describe the setting and create a sense of mood while also adding movement to an otherwise immobile scene. It's like an optical illusion, creating activity where there is none. Overall, it's a great technique for bringing quieter scenes to life.

USE CONTRAST FOR WIDE ANGLE SHOTS

Nature and landforms—particularly large ones such as swamps, forests, and oceans—can be difficult to describe well because of their scale. They're just so big; the size is hard to articulate. To adequately describe their immensity, it's best to use contrast. Use something small in the foreground or nearby to provide a comparison and a sense of proportion.

> The plains here weren't flat like people claimed. They sloped and rolled,
> gentle-like. And the wind in the grasses made a rippling wave, like silky
> sheets humping and bumping in the breeze. But, Lord, how this land did go
> on. I shaded my eyes and cast my gaze as far as it would go—past the lone
> cottonwood, past our barn, which was spacious by anyone's standard but looked
> like an outhouse in this grassy world. The plains were beautiful in their way but
> I couldn't help thinking God had gone a little overboard with it all.

Telling that the plains are huge is one thing. Showing it in comparison to something smaller helps bring the scale home to readers and gives them a better idea of just how enormous they are.

DO THE UNEXPECTED

Writing can be a difficult business on the best of days. Just finding the correct words can be exhausting. So when something comes to mind that even halfway works, it's easy to use it and move on. But as was mentioned earlier in regard to weather and the seasons, the things that come to mind often do so because we've seen them before. It's tempting to fall back on common clichéd setting choices, but it's almost always better to push past the obvious ideas and come up with something fresh that exactly fits your story and character.

A church, for example, can be a soothing place that bolsters a character's spirit. But it could also be an oppressive one for someone struggling with guilt, or a place associated with boredom for someone who is forced to attend. If your character is a con man, this setting might be one of opportunity rather than spirituality. We also tend to associate churches with people of faith. But why can't it be a favorite spot for someone unexpected, such as a little boy who goes there to escape the ghosts that plague him (*The Sixth Sense*)?

When you're choosing a setting for each scene, don't settle on the first one that comes to mind. Think about how you can mix things up, considering your character, the mood you want to create, and where the story is headed.

GIVE EVERY SETTING ITS DUE ATTENTION

In the author's mind, not all settings are created equal. We spend more time describing the places that are interesting, beautiful, or have significant value to us. The common, everyday ones don't get as much love: the bathroom, a cow pasture, the playground at the elementary school. In the case of fairly common settings like these, we gloss over the description or ignore it completely, thinking that readers already know what it looks like, so there's no point wasting words on it.

But the truth is that every setting can hold value. Every location can add something to the scene. Characterization can be made with the observation of one object. Mood can be set with the condition of the wallpaper in a house or the way a room smells. Foreshadowing can be achieved just as easily.

So the next time you find yourself skimming over the description for a common or seemingly boring locale, take a moment to think about what could be interesting about that place. What could your narrator notice that would add to the scene? Personalizing the setting can also help reveal a character's layers. Consider the techniques that have been explained thus far and see what quick mention could be made to bring that scene to life and make it memorable or meaningful.

FINAL THOUGHTS FROM THE AUTHORS

While we have tried to include a strong representation of the most common fictional settings between the urban and rural volumes, by no means is this thesaurus complete. Including every possible setting would have made these books very large and very expensive. Because many settings are similar to one another, we chose to profile some as a way of covering a range of possibilities. If you can't locate the exact setting you're hoping to find, look to other locations that are similar, since they may have the descriptive details you need.

As you're browsing the entries, you may also find seeming contradictions in each; for instance, in the marina entry, *waves* are referenced, and so is *still water*. Obviously, both are possible, depending on the presence of wind, the amount of activity on the water, nearby marine life, and other factors. Settings will vary from day to day and hour to hour depending on the conditions that are present. To give you a variety of options, we've covered as many possibilities as we could.

Likewise, you will find that not all the details included in a given entry are universal to that location. Personal settings will be influenced by a character's culture, religious beliefs, personality, education level, and financial means. Rural areas will also have a different look and feel depending on the location, climate, season, and amount of human influence. If your setting is a real place, we recommend investigating the area to ensure your description lines up with that part of the world.

Also keep in mind the importance of describing settings from the point-of-view character's or narrator's perspective, since you'll need to remember this as you peruse the information in each entry. For instance, while it makes sense for a jockey at a racetrack to reference the smell of horses, a spectator in the stands will be too far away to notice such a thing. As always, choose your setting details carefully, and make sure they're a fit for whoever's doing the describing.

When it comes to your settings, never forget emotion. Filtering the description through your viewpoint character's feelings will influence what he notices about where he is and how he feels about it. Emotions can create bias regarding a place, good or bad, and this bias is passed on to readers, helping them to feel more connected to the character and his world.

Finally, we recommend using this book in tandem with *The Urban Setting Thesaurus*, since the lessons there will give you an even greater command of setting elements, allowing you to bring readers more deeply into each scene. If you would like to see a list of the settings explored in the urban companion, there is one included at the end of this book.

THE
RURAL SETTING
THESAURUS

At Home

ATTIC

SIGHTS
Dusty floorboards, exposed wooden beams with visible pipes and wiring, an exhaust fan, a porthole windowsill covered with grime and dead flies, a hatch door and fold-down staircase, a lightbulb and pull string, sunlight filtering in through cracks near the eaves, airflow tubing, mouse or small animal scat on the floorboards, spiderwebs drifting off the beams and straddling old rocking chairs or coat stands, old faded boxes with contents written on the side, peanut barrels, rickety furniture, a broken vacuum, a corner filled with old children's toys and Christmas decorations, dusty sheets covering antiques, motes of dust dancing in the shaft of light coming in through the air vent or small window, stacks of old board games, rolled-up rugs, dusty picture frames and paintings stacked against the wall, animal tracks in the dust, dead moths on the floor, a fly bumping against the porthole glass searching for a way out, mildew stains on boxes from a leaky roof or window, taxidermy collections, a dressmaker's dummy, old clothing stored in garbage bags, trunks with war memorabilia (a soldier's uniform and gear) or wedding items, boxes of books and school manuals, a record or cassette tape collection, storage tubs of old clothing

SOUNDS
Creaks, squeaking mice, scampering feet, claws against the floorboards, the tug of a light cord as one switches it on, fabric crinkling, the wind beating against the house, a bird pecking at bugs in the eaves, voices heard through the attic floor, footsteps, music or movement floating up through air ventilation, rain or hail against the roof, thunder, the scrape of branches against the house, water running through the eaves, the steady drip of a leaky roof

SMELLS
Insulation, dust, mold, mildew, sawdust, damp wood, dry rot, rotten fabric, wet cardboard, old books

TASTES
Damp or stale air, dust, the ozone tang of cold metal flavoring the air

TEXTURES AND SENSATIONS
Balancing on a wobbly ladder, splintery rough beams, pulling a light cord on a bare bulb wired to a ceiling beam, dust-coated drop cloths, the smooth grooves of a cherished toy or item, wet cardboard flaps, a cold metal hinge on a trunk, shoving a heavy lid up, coughing on dust, waving a hand in front of one's face to ward off dust, the slight give of loose or warped floorboards, jumping or flinching at the sight of a mouse, a lacy coverlet, the felt softness of an old hat, the weight of a box as one carries it closer to the window to see what's inside, bumping one's shins against a trunk in the dark, jarring an elbow or accidentally scraping one's arm in a tight space, the rusty give of a metal key turning in a lock, sorting through contents in a box or plastic storage container

POSSIBLE SOURCES OF CONFLICT

Hearing something moving around in the dark

A light that only reaches so far

Soft spots in the floor that could give way

Finding hidden family photos that suggest one of one's parents has a second family

Hearing someone on the floor below when one is alone in the house

Discovering a family secret in one of the old trunks

Finding something disturbing hidden in a trunk (a collection of locks of hair, jars of teeth)

Smelling something that has died

Discovering mold or some other health hazard

A leaky roof that threatens the items in one's attic

Visiting the attic and finding that some items have moved from their original positions

The power going out

Finding holes drilled through the roof that create spy holes into the bedrooms below

Feeling claustrophobic in the tight, airless space

Having one's allergies triggered by dust

Visiting the attic to put something away and finding evidence that someone is living up there

Needing to hide in an attic with a squeaky floor

Finding footprints in the dust when one lives alone in the house

Discovering adoption paperwork in an old trunk

PEOPLE COMMONLY FOUND HERE

Construction workers during renovations, homeowners, insurance adjustors, repairmen

RELATED SETTINGS THAT MAY TIE IN WITH THIS ONE

Rural Volume: Basement (38), secret passageway (84)

Urban Volume: Antiques shop (156)

SETTING NOTES AND TIPS

When describing the attic, think about the age of the house and the current or previous occupants. This will give insight into what sort of things might be stored in the attic, if anything at all. Consider using items for symbolism opportunities to reflect your character's circumstances, highlight her worries, or act as a mirror to her emotions.

SETTING DESCRIPTION EXAMPLE

Slumped against an old vacuum, the one-eyed doll faced the back of the shadowed attic, home of the intermittent thumping noise. My flashlight shook. In the tremor of light, her rotten stitch smile seemed to widen, like she knew something I didn't.

Techniques and Devices Used: Light and shadow, multisensory descriptions, personification

Resulting Effects: Establishing mood, foreshadowing

BACKYARD

SIGHTS
Sparkling dew-drenched grass, a doghouse with a peaked roof, a shiny red swing set and matching slide, a tree house settled high in the branches of a giant oak tree, a green hose snaked across the lawn with the sprinkler fanning water, wild rose bushes flush with pastel blooms, sun-bleached garden gnomes or painted rocks speckling the flowerbeds, decorative garden lanterns or blown glass catching the light, dandelions and clover poking through the grass, a shed at the back of the yard, trees casting shade on the ground below, butterflies, mosquitoes, flies, ladybugs crawling over the foliage, toys or bikes leaning against the fence, ants crawling across the cement sidewalk, chew toys and dead spots in the grass from dog urine, a patio with chairs, air shimmers and smoke wafting up from a lit barbeque, a fire pit, a hammock strung between two trees, ferns, peony bushes with bright pink heads, children tossing a football or chasing the dog, decorative pots filled with bright flowers, white daises creeping through the fence slats from the neighbor's adjoining yard, a lone tire swing hanging from a thick oak branch, a pool (inground, aboveground, a child's blow-up pool), birds splashing in a birdbath and flying in and out of their nests in the trees, a cluster of mushrooms blooming through the grass after a big rain, a squirrel running along the fence, a string of decorative patio lights, a bird feeder hanging from a wooden post, a trampoline or sandbox, pine cones littering the grass below a pine or spruce tree, dandelion fluff floating on the air

SOUNDS
Grasshoppers or crickets, the drone of mosquitoes, the whine of flies, a radio plunking out a song from a neighbor's yard, kids laughing or squealing as they run through the sprinkler, bees buzzing, a breeze ruffling leaves, cars driving past on the street, doors slamming, a married couple arguing in the house next door, far-off hammering from a home improvement project, beer bottles clicking together, the chatter of a squirrel, the hum of hornets circling a flower bush, the burble of a nearby creek, frogs croaking, the snap of flip-flops across a walkway, the hiss of water through the hose

SMELLS
The clean scents of mown grass and new leaves, fresh floral odors (from blooming lilacs, roses or sweet pea vines), earthy moist soil, the charred scent of a barbeque, smoke from the fire pit, rain, coconut-scented sunscreen or tanning lotion, sweat, dust, dog poop

TASTES
Sweet peaches or watermelons, yeasty cold beer, the bitter char of meat mixed with sweet barbeque sauce or marinades, tart lemonade, iced tea, the cold numbness of a popsicle, water from a hose

TEXTURES AND SENSATIONS
Popsicle juice running down one's arm, a dog's coarse fur, the slap of one's bangs against the forehead when jumping on the trampoline, sticky sweat, sitting against the hard boards of the back steps, the prickle of grass on the feet, the tickle of an insect crawling over one's arm, the kiss of sun against the skin, a sharp rock hidden in the grass, clothes sticking to one's back in the

summer heat, a chill on one's skin once the sun goes down, the velvety smoothness of a rose petal, the spray of the water hose on a hot day, cool garden soil clinging to one's fingers

POSSIBLE SOURCES OF CONFLICT

Noisy or snooping neighbors

A property dispute (a neighbor's tree dropping rotten fruit into one's yard, fence lines cutting into one's property, etc.)

Being a hoarder or living next to one

Loud parties that go on all night

A fence or shed collapsing

Tree damage after a storm

An unsafe tree house

A neighbor's child falling out of a tree house and suffering injury

Finding boot prints near the windows that don't belong to anyone in the family

The family pet escaping through an open gate during a child's birthday party

PEOPLE COMMONLY FOUND HERE

Friends and neighbors, gas or electric meter readers, party guests, property owners and their family, prowlers

RELATED SETTINGS THAT MAY TIE IN WITH THIS ONE

Birthday party (42), flower garden (52), outhouse (78), patio deck (80), tool shed (88), tree house (92), vegetable patch (96), workshop (102)

SETTING NOTES AND TIPS

Climate and location are big factors when it comes to a backyard. Some areas are suitable to greenery, while others are more arid, meaning only the hardiest plants can grow. Backyards often reflect their owners. Well-tended yards likely indicate people who live a balanced life, enjoying the outdoors and taking pride in their home. Neglected yards that are patchy or overgrown most likely belong to people who do not place the same value on their outdoor space or who are unable, for whatever reason, to deal with the upkeep. Some people use their backyards for social activities and family time while others use it as a dumping ground for broken housewares and half-finished projects. Use the backyard in your scene to characterize house occupants and set the mood for the scene.

SETTING DESCRIPTION EXAMPLE

Mia's flashlight beam shot here and there, slashing the night like a light saber as she searched for kids to tag. A low-hanging branch knocked her party hat loose and she pulled it off. The band snapped so loud, she barely heard the giggle near the hydrangeas. Mia clicked off her light, smacked a mosquito, and crept through the grass. As she closed in on the gangly flower bush, she squeezed a hand over her mouth, stifling her own giggle.

    Techniques and Devices Used: Multisensory descriptions, simile

    Resulting Effects: Reinforcing emotion

BASEMENT

SIGHTS

Worn wooden steps descending into the dark, a cement floor with mildew cracks snaking across it, a rusty floor drain, a bare bulb with a pull string, an electrical panel board, a scratched washing machine and dryer sitting against the wall, a trash can full of old dryer sheets and colorful lint clumps, a shelf holding laundry soap and stain removers, small grimy windows with dead flies on the sill, old boxes and storage items (decorations, keepsakes, books, clothing, and collectibles), bins for recycling, ugly mismatched furniture waiting to be refurbished or repaired, utility shelves (laden with food cans, preserves, cases of lightbulbs, toilet paper, paper towels, and other bulk household supplies), a laundry tub or sink, a pile of rags, shadowy corners behind piles of boxes, a jumbled row of paint cans, spiders spinning webs in the corners or crawling into the floor drain, bare beams and fuzzy insulation, a grungy mat placed in front of the washer and dryer, a furnace and clunky hot water tank, old rolls of extra carpet or linoleum from past home repair jobs, an electrical box, pipes running across the open ceiling, dust and dirt, damp spots on the walls, mold, broken lamps, storage cupboards, an ironing board, boxes of old photos, camping gear and sporting equipment, a children's play area (toys, a rug, a giant cardboard box fort, an easel and painting supplies, remote control cars lying on the cement)

SOUNDS

The murmur of voices and footsteps from overhead, zippers clinking against metal inside the dryer, a chugging washing machine, creaky steps, the raspy noise of a cardboard box being dragged across the floor, the click and thump of a furnace pilot light catching, the ticking of cooling metal as the furnace shuts off, gurgles of water in the pipes when someone flushes a toilet above, unidentifiable scratching noises and creaks, the groan of a shifting wooden beam, the dryer's buzzer going off, the slam of a dryer door or washer lid, the fast thump of footsteps up the stairs once the light is shut off, moths flapping around the bare lightbulb

SMELLS

Musty air, mold and mildew, scented dryer sheets and laundry soap, bleach, cleaners and supplies, hot clothing fresh from the dryer, damp clothes from the laundry, wet boxes, rot, an ozone-like tang from metal and cement, a foul odor coming from the drainage grate

TASTES

Some settings have no specific tastes associated with them beyond what the character might bring into the scene (chewing gum, mints, lipstick, cigarettes, etc.). For scenes like these, where specific tastes are sparse, it would be best to stick to descriptors from the other four senses.

TEXTURES AND SENSATIONS

Running a hand along the cold wall for balance on the stairs, the slight give of an old step, a shaky banister, the thin string of the lightbulb cord, bumping into boxes, dusty cardboard, the weight of a box or other item as one carts it up or down the stairs, the heaviness of a full basket of clean laundry, dust sifting into one's face when someone pulls something off a high shelf, warm laundry being folded, the clammy chill of wet laundry, cold air on the skin, a cold cement wall, shuffling one's feet in the dark so as not to bump into anything, the tickle of a hanging spiderweb, itchy insulation on one's skin, dust and grit under one's bare feet, swiping spilled laundry detergent granules off the washer

POSSIBLE SOURCES OF CONFLICT
Fears of the dark and a lightbulb burning out
Being trapped when a door with a sticky lock closes
Having to hide from intruders or an angry older sibling after a prank goes wrong
The washing machine overflowing
Finding a trapped animal or rodent that has made the basement its home
The sewer backing up
A pipe bursting right above the electrical box
Huddling in the dark as a tornado or storm shakes the house
Going to retrieve a cherished item from the basement only to find one's spouse has tossed it
A valuable collection being ruined by an unnoticed leak or a mold issue
Cracks in the foundation that threaten the house's stability

PEOPLE COMMONLY FOUND HERE
Homeowners, repairmen

RELATED SETTINGS THAT MAY TIE IN WITH THIS ONE
Attic (34), root cellar (82), secret passageway (84), workshop (102)

SETTING NOTES AND TIPS
A basement can be creepy or homey; it's all up to you. Many people use this room as a recreation space, not just for storage. Still, most basements—especially unfinished ones with unlit crawlspaces—have unusual nooks and crannies, making them excellent spots to hide things.

SETTING DESCRIPTION EXAMPLE
I hit the switch at the top of the stairs but nothing happened. Dad yelled at me to hurry up, that the toolbox was right under the shelf with all of Mom's canned fruit. I could picture it in my mind, just a few steps into the darkness at the bottom of the stairs. I swallowed and started down the creaky steps, trying not to think about how the sloshing, burping washing machine sounded like a monster enjoying a tasty meal.

Techniques and Devices Used: Multisensory descriptions, personification, simile
Resulting Effects: Establishing mood, tension and conflict

BATHROOM

SIGHTS
A narrow doorway, matching glazed fixtures (toilet, shower, tub, sink), a colorful shower curtain, a sink and countertop, mirrors, a medicine cabinet, cupboards or a shelving unit with rolled-up or stacked towels, a towel bar and door hook for robes, matching soap and lotion dispensers, clear glass jars holding makeup pads and cotton balls, a dented toothpaste tube with crusty bits leaking out of the cap, different colored toothbrushes in a cup on the counter, smears of dried soap or toothpaste froth on the faucet, fingerprint smudges on the mirror, hair curls in the sink, toothpaste spots on the mirror, cutesy wall decorations (popular sayings about home and family, pictures of flowers or nature, a collection of seashells), a floor rug pocked with white fluff, a can of deodorizer by the toilet, a dusty old candle that no one uses, a drawer full of makeup and hair products, a toilet paper roller, a plunger, a stack of magazines on the back of the toilet, a blow dryer on a wall stand, a round makeup mirror, a mouthwash bottle, steamy mirrors and condensation-streaked walls after showering, hairbrushes and combs, razors, a bathroom scale in the corner, discolored grout around the tub, dusty floorboards and grunge around the bottom of the toilet, hairballs collecting in the corners, stray clothing kicked against the walls

SOUNDS
Water running, a toilet flushing, someone singing in the shower, the burp of a mostly empty shampoo bottle, coughing, nose blowing, spitting after brushing one's teeth, the drag of shower curtain rings on metal as one pulls the curtain back, the squeak of a shower door opening or closing, pipes shaking and gurgling in the wall, water from a turned-off shower dripping onto wet tile, a damp towel falling to the floor, kids banging on the door or yelling through it, the squeak of a tap being shut off, drawers opening and closing, the snip of nail clippers, the spritz of hairspray, a noisy blow dryer, a cat or dog scratching at the bottom of the door wanting to come in

SMELLS
Shampoo, body spray, air freshener, astringent cleaners, hairspray, mildewed towels and mats, perfume, unpleasant bathroom odors

TASTES
Toothpaste, water, harsh mouthwash, mint-flavored dental floss, accidental spritzes of bitter hairspray

TEXTURES AND SENSATIONS
Soft towels, creamy soap and lather on one's skin, a fluffy mat underfoot, cold shower tile, water gradually going from cold to hot, thick and steamy shower air, heat that reddens one's skin, the prickle of goose bumps, the careful scrape of a razor blade across the skin, being immersed in a hot bath, lather sliding down one's back as one rinses off, greasy hair conditioner, the pull and painful snag of the hairbrush, sticky hair gel, water dripping down one's neck, smoothing lotion or oil over one's skin, the sting of a cut while shaving, papery tissues, hot pain caused by a blow dryer as it accidentally heats up one's necklace

POSSIBLE SOURCES OF CONFLICT
Slipping in the shower
An overflowing toilet
Losing an earring down the drain
Getting caught snooping through someone's medicine cabinet
Running out of toilet paper
A door that doesn't lock in a house full of people
Gastrointestinal issues caused by food poisoning or allergies (especially at someone else's house)
A bathroom window that looks directly into a neighbor's house
A bathtub that won't hold water
A botched home hair color or haircut
Not having enough time to get ready
Running out of makeup or hair items while preparing for an important event
A hot water tank blowing mid-shower
Messy roommates who refuse to take a turn cleaning the bathroom
Walking in on someone because one believed the bathroom was unoccupied
An accidental drowning (children left unattended, an adult passing out in the tub)

PEOPLE COMMONLY FOUND HERE
Homeowners and their families, invited guests, plumbers

RELATED SETTINGS THAT MAY TIE IN WITH THIS ONE
Child's bedroom (50), teenager's bedroom (86)

SETTING NOTES AND TIPS
Bathrooms are great places to show personality. Militarily neat or a collage of hair, makeup and grunge, these rooms can reveal the inner landscape of your character to readers. Keep in mind, though, that a powder room frequently used by guests may look much different than one's own personal bathroom.

SETTING DESCRIPTION EXAMPLE
I shook my hands in the sink and glanced about for a hand towel. Bright pink and embellished with stitched shells and lace, it dangled from a fragile brass stand. Just past it, two matching full-sized towels hung from dainty hooks on the door. I grabbed the hand towel and my gaze wandered, taking in the rest of the room. Doilies and potpourri bowls, flowers stencilled around the mirror, pink cherub-shaped soaps in a basket—wow. Did a Martha Stewart ad throw up in here?
    Techniques and Devices Used: Hyperbole, simile
    Resulting Effect: Characterization

BIRTHDAY PARTY

SIGHTS
A driveway filled with cars, balloons tied to a mailbox, streamers taped to the walls and dangling from lights, party hats, confetti scattered across tables, brightly wrapped presents with bows, colorful envelopes, gift bags sprouting tissue paper, theme-based paper products and tablecloths, a banner, birthday cake, cookies and brownies, bowls and platters of snack foods (chips, pretzels, bite-sized fruit, carrot sticks, cubes of cheese, crackers), a bounce house in the backyard, water or sprinkler toys, a piñata, doors standing open, kids running in and out, scattered toys, light shining from the TV in the background, kids dancing, parents chatting and eating, crumpled wrapping paper and open boxes strewn about, bows stuck to someone's head or clothing, an overflowing garbage can, plates of half-eaten cake and melted ice cream left on counters, a messy kitchen (empty food containers, serving utensils on the counter, food spills, half-empty juice boxes or water bottles, dirty dishes in the sink or piled up to be loaded into the dishwasher), dirty handprints on glass doors, a cooler on the floor surrounded by water spatters and ice cube puddles, plastic cups with names written on them in marker, bits of trash on the floor (straw wrappers, pieces of torn wrapping paper, cookie crumbs, a crushed chip), decorations fluttering in the breeze, kids with cake mouths and parents swooping in with napkins to clean them up

SOUNDS
A ringing doorbell, kids shouting out a welcome, kids laughing, parents talking, doors slamming, pounding feet, noisemakers and whistles, the fluttering of paper decorations, blaring music and TV noise, shrieks from outside in the backyard, kids arguing over toys and games, voices singing, candles being blown out, kids talking with their mouths full, the scrape of plastic forks on paper plates, tearing paper, exclamations as presents are opened, the whir of the bounce house machinery, electronic toy noises, a stick smacking the piñata, cheers when the piñata breaks and candy rains down, competing voices during a party game, people talking in helium voices, balloons popping, kids crying and protesting at departure time

SMELLS
Cake and cookies baking, just-cleaned floors, scented candles or air fresheners, other specific house smells (cigarette smoke, dog or cat, potpourri), sweaty children, coffee, a match being struck, extinguished candles

TASTES
Too-sweet icing, moist or dry birthday cake and other desserts, salty chips, candy from gift bags, ice cream, waxy drink cups, juice, water, soda, coffee, the plastic taste of an inedible cake topper

TEXTURES AND SENSATIONS
A breeze from open doors and windows, a blast of cool or hot air from the air conditioning or heat, hard plastic dishware, a cake server sinking into a new cake, sticky icing, cool drinks, cake crumbs on the table, soft melting ice cream, rubbery balloons, the scattered paper feel of confetti, an elastic party hat band biting into one's neck, a hat crookedly balanced on the head, shaking a gift to try and guess what's inside, glossy wrapping paper, melting ice around the drinks cooler,

the contraction of a juice box as the drink is sucked out, condensation on a water bottle, being bumped by excited children

POSSIBLE SOURCES OF CONFLICT
Children being injured or having allergic reactions to the food
Kids fighting over toys
Hurt feelings from people who weren't invited
Financial strain caused by an extravagant party
Spoiled kids upset over the gifts, party events, food, or treat bags
Bullying between peers
A car being dented or dinged by a stray ball or bicycle
Other parents upset by goings-on at the party (parents smoking or drinking, an inappropriate movie being shown)
Gossipy parents who rip one another down or spill secrets about others
A collapsing bounce house
A miscalculation that results in too few gift bags
An entertainer showing up who is creepy, unprofessional, or behaves in a way that is unsuitable

PEOPLE COMMONLY FOUND HERE
Children, entertainers (clowns, princesses, pirates, magicians, celebrity look-alikes), parents, relatives and family friends

RELATED SETTINGS THAT MAY TIE IN WITH THIS ONE
Rural Volume: Backyard (36), child's bedroom (50), kitchen (66), patio deck (80), tree house (92)
Urban Volume: Bakery (136)

SETTING NOTES AND TIPS
Anyone with a child knows that there's no longer a standard for kids' birthday parties. They can take place at home or at a public venue like a playground, bowling alley, movie theater, or amusement park. There might be five guests or fifty. The party can be themed and planned as thoroughly as a wedding or it could be a simple, whatever-goes affair. The event should in some way reflect the birthday boy or girl, but, sadly, it often ends up saying much more about the person throwing it.

SETTING DESCRIPTION EXAMPLE
Lightning forked the sky, sending wet kids scrambling out of the pool and into the house. Thunder boomed and the girls screamed, throwing water every which way. The streamers sagged. Water pooled in half-a-dozen places on the hardwood floor. I racked my brain for a way to salvage Annie's party while she stared into the lowering sky, her palms pressed to the window trickling pool water tears.
Techniques and Devices Used: Multisensory descriptions, weather
Resulting Effects: Establishing mood, reinforcing emotion

BLOCK PARTY

SIGHTS
Houses sitting side-by-side or curved around a cul-de-sac, cement sidewalks, balloons tied to mailboxes, barricades and cones set up to stop traffic, tables lining the street holding casserole dishes and crock pots, food in warming trays, a grill with hamburgers and hot dogs cooking, a barbeque smoker sending tendrils of heat shimmering into the air, ears of corn boiling in a tall pot, coolers brimming with drinks (sodas, water bottles, beer, drink pouches for the kids), ice melting into puddles on the ground, people eating off paper plates, garbage cans at periodic intervals, neighbors visiting (standing around and chatting, sitting on hay bales or lawn chairs, lined up to get food), families sharing a blanket on the grass, kids playing ball in the street or riding scooters and bicycles, a bounce house, a game of pick-up around a neighbor's basketball hoop, a horseshoe pit, beanbag games, people coming in and out of houses, babies strapped into strollers or playing on the grass with their parents close by, leashed dogs panting in the heat, flies buzzing around the food

SOUNDS
Music playing from a sound system, laughter and voices, kids yelling, soda cans being opened, running footsteps, leaves and acorns being crunched underfoot, garbage being crumpled and thrown into a can, lost napkins fluttering along the sidewalk until the owner steps on them to stop them, tinfoil being folded back or removed from dishes, the hiss of a grill, doors slamming, the squeak of bicycle wheels, the wind in the trees, chairs scraping on the sidewalk, babies crying, horseshoes thumping into the grass, a football bouncing off the asphalt, dogs barking, a neighborhood organizer making announcements or thanking everyone for coming, tablecloths flapping in the breeze, flies and mosquitoes buzzing, an ice cream truck's musical jingle

SMELLS
Smoke from the grill, food cooking, sweaty kids, blooming flowers, hot pavement, food and drink, insect repellant, cigarettes, fresh-mown grass, hay, boiling corn, beer or onion breath

TASTES
Hamburgers, hot dogs, bratwurst, chicken wings, barbeque sauce, ketchup, chips, potato salad, macaroni salad, coleslaw, lasagna, casseroles, fruit salad, watermelon slices, lemonade, soda, water, coffee, beer, juice, brownies, cookies, cake, pie

TEXTURES AND SENSATIONS
Wind teasing the skin, heat from the sun, a warm plastic chair, the woven fabric of a folding lawn chair against the back of the legs, heaving oneself up and out of a chair that's low to the ground, a cold bottle or can in one's hand, wet drink containers, drips of icy water sliding down a wrist, stepping in dog poop or dropped food, sweating over the grill, a horseshoe's metal heft, a bumpy leather football, balancing a flimsy plastic plate of food on the lap, thin paper napkins, using a sanitary wipe to clean a child's face, slapping at a mosquito, neighbors who have a bit too much to drink and get "handsy"

POSSIBLE SOURCES OF CONFLICT
Spoiled food or allergic reactions
Children getting hurt (running too fast, burns from getting too close to a grill, falling down steps)
Insulting someone's cooking skills
Burning oneself on a grill
Getting brained with a horseshoe or football
A diaper explosion
Bad weather that ruins the event
Disagreeing with someone's parenting style
Marital discord displayed in a public fashion
People drinking too much and speaking too freely
A neighbor caught ogling someone else's wife
Neighborly disputes escalating thanks to alcohol
Banter turning sexual and going too far, angering a neighbor or a jealous spouse
A child wandering off
A child abduction
A rash of break-ins as opportunists take advantage of the event

PEOPLE COMMONLY FOUND HERE
Babies, bikers, children, couples, families, neighbors, people out walking their dogs, runners and joggers

RELATED SETTINGS THAT MAY TIE IN WITH THIS ONE
Rural Volume: Garage (54), patio deck (80)
Urban Volume: Small town street (120)

SETTING NOTES AND TIPS
Block parties can be thrown for an individual street, a neighborhood, or a town or city. They can take up the space in front of three houses or cover a city block. These parties may be informal, with people bringing their own food, drink, and chairs, or they might be highly organized, with catered food and live music. Because the weather is an important factor, these parties tend to happen in the spring or summer, once cold temperatures have safely passed.

SETTING DESCRIPTION EXAMPLE
The neighbors kept up a steady stream of chatter and Marcy nodded in the right places but where the heck were her kids? The twilight made it difficult to see; the street lamps hadn't come on yet and the lights from the houses were too far away to help. She smacked at a mosquito, then spotted Ben halfway up the Nelson's oak tree, his white shirt bright against the bark. That made it easy to find Matty at the tree's base, scrabbling for a low branch and getting ready to shriek at being left behind. Marcy relaxed back into the plastic chair and, one eye on the boys, turned her attention back to her neighbors.
Techniques and Devices Used: Contrast, light and shadow
Resulting Effects: Characterization, reinforcing emotion, tension and conflict

BOMB SHELTER

SIGHTS

Reinforced hatch entrances (a primary and an escape hatch) with blast-proof caps made from corrugated metal, a ladder descending into the bunker, a sparse decontamination area with shower and drain, a secure hatch to the main compartment that locks from inside, a small toilet with a hand pump or gravity feed, several sleeping bunks, a weapons storage area with locked cabinets, separate storage for ammunition and gun cleaning supplies, food and water lockers beneath the floor, storage niches holding blankets and clothing, a small living area with chairs, a kitchen (with a sink, cupboards, a microwave and fridge), a radio, drawers for personal items, medical supplies, a battery bank that is either solar- or generator-powered, plain corrugated metal walls, fold-up tables and chairs for space conservation, shelving units filled with canned items and packaged food, a climate-controlled air filtration unit, fans, tools, rope, pots and pans, games, books, cards, a TV and movie player, overhead lighting, people lying on the floor or in bunks, dirt clumps from shoes and boots on the floor, crying children, frightened faces, people whispering and pacing in small spaces, flickering lights

SOUNDS

Tinny echoes of voices, footsteps crossing the floor, metal cans being opened or moved around, the hiss of air circulation, the gurgle of running water, the toilet flushing, metallic and pressure echoes as hatch doors are secured, the snap of a secret storage area being opened, people breathing, a radio playing, children crying and parents attempting to console them, someone inventorying food and water, tools banging, the buzz of a spotty electricity connection

SMELLS

Canned air, metal, stale bodies and sweat, food, soap, gun oil and gunpowder

TASTES

Metallic water from the pipes, bottled water, tasteless packaged food rations, sweat, a sour mouth if one is unable to brush one's teeth

TEXTURES AND SENSATIONS

The bumpiness of corrugated metal walls, a thin mattress pad or hard floor to sleep on, thin blankets, cold tin cans, dirty clothing that chafes, greasy hair that itches, hot feet in shoes and boots, the splash of water over the skin in a shower or makeshift sponge bath in the sink, turning pages of a book that one's read many times over, flipping through a glossy magazine to see pictures of the outside world as it used to be, feet hitting the floor as one exercises in place, running a cloth over parts of a gun to clean it, disassembling and assembling one's rifle or handgun, too many people in a small space, fiddling with a radio knob in hopes of catching a broadcast

POSSIBLE SOURCES OF CONFLICT

The occupants getting cabin fever
Running out of food or water

Being in an enclosed space with people one does not like
Disagreements about when or if the hatch should be opened
Being unable to open the door
A serious illness that requires medication
Paranoia and PTSD
The shelter being damaged in the blast or emergency (blocking the ventilation, breaking a seal)

PEOPLE COMMONLY FOUND HERE

A combination of military personnel and civilians (if the shelter is owned and manned by the military), bomb shelter owners and their immediate families, possibly family or neighbors

RELATED SETTINGS THAT MAY TIE IN WITH THIS ONE

Underground storm shelter (94)

SETTING NOTES AND TIPS

Bomb shelters are usually placed deep underground, reinforced to withstand specific dangers (air raid bombings, chemical, biological or nuclear fallout) while providing what is needed to survive. The shelter described in this entry is professionally manufactured, but bomb shelters can be more hastily built or rudimentary in nature, with limited lighting, space, storage, air control, and filtration. Shelters may be civilian-built (often by those with military and engineering backgrounds) using metal, cement, tarps, wood supports, and earth, and can house either a single family or larger groups. Others are designed and built by the military to hold large forces or a combination of civilians and military personnel.

SETTING DESCRIPTION EXAMPLE

Wedged under a tiny metal table, Fiona clutched her sister close, stroking her hair. With each explosion, the room shook, and more tears tracked Lena's soot-covered cheeks. Her mom stood at the porthole door, shining a flashlight through its thick circle of glass. The beam jerked with each blast, and her hiccupping sobs echoed along the corrugated roof, loud and terrifying. Dad had promised he'd be right behind them. Where was he?

    Techniques and Devices Used: Multisensory descriptions

    Resulting Effects: Foreshadowing, reinforcing emotion, tension and conflict

CHICKEN COOP

SIGHTS
Weathered wood framing and chicken wire creating a yard enclosure, grass growing along the edges, a narrow door with a latch, a collection of fluffy chickens (crossing the yard in jerks and stops, digging holes, pecking for bugs and stray feed, eating grass, preening), weeds poking up through beaten earth, a dusting of wood shavings on the ground, rocks, a tin pan with multicolored seed and grain feed, a plastic water feeder, a board rising on a slant and leading to a raised platform and coop door, straw or wood shavings spilling out past the exit and onto the platform, enclosed nesting boxes, roosting poles, half-hidden eggs (brown, white, or tan) in the golden straw, dark bits of chicken poop lying on the plywood floor, air vents, a lightbulb heater in cold climates, a door slider to protect chickens at night and keep the coop insulated from wind

SOUNDS
Watery clucking and vocalizing, claws scratching against the ground, a fluttery ruffle as a chicken preens, the creak of a door hinge, a hook latch clinking as it's disengaged, the click of claws across plywood, wind sliding through the grass, a beak hitting a tin feeding pan, screeching that rises in pitch and frequency when chickens are anxious or a threat is nearby, a rooster's crowing, the soothing voice of someone collecting eggs or cleaning the coop, peripheral sounds (a dog barking, doors slamming, children running, voices coming from a nearby house, traffic), a loud scuffle between hens as the pecking order is established

SMELLS
Straw, dusty feed, stagnant water, dirt, chicken feces

TASTES
Dust in the air, straw fragments

TEXTURES AND SENSATIONS
Pebbly grain feed, uneven ground, rocks underfoot, the smoothness of a fresh egg, scratchy straw or wood shavings, grass tickling one's ankles, rain, a breeze fluttering one's clothing, a metal handle from a tray digging into one's palm when carrying feed or water, soft chicken feathers, the peck of a beak against one's hand or ankle, the weight of a few eggs in a pail or collected in a shirttail

POSSIBLE SOURCES OF CONFLICT
A wild animal accessing the coop
An angry neighbor poisoning the water supply or letting the chickens out
An especially cold winter
A hoarder owning chickens that have squalid living conditions and are prone to disease
Disgruntled suburb neighbors who petition the community to have the coop removed
Chickens that won't lay
Chickens digging their way out or otherwise going missing
Having a child or person on the property with a bird phobia

PEOPLE COMMONLY FOUND HERE

Customers purchasing farm fresh eggs, family members, neighbors, the coop's owners, visitors

RELATED SETTINGS THAT MAY TIE IN WITH THIS ONE

Backyard (36), barn (148), farm (160), farmer's market (162), vegetable patch (96)

SETTING NOTES AND TIPS

As more people grow interested in sustainable living, raising chickens has become a popular activity. No longer confined to country and farm life, backyard coops are springing up in suburbs and cities (where sanctioned). They range from rudimentary wooden and wire structures to designer coops. Some may have automated feeding and watering systems and be built from repurposed materials, ranging from an old greenhouse or shed to the rusted-out skeleton of a Volkswagen bug. Chicken enthusiasts may also choose to beautify their structures with bright paint, chicken name plaques, or trendy antique signs. Don't feel hemmed in when designing a coop; let it match the owner's personality.

SETTING DESCRIPTION EXAMPLE

I moved through the coop, working fast and listening hard. The wind whistled through the warped boards and hens scratched outside, but there was no sign of the rooster's rough cluck. I snatched eggs from nests. Didn't mean he wasn't there, though. You thought you were safe, then there he'd be, gurgling under his breath, head twitching, staring at you with those predator eyes. A squawk sounded from outside, and I jerked. Jeez, he gave me the creeps.

    Techniques and Devices Used: Light and shadow, weather

    Resulting Effects: Establishing mood, tension and conflict

CHILD'S BEDROOM

SIGHTS

A narrow bed, a dresser (holding medals, awards, trophies, and small collectible toys from fast food kids' meals), a desk with art supplies (pencils, pens, crayons in a jar, paper and doodles), a handheld gaming or music device, a wall shelf or bookcase holding books, a corkboard (pinned with drawings, a key chain collection, pictures, school programs), a scuffed backpack leaning against the wall, rumpled clothes on the floor, a closet (packed with dirty clothing, toys, and games), movie and cartoon posters pinned or taped to the wall, graphic T-shirts boasting cartoon characters or popular statements, a floor rug, balled-up socks hiding under the bed, sports equipment lying in a pile, a small window with curtains or blinds, a pet goldfish or hamster in a cage, an overflowing trash can, empty glasses and plates scattered about on surfaces, fingerprints and dirt smudges on the door and around light switches, a secret candy stash

Girl-centric: a stuffed animal collection displayed on a shelf or ledge, bins of dolls and clothing, sports equipment, nail polishes, hair bands, barrettes, a hairbrush, dress-up clothes, a brightly colored bedspread with matching pillow, pastel décor (curtains, wall paint, etc.), a vanity mirror, a collection of perfume or body sprays, sequined T-shirts in drawers, a jewelry box

Boy-centric: sports equipment, a bin full of Legos, collectible toy cars and remote control toys, a shelf full of action figures, water guns or cap guns, a mini basketball net on the back of the door, bedding and décor that is darker in color or follows a sports theme or iconic movie, several baseball hats, posters of celebrities (sports teams, athletes, superheroes from movies)

SOUNDS

Music, laughter, the tick of a wall clock, drawers opening and closing, the child talking out loud to him or herself, the bed creaking as one throws oneself onto it, digging through drawers, hangers swiping side to side in the closet, a ball bouncing against the floor, thumping and bumping as things are moved and knocked over, the *scritch* of pencils or crayons coloring in a picture, the scratch of a hamster's claws in a cage, singing or humming along with a favorite song

SMELLS

Dust, carpet, markers, crayons, dirty socks, sweat

TASTES

Snacks brought upstairs (a sandwich, chips, a granola bar, sweets), candy from a stash (gum, hard candy, chocolate bars), drinks (juice boxes, soda, milk)

TEXTURES AND SENSATIONS

The soft fur of a teddy bear, a fluffy warm comforter, the cold doorknob, bouncy bed springs that give when one flops onto the bed, a plush carpet or rug underfoot, the cold slick of polish sliding across a nail, a breeze sliding past fluttering curtains and brushing one's cheek, a brush or comb catching on knotted hair, yanking a T-shirt over one's head, the sharp jab of pain from hitting the edge of a desk or nightstand, a jarring thud after falling off the bed, sinking into a beanbag chair while reading a book, a firm wooden desk chair at a desk

POSSIBLE SOURCES OF CONFLICT
Siblings being in one's bedroom uninvited
Siblings touching or borrowing things without permission
Losing something treasured or borrowed
An argument with a playmate
Feeling threatened by a family member or friend
Having bad dreams
Being afraid of the dark
Overhearing arguments or phone calls where a secret is revealed
An item going missing after a friend was over
An ant infestation from sugary snacks shoved under the bed and forgotten
Being jarred awake and smelling smoke
Waking up to discover someone is in one's room in the dark
A tapping at the window that wakes one up
Hearing someone calling one's name but there's no one there

PEOPLE COMMONLY FOUND HERE
A cleaning lady, friends and siblings, parents, the owner of the bedroom

RELATED SETTINGS THAT MAY TIE IN WITH THIS ONE
Bathroom (40), teenager's bedroom (86)

SETTING NOTES AND TIPS
The gender suggestions in this entry are simply broad strokes for those needing some brainstorming help. It is important to remember that each character—boy or girl—is unique in regards to his or her interests, likes, and dislikes. The child's personality, not his or her gender, should dictate the room's décor. To set your child's room apart, think about collections they might keep that will speak to their interests, musical instruments they may like to play or other equipment that speaks to a talent or skill, and a secret space (a drawer, a hidden box) where they keep things that are the most special to them.

SETTING DESCRIPTION EXAMPLE
From the doorway, I watched my nephew sleep, relieved by how much more bearable his room was at night. With the window open to pull in a cool draft and shadows turning the piles of clothing, dirty glass collection, and overflowing trash can into vague lumps, I could almost pretend a vacuum had seen this space sometime in the last century. I loved my free-spirited sister, but I wished that cleanliness was a value she had chosen to instill in her child.

Techniques and Devices Used: Light and shadow, weather
Resulting Effects: Characterization, reinforcing emotion

FLOWER GARDEN

SIGHTS
Sunshine glancing off dew-bright leaves, bursts of color from other flowers (red roses, spiny-leaved yellow lilies, brown-eyed Susans, blazing stars, marigolds, cone flowers, sunflowers, lungwort, lavender), flowering trees and bushes (snowball-sized bursts of blue or white hydrangea, heavy purple cones of fragrant lilac), stepping stones hidden in the grass, meandering walkways, a park bench or set of Adirondack chairs on a small stone patio, climbing vines that enfold sheds and claim sheets of lattice, a water hose left out on the path, watering cans, bags of potting soil, a bucket of weeds that have been pulled and are starting to wilt, gardening gloves, a sprinkler gently misting the greenery and creating water rainbows, bees crawling across flower petals, beetles and ants meandering over the soil, spiders spinning webs between plants, small snakes, a fish pond, a bird bath, a rolling lawn, birdhouses with birds darting in and out, birdseed scattered beneath a feeder, empty sunflower seed husks, a papery wasp nest attached to the underside of the shed roof, bird poop, garden tools (a rake, pruning shears, shovel, gardening gloves, a lawn mower), fertilizer, trellises covered in flowers, moss, a water feature, a smattering of clover, painted rock gifts from one's children or grandchildren, dragonflies landing on sun-dappled leaves or hovering over a decorative pond

SOUNDS
The hiss of a running sprinkler, the rapid slicing of lawn mower blades, the snip of shears, the hum of bees, birdsong, skittering squirrels or mice, the flutter of wings as birds squawk over space in the bath or feeder, a hose splashing water on pavers, a screen door slamming on the porch, leaves shuddering during rainfall, a breeze rustling the leaves, a shovel blade scraping against rock while digging, the thump of a shovelful of dirt being dumped on the ground, flies buzzing, the whine of mosquitoes, a gardener humming or speaking softly to the plants, children playing nearby, a dog's panting, voices from a neighbor's yard, the tinkling of wind chimes

SMELLS
Sweet flower perfume, freshly mown grass, damp earth, the tang of ozone before or after a storm, warm earth, dust, kitchen scents wafting outside, smoke from a nearby fire pit

TASTES
Chewing on a stalk of grass, sucking on a popsicle on the steps, taking a drink from a glass of lemonade or water bottle before getting back to weeding, enjoying a bitter or sweet morning coffee on the garden bench

TEXTURES AND SENSATIONS
Satiny petals, crumbly earth, cold water leaking from the sprinkler or hose, the hot sun beating on one's neck while weeding and pruning, the coolness of a breeze in the shade, sweat gathering on one's brow, stiff gardening gloves, powdery dirt on one's palms, errant thorns catching one's flesh, knees pressing into the dirt while one weeds, the smoothness of a shovel handle, cradling the root system of a plant being moved, a shrub's rough bark, sticky sap from a cut branch or stem, dusty pollen

POSSIBLE SOURCES OF CONFLICT
Over-fertilizing or using the wrong kind, killing one's plants
A heat wave or drought that kills one's plants
An angry neighbor or enemy who destroys one's garden out of spite
An infestation of aphids
Being expected to carry on the legacy of gardening but secretly hating it
Having to care for someone else's garden (an elderly parent or grandparent) and having no time to care for one's own
Deer or other pests destroying one's efforts
A dog who insists on burying things in the garden or lying in the warm dirt
Water restrictions making it difficult to nurture one's garden
Always being one-upped by the next door neighbor's gardening efforts
An annoying neighbor who is always suggesting changes or telling one what to do to make the garden better

PEOPLE COMMONLY FOUND HERE
Children and other family members, landscape or lawn maintenance personnel, neighbors or visitors, the garden owner

RELATED SETTINGS THAT MAY TIE IN WITH THIS ONE
Backyard (36), greenhouse (56), tool shed (88), vegetable patch (96)

SETTING NOTES AND TIPS
Gardens provide an excellent opportunity to characterize and set the mood. A barren wasteland of clumped weeds, wizened bushes, and broken walkway slabs can paint a very lonely picture, whereas a well-tended, weed-plucked oasis gives readers a bounty of beauty that reinforces happiness and prosperity. Need to show your perfectionist and controlling protagonist without telling readers what he is? Consider what his garden might look like: carefully pruned symmetrical bushes, vines bound by wire so they grow a specific way, and color-coded flowers spaced at exact intervals along an immaculately swept pathway. A description like this might just do the trick.

SETTING DESCRIPTION EXAMPLE
I'd fled the house and all of its death sounds—the beep of the monitors, everyone talking in whispers—but it was no better out here. Even in spring, the flower garden was a brown wasteland: leafless branches, skeletal twigs, dead leaves for ground cover. A stale breeze stirred the detritus, filling the air with the smell of decay and providing the only noise. No insects hummed, not a single bird sang. Even the sound of my footsteps sank quietly into the dusty ground.
Techniques and Devices Used: Metaphor, seasons, symbolism, weather
Resulting Effects: Establishing mood, reinforcing emotion

GARAGE

SIGHTS
A concrete floor with kidney-shaped oil stains and meandering cracks, tire tracks, bits of gravel and pine needles scattered on the floor, muddy tracks, dust, a pegboard holding tools, rolls of orange extension cord hanging from nails on the wall, steps leading up to the house, rickety metal shelving, power tools (a drill, a circular saw, a sander), motor oil, tubs of nails, boxes containing old keepsakes or Christmas decorations, bottles of lubricants and additives, cans of paint and wood filler, a pair of bikes hanging from roof hooks, bins for recycling and bottle returns, garbage cans, bags of grass seed or fertilizer, ant traps, slug bait, wasp sprays, garden supplies stacked in a corner (shovels, a rake, shears, etc.), garbage bags filled with clothing to be given to charity, rubber boots lined up along a mat, toolboxes filled with household tools and gadgets, cans of screws and washers, a stack of winter or spare tires, a roll-up garage door, a garage door button and light switch, cupboards, a shop vacuum, sawhorses stacked up against the wall, a workbench, a car or truck parked on the cement pad, dead flies and wasps lying on the windowsill, handprints and scuff marks on the walls, spiderwebs in the corners, a bin full of colorful kids' toys (water guns, buckets and shovels, cars and trucks, remote control cars, sidewalk chalk), sporting equipment (basketballs, hockey sticks, a baseball glove, stray golf balls), jugs of pink or blue window washing fluid, an extra gas can, ladders clamped to the wall, a bike pump, wood stacked in a corner

SOUNDS
The clacking and grinding of the garage door opening or closing, a ripsaw slicing through wood (when the garage is being used as a workshop), the squeal from a power drill, hammering, a storage tub being dragged across a dirty floor, flies or wasps bumping the glass window, tools being tossed into a metal chest, footsteps scuffing the floor, car doors opening and closing, vehicles starting up, a motor pinging as the engine cools, footsteps on the stairs, music from a radio, voices, noise from the street (cars, kids playing, lawns being mowed), the swish of broom bristles against the floor during cleanup, a lawn mower roaring to life, a basketball being bounced on the cement, drawers opening and closing, a grunt as someone lifts a bike off its hooks, cardboard flaps being pulled back as one goes through boxes, a dustpan being banged against the trashcan, the hiss of bike tires being inflated

SMELLS
Motor oil, gas, grease, hot motors, sweat, dust, cold cement, fresh-cut grass, garbage that's starting to rot

TASTES
A cold beer (or coffee, pop, water) while one is working on a project, dust that's been stirred up, a lunch brought out from the kitchen

TEXTURES AND SENSATIONS
Powdery dust on one's fingers, a stiff rag used to wipe one's hands, slick grease, the cold steel of a wrench, a rubber tool grip, pain from blisters and scrapes, sweat gathering on the forehead and

clinging to one's neck, sneezing from dust in the air, vibrations from power tools, sweat sealing a pair of safety goggles to one's face, hair falling into one's eyes, lying on a mat or runner on the floor to work under a vehicle, the weight of a tool in the hand, splintery lumber, raspy sandpaper against the fingers, rubbing dirt off cans or bottles to read the labels, cold concrete under one's bare feet, rummaging through a tub to find the right screw or bolt, wind gusting in when the door opens, a burning hot engine or motor, squeezing into a narrow space to get what one wants, stretching and reaching for something on a high shelf

POSSIBLE SOURCES OF CONFLICT
A fire
Theft of a car from the garage
Accidentally hitting the garage door while backing out or pulling in
A broken garage door that can't be raised
Overhearing one's neighbors discuss something private
Kids not putting tools back where they belong
Scattered toys making navigation difficult
Poorly maintained tools that become dangerous
A chemical leak that damages special items (old mementoes, an expensive collection of comics)
A garage packed with so much clutter that it's causing friction in the family or neighborhood
Being attacked from behind and falling unconscious

PEOPLE COMMONLY FOUND HERE
Adults, children, family friends, neighbors

RELATED SETTINGS THAT MAY TIE IN WITH THIS ONE
Basement (38), tool shed (88), workshop (102)

SETTING NOTES AND TIPS
Garages can become a dumping ground for storage or a workshop for home projects. Some are even converted into workout rooms or man caves. So in your story, think about the interests of the homeowners and what use they might have for their garage. It might not even be used for its intended purpose of storing vehicles. A garage doesn't have to be just a garage; what it does and how it looks can say a lot about the people living in the house, so make choices that help characterize.

SETTING DESCRIPTION EXAMPLE
I flicked on the light switch and scanned the mounds of tomato cages, Christmas decorations, old tires, and bike parts. A spot of color caught my eye near a haphazard tower of old linoleum rolls, but no. It was just Ryan's old kite. Then I saw it on the far side of the garage, balanced on top of Dad's rusted golf clubs: my Super Soaker 9000. I blew out a breath. Now, how was I supposed to get it? This place was the Temple of Doom; I'd have to be Indiana Jones to make it across alive.

Techniques and Devices Used: Contrast, hyperbole, metaphor
Resulting Effects: Reinforcing emotion

GREENHOUSE

SIGHTS

A structure made of glass or of plastic sheeting on a wooden frame, seedling trays on wire racks with new shoots poking out, shelving units holding a variety of pots, a raised bed at floor level, herbs (basil, thyme, parsley, dill, tarragon), wooden counters with crumbles of potting soil, deep pots or long bins (for tomatoes, cucumbers, squash, peppers, zucchini), a watering can, hanging baskets full of strawberries and cherry tomatoes, a trowel, a bucket of pulled weeds, fertilizer, fruit flies and spiders crawling on the plastic, sun streaming through the clear roof and lighting up condensation beads on the walls, tags sticking out of pots to identify seedlings, yellow and white flowers on zucchini plants, bags of compost, a handheld broom and dustpan hanging off a peg, a silver kitchen bowl filled with harvested vegetables, intertwined vines running along the dirt, wide green leaves pressing against the plastic walls, a temperature gauge, coiled water hoses, dirt-stained gardening gloves on a wooden or metal tabletop, a bucket of water left out to boost humidity, a bin full of seed packets, water stains on the dirt or concrete floor, blooming flowers, aphids and ladybugs

SOUNDS

Rain tapping against the roof and walls of the greenhouse, the misting spray from a hose, flies buzzing, the wind shaking the walls or causing plastic to fluff and flap, the snip of scissors, the crackle of a dead leaf when it's stepped on, the snap of branches being pruned, outdoor sounds (wind in the trees, birds singing, kids playing in the yard, crickets chirping, bees buzzing), a pot being tapped against the counter to loosen the plant for transplanting, the thump of a full water can being set on the ground, a drippy hose, a trowel scraping the inside of a terracotta pot, potting soil being poured into a bin

SMELLS

Crisp and pungent tomato vines, clean and fragrant sweet herbs (basil, tarragon, sage, cilantro, etc.), sun-warmed soil, damp earth, mildew, humid air, fresh flower blossoms

TASTES

Lettuces, tomatoes, freshly picked berries, spicy peppers, juicy melons, crisp radishes, crunchy cucumbers

TEXTURES AND SENSATIONS

The prickly thickness of healthy squash leaves, warm wet soil, crumbly fertilizer, powdery bone meal, smooth peppers, the warmth of moist air on the skin, soil clinging to one's fingers, a ripe tomato skin with a slight give to it, the weight of shears in one's hand, water running off a leaf and dripping onto one's skin, a leaky nozzle sending a drizzle of cold water into one's gardening glove, the heaviness of a full watering can, the brush of leaves against bare skin, stiff gardening gloves encasing one's hands, the dry and papery feel of dead leaves, sharp thorns, being poked by a twig

POSSIBLE SOURCES OF CONFLICT

Hailstorms that damage or rip holes in the structure
Bugs and other destructive pests
Plants overheating or not getting enough water
An animal that gets into the greenhouse and digs up plants
Using fertilizers or chemicals that upset the soil chemistry
A late frost that damages plants
An exceptionally hot year where plants overheat

PEOPLE COMMONLY FOUND HERE

Family members, gardeners, neighbors tasked with watering on vacation

RELATED SETTINGS THAT MAY TIE IN WITH THIS ONE

Backyard (36), flower garden (52), tool shed (88), vegetable patch (96)

SETTING NOTES AND TIPS

Some greenhouses are simple structures of plastic stretched over a frame, while others are constructed of metal and heavy glass or hard plastic that allows light in and traps heat. More sophisticated greenhouses may have electricity to run a sprinkler system, heating mats, fans, grow lights, mist timers, and cooling units. Commercial greenhouses, of course, have all the bells and whistles, as well as staff to manage the plants and equipment. But the biggest determining factor in what kind of greenhouse you'll have is the character who owns it. Think about your character's gardening IQ before deciding how simple or complex the greenhouse will be. Location is also a factor. While most greenhouses are used to start plants growing before transplanting them outside, some plants remain within the greenhouse because it is a more suitable growing environment. If any of these plants require fertilization through bee pollination (squash, for example), this will need to be done by hand by the gardener.

SETTING DESCRIPTION EXAMPLE

Glen's love of geometry ruled pretty much every aspect of his life, and the greenhouse was no exception. Marigolds and pansies rose in peaks and valleys, forming chevrons along the back wall; thick bean vines climbed a diamond lattice; red leaf lettuce squatted in round pots, and the tomato plants marched down the middle of the space in a series of rectangular beds. The hose lay in a neat coil near Glen's garden gloves, which were splayed out in a fan—even the beads of condensation lined up on the plastic sheeting played along. I grinned, wondering who was nerdier, my brother for doing this in his greenhouse, or me for noticing his handiwork.

Techniques and Devices Used: Personification
Resulting Effects: Characterization

GROUP FOSTER HOME

SIGHTS
Simple furnishings, a whiteboard on the kitchen wall with assigned chores written on it, posted house rules, signs in various places to remind residents of usage rules, ragged books on the shelf left behind by other children, well-used toys and games, shared bedrooms (with bunk beds, a closet, and shared drawer space), duffle bags or luggage in the closet, rotating staff members supervising children and running the household, an occasional therapist or social worker visiting, locks on certain doors or cupboards, a large common room for meetings, a dining area with a long table for all the residents at mealtimes, older children taking turns cooking meals and helping with cleaning, shared bathrooms, older kids packing up to leave once they have aged out

SOUNDS
Music coming from behind closed bedroom doors, a staffer calling for lights out or reprimanding a child for a rule infraction, kids bullying other kids, arguments over what to watch on television, the scratch of pencils on paper during the homework hour, dishes clanging in the kitchen around mealtimes, newer kids crying at nighttime, kids avoiding pain by telling lies to one another and themselves about going back home or being adopted soon, angry outbursts and shouting, laughter, whispered conversations between roommates at bedtime, a knock on the door from a staffer when it's time to get up, the flick of a lighter as someone lights a cigarette in a hidden corner of the yard, drawers opening and shutting, a shower running, bedroom doors slamming, a car pulling into the driveway to take a child to a visit with parents or return him or her home

SMELLS
Meals being cooked in the kitchen (chicken, spaghetti, hamburgers, hot dogs, eggs, roast), coffee brewing, cleaning supplies, shampoo, cigarettes, pot, sweaty kids, old carpet

TASTES
Typical meals that can easily be adapted for a crowd (French toast, oatmeal, scrambled eggs, pancakes, sandwiches, spaghetti, hamburgers, hot dogs, casseroles, stews)

TEXTURES AND SENSATIONS
Stroking a cherished object from one's past for comfort (the soft fur of a teddy bear, the pilling fabric of a doll's skirt, the smooth picture frame of one's brother or sister at another home, the bumpy links of a bracelet given as a gift by one's parents in better times), the fraying edge of a collar or shirttail, clothing that pulls or pinches because it no longer fits well, a couch that has lost its support, hot and soapy dishwater, the prickle of grass beneath one's bare feet in the backyard, painful bruises, burns and cuts that flare with movement or at the rub of clothing

POSSIBLE SOURCES OF CONFLICT
Abusive or neglectful caregivers
Children acting out as a way to cope
Having one's possessions stolen

Being set up by an enemy and losing one's privileges
Medication changes or misdiagnoses that create further behavioral problems
Living with other kids who are violent or cruel
Trust issues; becoming jaded
Staff members that play favorites
Being separated from one's siblings
Stressful visits with one's biological parents
Having mixed feelings about returning home
Nightmares and PTSD
Dealing with stigma at school for being in the system
Struggling with a lack of privacy
Feeling unworthy and suffering low self-esteem
Being a target for bullies (because of one's clothes, having no family, etc.)
Wanting what others kids have (love, a family, nice clothes, family vacations and activities)

PEOPLE COMMONLY FOUND HERE
Family members, foster care children and teens, police officers, social workers, staff workers or a house parent, visiting psychologists,

RELATED SETTINGS THAT MAY TIE IN WITH THIS ONE
Bathroom (40), kitchen (66), living room (68)

SETTING NOTES AND TIPS
Group homes run the gamut. Some strive to create a healthy, happy environment for the children and work hard to break down walls built up through years of abuse or neglect. Some facilities encourage closeness, with staffers who offer children hugs if they want them while giving them a stable, safe place to live. Others are claustrophobic minefields: children lose privileges over the slightest infractions, access to everything—even food—is restricted and monitored, and little or no attempt is made to offer them love or stability beyond the basic necessities. It's a sad fact that both kinds of homes exist; whether the residence in your story will be supportive, abusive, or somewhere in between is up to you.

SETTING DESCRIPTION EXAMPLE
The new girl sobbed into her pillow, sounding like a toddler who'd just been left at preschool. Beverly sighed and counted the flashes of light that slid across the wall as cars drove past, glad she wasn't so soft anymore. Once upon a time that had been her, back when she was taken from her mom's apartment, back when she still thought she'd only be gone a week or so. After three years of being shuffled around, ignored, bullied, and abused, she understood that it was tears or survival. You couldn't have both. Beverly closed her eyes and rolled over, burrowing into the warm blanket. The new girl would figure it out eventually.

    Techniques and Devices Used: Multisensory descriptions, simile
    Resulting Effects: Characterization, hinting at backstory, reinforcing emotion

HALLOWEEN PARTY

SIGHTS
Pumpkin luminaries lining the sidewalk or driveway, a jack-o-lantern, spooky decorations (fake cobwebs, hanging bats and spiders spread across windows, tombstones, bones and dismembered body parts scattered across the lawn, smears of fake blood, ghouls and ghosts hanging from bushes and trees, skeletons and grim reapers decorating porches and doors), a bubbling cauldron of dry ice on a table, candlelight, a Halloween banner and paper posters of witches and black cats, strings of pumpkin or ghost lights, hay bales and fall flowers outside in the yard, balloons, dry ice, smoke from a smoke machine, strobe lights, black lights, streamers and cobwebs fluttering in the breeze, Halloween-themed food and drinks, black or orange plasticware, people in costumes, guests dancing and drinking

SOUNDS
The doorbell ringing as guests arrive, hosts calling out greetings, the door opening and closing, background music that plays iconic horror movie soundtracks or creepy noises (groans, screams, tombstones creaking open, ominous footsteps, owls hooting, the wind moaning), guests shrieking as a motion-activated decapitated hand rushes across the floor, laughter when they see a friend's costume, people greeting each other in character, guests talking, dance music, the rustle and crinkle of fabric costumes, beer and soda cans hissing open

SMELLS
Incense, scented candles, hairspray, face paint, the rubbery inside of a mask, food, dusty decorations

TASTES
Typical Halloween fare (candy corn, gummy worms, cookies, cake and cupcakes, sandwiches, pizza, chips and pretzels), homemade treats made to look like Halloween decorations (eyeballs, fingers, tombstones, spiders, ghosts, mummies, witch hats), alcoholic beverages, soda, water, punch with plastic bugs frozen into ice cubes floating in it

TEXTURES AND SENSATIONS
Hanging decorations brushing the top of one's head, the stiffness of a brand new costume, a costume that is too small or doesn't fit well in places, the too-tight strap of a hat or headpiece under the chin, chill October air on one's exposed skin, warmth from burning candles or a fire, the rush of adrenaline at being frightened by something, sitting on a scratchy hay bale, dry face paint that makes one's skin feel tight and cracked, an itchy wig, a hot costume that makes one sweat, trying to dance while holding props, trying to eat or drink without smearing one's makeup or face paint

POSSIBLE SOURCES OF CONFLICT
Showing up wearing the same costume as someone else
Showing up in costume and realizing that it's not a costume party

Pursuing someone who is interested in someone else

Drinking heavily despite being the designated driver

Discovering that one's designated driver is drunk

Getting caught in the rain and having one's costume ruined

Having an allergic reaction to one's makeup

Being targeted by a prankster

Tripping in the dim lighting

Candles lighting one's costume on fire

Having one's drink drugged

Feeling uncomfortable because everyone is in masks and it's difficult to know who they really are

Feeling stared at or observed but not being able to pinpoint who's doing it

Feeling insecure about one's costume after seeing everyone else's

Being separated from one's friends by someone one doesn't know well and feeling unsafe

Witnessing something uncomfortable (a neighbor kissing someone else's spouse, for example)

Seeing one's friends making bad choices and being unsure about intervening

Wearing a costume that people don't "get" or that causes offense

Damage or theft of property

Guests inviting others that one would rather not be there (an ex-partner, a rival, a loathed co-worker)

PEOPLE COMMONLY FOUND HERE
Caterers, delivery people, family members, party crashers, party hosts and guests

RELATED SETTINGS THAT MAY TIE IN WITH THIS ONE
Bathroom (40), kitchen (66), living room (68), man cave (70), patio deck (80)

SETTING NOTES AND TIPS
Halloween parties run the gamut from lighthearted and fun to dark and dirty. Everything's a little bit creepier this one day of the year, so a Halloween party is a great vehicle through which to up the tension and possible conflict for an unsuspecting character. Emboldened by a costume and mask, characters might also say or do things that are more outgoing and direct, or take risks in a way they normally might not.

SETTING DESCRIPTION EXAMPLE
Jason's pirate boots squeaked as he climbed the porch steps. Bats hung from the overhead beams and strings of cobwebs fluttered in the breeze. Laughter and excited voices leaked out the screened door, and inside, music boomed. A skeleton in a rocking chair had been placed under a red porch light, wearing a pink hair bow and several strands of Mardi Gras beads. Cute, but not exactly scary—and he'd expected Lisa to go all out after her big talk at work. He reached for the door handle and the skeleton screamed and lurched forward. Jason jumped back and then burst out laughing, clutching his chest. *Nice one, Lisa.*

Techniques and Devices Used: Contrast, multisensory descriptions, weather

Resulting Effects: Reinforcing emotion, tension and conflict

HOUSE FIRE

SIGHTS
Smoke drifting at the ceiling level and sliding under doors, billowing plumes darkening to sooty black as paint and other chemicals are consumed, flames licking the walls and sweeping across the ceiling, ropes of fire chewing through curtains, fire spreading across the floor in rippling sheets, windows bursting, roof beams caving in, brighter flashes as combustibles explode, timbers charring and blackening, a smoke haze coating the room, sparks drifting and swirling in the air drafts, ash drifting down, paint bubbling, bits of curtains crumbling, parts of the electrical system (wires, bulbs, sockets) flickering and then shorting out, patches of carpet melting, plastics shrinking and melting, wood warping, stair spindles turning into pillars of flame, metal becoming red hot, furniture transforming into beds of fire, a shower of sparks as a cabinet collapses, light fixtures falling from the ceiling, people crawling along the floor as they gasp for breath, firefighters with oxygen tanks strapped to their backs, water dousing flames, heavy-duty fire hoses (spraying, creating water vapor, snuffing out fire), plastic melting into liquid flame drops that stream down the object's surface, a flickering orange glow, the welcome silhouette of a firefighter striding through the clotted haze, blackened stumps of timber and furniture, shattered glass

SOUNDS
The crackle of flame, the *woof* sound as something catches fire quickly, plastics melting and dripping into hissing puddles, the creak and groan of timbers contracting, cries for help, the roof caving in, sounds made by someone trapped inside (banging on a door, shouting out a window, crying, gasping for breath, coughing uncontrollably), doors and stairs shifting, tables collapsing with a crash as the legs turn to charred stumps, exploding glass, the hiss and squeal of liquids turning to steam, firefighters smashing down the door and tromping through debris, bottles of liquid exploding, the fire alarm blaring, sirens outside wailing, axes cutting through walls, lights crashing to the floor or smashing through from the floor above, curtain rods clanging to the ground, screams, the pop of glass splintering inside picture frames

SMELLS
Smoke will pick up smells at different stages of burning. Walls and furniture will have a smoky campfire smell at first, while plastics will give off a sharp, chemical odor that burns the nose and throat. As the fire progresses, smells mingle and the air grows increasingly toxic, burning the lungs.

TASTES
Ash, thick phlegm, the occasional gulp of fresher air as one leans out a window

TEXTURES AND SENSATIONS
Stepping across uneven rubble, cutting one's feet on glass or wood splinters, painful burns, searing heat, palms that grow slick from popping blisters, the press of suffocating cotton as one holds a towel or shirt to the mouth and nose, wrapping shirts around one's hands to protect them, knees bruising as one crawls across the floor, knocking into furniture, smoke burning one's nose and throat, ramming a blocked door with a shoulder, stumbling or half-slipping down

stairs, the dead weight of an unconscious child in one's arms, the coolness of wet fabric as one wraps a loved one in wet towels or blankets, a raw throat and nose, wheezing breaths that rip at one's throat, clutching one's middle as one doubles over to cough, pounding weakly at a door, tears that douse one's soot-stained face with wetness, sweat that turns one's hands slippery, the heaviness of fatigue, pinpoint pains as sparks burrow into clothing, feeling faint as one begins to lose consciousness, slicing pain as one breaks a window and cuts one's skin

POSSIBLE SOURCES OF CONFLICT
Doorknobs too hot to touch or obstructions blocking the exit
A home renovation that supplies the fire with added fuel (flammable chemicals and accelerants)
Smoke inhalation making one weak and messing up one's vision
Fearful children or pets hiding during a fire
The fire breaking out when one has extra houseguests (relatives in town, a sleepover party)
Not knowing if everyone has gotten out safely
Having an occupant that is bedridden, such as an elderly parent or a family member with a serious illness
Diminished critical thinking skills and responses due to painkillers, a sleep aid, or alcohol
Guilt from being the one to accidentally start the fire
Learning that the fire was caused by arson

PEOPLE COMMONLY FOUND HERE
Firefighters, homeowners and their families, paramedics, police officers

RELATED SETTINGS THAT MAY TIE IN WITH THIS ONE
Urban Volume: Ambulance (254), condemned apartment building (50), fire station (64), run-down apartment (116)

SETTING NOTES AND TIPS
During a fire, smoke can obscure the landscape enough to make it difficult to navigate, even if one knows the area quite well. Smoke inhalation affects brain function, making memory recall and problem solving more difficult. This, along with poor visibility, can cause victims to be unable to find their way to safety, even if it is only steps away. Strength and will both factor into how a character fares against shifting smoke and debris blocking his path, but without help, his survival will depend on his ability to think quickly.

SETTING DESCRIPTION EXAMPLE
I pushed tight into the corner so the flames couldn't find me in the dark. Bear's hard plastic nose dug into my chest but I didn't let go. Across the room, the dolls on the shelf started to change, their curly hair shrinking into frizz and crumbling to dust. They stared at me, growing sadder and sadder as their smiles drooped and plastic tears dripped off their faces. Shaking, I breathed in Bear's cotton fur and pretended I was at Grandma's house hiding in the linen closet, waiting for her to find me.

    Techniques and Devices Used: Multisensory descriptions, personification
    Resulting Effects: Foreshadowing, reinforcing emotion, tension and conflict

HOUSE PARTY

SIGHTS

Inside: Packed hallways and rooms, people sitting on the stairs, beer cans and bottles left on tables, a blasting stereo, haze from cigarettes or pot, strung lights that shed colors across living room furniture, popcorn and chip fragments ground into the carpet, people forming a line to use the bathroom, people crowding onto couches and chairs or jumping chaotically to the music, groups standing around a pool table and cheering players on, snack bowls (chips, pretzels, popcorn) left on tables, steady traffic to the fridge in the kitchen or coolers in the garage, drink spills on the counters, a bag of ice sitting in the sink, discarded red plastic cups everywhere, girls sitting on the kitchen island, pizza boxes stacked on a counter or living room table, couples standing close together (flirting, arguing, making out, etc.), someone throwing up, a beer keg and funnel, empties piled in the sink, an overflowing trash can, someone making the rounds with a tray of colorful shooters or Jell-O shots, broken figurines or picture frames that have been knocked over, locked bedrooms that have been jimmied open

Outside: Puke on the lawn or in a bush, people smoking on the deck or in the backyard, cigarette butts mashed out on the walkway, someone passed out in a deck chair, couples making out in the shadows, partygoers stumbling out the front door, a bonfire, cars parked up and down the street, people sitting on the front step or hanging out in doorways, empty cups and beer cans littering the front steps, fights in the front yard, angry neighbors banging on the door, flashing lights from police cars, people rushing to leave

SOUNDS

Loud music, people (laughing, yelling over the music, crying, screaming, arguing), glass breaking, a smoke alarm going off, doors opening and closing, beer bottles on the fridge door clinking together every time it's opened, glasses thumping onto a tabletop, drunken whooping, the click of pool balls hitting each other and falling into pockets, cries of indignation as people are bumped and drinks are spilled, someone pounding on a bathroom door, the crunch of chips, slurping on beers and drinks, cell phones going off, people calling out for more beer, feet running up and down the steps, creaky spots in the floor, the TV blasting a hockey game, bowls of chips overturning, things being knocked over and smashed, horns honking outside, neighbors pounding on the door, police sirens, drunks (singing, hooting, swearing, falling down)

SMELLS

Spilled beer, a cloying mix of hair products and strong aftershave, alcohol, salty chips, popcorn fresh from the microwave, pizza, pot, cigarette smoke, vomit, sweat, beer breath

TASTES

Hard liquor (rum, whiskey, vodka, gin), pop, water, cigarettes, pot, gum, mints, chips, popcorn, pretzels, pizza, beer, coolers

TEXTURES AND SENSATIONS

Sticky counters, crunchy chips under foot, being shoved or jostled in a crowd, squeezing up a tightly packed stairway, an anonymous pinch or grope in a crowded room, the unwelcome embrace of a sweaty drunk, brushing against others as one dances in a crowded space, a cool beer cup against the palm, wet lips after taking a swig, a splash of beer spilling down the front of one's shirt, slipping on a spill in the kitchen, balancing on the edge of a chair or the armrest of a couch, salt from chips coating one's fingers, the shock of cold as one digs through a cooler, clinking shot glasses with someone, a pool cue sliding along fingers, fending off drunks, kissing, holding hands, cool grass on one's bare feet in the backyard, hot air against the skin as one sits around a bonfire, clothes sticking to skin, taking a drag of a cigarette or joint, the shock of cold liquid against an eyeball when using eye drops to clear redness, fumbling with a smooth doorknob in the bathroom, the hard linoleum or tile floor against one's knees as one barfs into the toilet, the sensation of dizziness or vertigo, prickly grass against the skin as one lies in the yard, falling into other people in giggling fits

POSSIBLE SOURCES OF CONFLICT
The police showing up or one's parents coming home
Theft, vandalism, or property damage
Drugs being sold, used, or put into someone's drink
Sexual assault
Fights breaking out between rivals
Drunks revealing secrets to others or saying something that can't be taken back
The party being crashed by an unwelcome group of people

PEOPLE COMMONLY FOUND HERE
Angry neighbors, parents arriving home early, partygoers, police, younger siblings

RELATED SETTINGS THAT MAY TIE IN WITH THIS ONE
Backyard (36), bathroom (40), kitchen (66), living room (68), patio deck (80)

SETTING NOTES AND TIPS
Parties are only as crazy and destructive as the people attending them. If the person throwing the party has friends who are generally respectful and restrained, events likely won't get too out of hand. If, however, one's friends are looking to really let loose or are indiscriminate with their invites, things can easily spiral out of control. Adding alcohol or drugs to the mix, wanting to fit in, or the desire to attract a specific person's attention can also lead to impaired judgment.

SETTING DESCRIPTION EXAMPLE
Greg's wide shoulders came in handy on the packed stairway, and Jenn followed closely in his wake before the gap around him closed. The air was tight and hot, flavored with the skunky odor of pot. Music shook the windowpanes and had her bouncing to the beat; by the time she reached the basement, she was full-on throwing down, shaking away the stress of Monday's finals, her broken curfew, and the fight with Allison. She'd deal with that crap tomorrow.

    Techniques and Devices Used: Multisensory descriptions
    Resulting Effects: Characterization, hinting at backstory, reinforcing emotion

KITCHEN

SIGHTS
Tile or patterned linoleum flooring, appliances (dishwasher, fridge, stove, microwave) in the standard colors (stainless steel, black, or white), a hanging rack with pots and pans dangling from it, appliances and dishware tucked away in cupboards (a blender, a toaster, a food processor, a can opener, plates, cups, cutlery, cookware, bake ware), frequently used items on the counter (a flowery ceramic jar with cooking implements poking out of it, a banged-up wooden block holding kitchen knives and shears, a set of canisters, brown-spotted bananas and apples in a fruit bowl, a coffeemaker perking a fresh pot), a shiny black-handled kettle on the stove, wooden chairs tucked around a well-used table covered with place mats, a vase of wilting flowers surrounded by orange pollen dust, herb pots soaking up light on a window ledge, a marked-up calendar on the fridge, a corkboard or dry-erase board with important items stuck to it (lunch menus, schedules, shopping lists, school reminders, coupons), a wet teabag left out on a spoon, spilled sugar or juice on a countertop, a greasy hood over the stovetop, a smelly garbage can crammed with trash because no one likes to empty it, dog dishes on a mat, a sink and faucet ringed with smudges and water droplets, flies, dirty dishes piled in the sink, cereal floating in a dish from breakfast, toast crumbs peppering the counter, pet hair and paw prints on the floor

SOUNDS
Bacon or oil sizzling in a pan, toast popping up, the whir of the fan over the stovetop, fresh coffee being ground, a microwave dinging, cooking timers going off, a fridge motor rumbling, the slosh and clank of a dishwasher, the grinding gargle of a garbage disposal, the gurgle and hiss of steam from the coffee maker, the shrill of a hot kettle, family members chatting and laughing, a knife chopping against a cutting board, eggs dropping into hot grease, the hiss of a pot boiling over, music or the TV playing in the background, a food processor grinding up food, cutlery clattering against the table or scraping a plate, the clink of glasses, the rumble of a can opener, the rattle of plastic wrap or tinfoil being pulled loose, a dog scratching at the door to be let out, a spoon tapping against a pot after stirring, the fridge door opening and closing, the rustling of chip bags being opened, squeaky pantry doors, chairs scraping over the floor, pot lids banging, the patter of cereal pouring into a bowl

SMELLS
Garlic wafting off tomato sauce, salty bacon frying in the pan, spices (basil, rosemary, curry powder, pepper, salt, fennel, cinnamon, pumpkin spice, ginger), yeasty bread rising in a pan, onions frying in butter, steam wafting up from a pot of boiling pasta, smoky burned toast, popcorn in the microwave, rotten food funk in the fridge, decomposing root vegetables in the pantry (potatoes, onions, turnips), garbage that needs to be taken out, a fragrant candle, the charred smell of burned steaks or sausage, cleaners and soap, musty cloths needing to be laundered, wet dogs rushing in from the rain

TASTES
Staple foods and drinks: fluffy pancakes drenched in maple syrup, cheesy lasagna, spicy stir-fries or curries, sweet fruit, vegetables bursting with freshness, mounds of sweetened whipped cream

on chocolate cake, gooey cookies pulled from the oven, bitter coffee, robust wines, an afternoon beer, herbal teas, ice cream, the metallic taste of a spoon in the mouth, buttery crackers right from the box, grilled meats, pastas, pulled pork on buns

TEXTURES AND SENSATIONS
Warm water rushing over rubber gloves while one washes the dishes, the softness of soap suds against the skin, sugar granules and crumbs from the floor sticking to one's bare feet, a smooth broom or vacuum handle in one's hand, condensation beading on a cold glass, steam rising from a recently run dishwasher, wet tea towels, a hot coffee mug, pain from a knife cut while one chops vegetables, stinging burns or a scalding, scrubbing at the stovetop with a sponge, the weight of metal cutlery, a cloth napkin against the lips, spongy dough, flour dusting one's fingers, warm dinner rolls, a burned tongue from a too-hot bite of food

POSSIBLE SOURCES OF CONFLICT
Teenagers who demolish a special dessert for their afternoon snack
Arguments at the dinner table
Appliances that break down or bad plumbing that causes water damage
A kitchen overtaken by clutter (paperwork, mail, homework supplies, gloves and hats, etc.)
A secret coming out at the dinner table

PEOPLE COMMONLY FOUND HERE
Extended family and friends, family members, neighbors popping by for a visit, repair technicians

RELATED SETTINGS THAT MAY TIE IN WITH THIS ONE
Living room (68)

SETTING NOTES AND TIPS
Because kitchens are often the heart of a home, they provide many opportunities to show (rather than tell) who lives there. By introducing clues that highlight dysfunctions, hint at backstory, and reveal the closeness or distance between family members, authors can easily use the kitchen to characterize the people who call it home.

SETTING DESCRIPTION EXAMPLE
The invite for tea couldn't have come at a better time; Dale and I had just finished pulling the last box off the moving truck and needed a break. My new neighbor led us to her kitchen, where my steps faltered. Plates crusted with last night's dinner were stacked next to a sink brimming with dirty dishes. The counter was a topographical map, its landforms made with globs of peanut butter and sticky smears of jelly. I winced with each crunching step—the floor might've been tiled with potato chips—but refused to look down. Instead, I smiled, sweeping crumbs off a chair as Donna poured tea into what I prayed were clean mugs.
    Techniques and Devices Used: Metaphor, multisensory descriptions
    Resulting Effects: Characterization, tension and conflict

LIVING ROOM

SIGHTS
Couches with colorful pillows, a TV on a stand or mounted to the wall, end tables holding lamps and coasters, a fireplace with a mantel, a recliner, an area rug on the floor, pictures and artwork on the walls, built-in shelves for books, toys scattered about, a pair of kicked-off shoes or slippers, a coffee table, throw blankets folded over the back of the sofa, half-empty glasses or beverage cans on the tables, windows framed by curtains or blinds to block out the light, living or artificial plants, speakers set into the walls and ceiling, an entertainment center (holding music and movie discs, board games, remotes, extra coasters, a DVD player, a gaming system, a stereo system), décor that matches the style of the inhabitants (vases, knickknacks, pictures in frames, family photos, artwork, scented candles, decorative bowls), unique or unusual items that indicate interests and values (an urn holding a family member's ashes, a framed flag from a fallen soldier's funeral, fossils and geode specimens under glass, masks purchased from different countries, trophies and medals, a collection of ceramic owls), a reading device or paperback book, a dog bed, a stack of magazines, a knitting basket with yarn and a half-completed project

SOUNDS
Voices from the television, music playing through a docking station or stereo system, the clank of a recliner closing or being opened, the squish of someone falling onto a sofa, people talking and laughing, family members arguing, the murmurs of conversations from another room, kitchen sounds (dishes clinking, food cooking, a fridge door closing), a phone ringing, footsteps clumping over hardwood floors or scuffing through soft carpets, rain thrumming against the roof, outside sounds drifting through an open window (kids playing in the backyard, a lawn mower, car doors slamming, traffic, sprinklers rotating, neighbors calling to one another, birds singing), the ring of a doorbell and a dog's reactive bark, lights clicking on, the rustling pages of a book or magazine, the air conditioning or heating unit thumping on, papers rustling in a cross breeze

SMELLS
Food cooking in the kitchen, rain, a fire burning in the fireplace, cigarette smoke, cologne and perfume, musty upholstery, garbage that needs to be taken out, sweaty kids, stale air, old carpet

TASTES
Meals being eaten in front of the television, takeout food, party foods (appetizers, pizza, wings, veggie platters, birthday cake, chips and salsa, desserts), beverages (water, soda, alcoholic drinks, juice, tea, coffee)

TEXTURES AND SENSATIONS
Smooth sofa upholstery, cheap leather sticking to one's skin, sinking into a cushy recliner, a fuzzy blanket over one's lap, the warmth of a fire, feeling in the dark for the right button on a remote, the rough stone of a fireplace hearth, smooth floors or plush carpeting under one's feet, a breeze brushing against one's skin from a fan or open window, pain at stepping on a stray block or dog toy, the comforting weight of a dog's head resting on one's foot, a cat purring in one's lap,

pushing back in a recliner to open it up, condensation on a glass of cold water, a warm mug in one's hands, breathing in the steam from a cup of coffee or hot cocoa

POSSIBLE SOURCES OF CONFLICT

Tension between family members
A burglary
Important items being misplaced (keys, a wallet, the remote, a cell phone)
A living room space that is too small for a large family
Having guests over and not having enough seating
Children roughhousing and knocking things over
Guests or relatives who overstay their welcome
Spills on the carpet or couch
Phone calls that bring bad news
A drunken guest spilling a glass of red wine and staining one's carpet
Power outages during a snowstorm or the heat of summer
Neighbors who drop by for a visit when one's living room is a mess
Entertaining guests only to discover the dog or cat has peed on the carpet

PEOPLE COMMONLY FOUND HERE

Contractors and repair technicians, family and friends, guests, neighbors, the homeowners

RELATED SETTINGS THAT MAY TIE IN WITH THIS ONE

Basement (38), kitchen (66), man cave (70)

SETTING NOTES AND TIPS

The living room of a home can have different purposes for different families. For some, it's the place where the family hangs out and spends time together. In other homes, it can be a very formal area, where guests are received and entertained. Still others might have multiple living rooms for various people, such as a rec room for one's kids and a man cave for adults. Knowing the purpose of the space and who primarily uses it will help you personalize it in a way that characterizes the residents and show the closeness (or distance) in their relationship.

SETTING DESCRIPTION EXAMPLE

The February wind rattled the crappy windows and blew icy snow against the panes. I could feel the cold creeping through the thin walls. Stacey brushed against me, tucking up her legs and pulling the thin blanket tighter around her shoulders. The threadbare couch sagged and creaked as I shifted my weight, putting my arm around her. I nuzzled her hair and she gave me a quick kiss before getting back to grading her papers. Sipping my coffee, I felt a little warmer—whether from the drink or Stacey's closeness, I don't know. With a sigh, I opened up my paperback. Maybe the spring would bring not only warmer weather, but a pay raise and a better place to live.

Techniques and Devices Used: Contrast, seasons
Resulting Effects: Hinting at backstory

MAN CAVE

SIGHTS
Sports paraphernalia (team jerseys on the wall, signed posters, beer glasses with team logos, signed balls or other collectables), a beer fridge, reclining chairs in front of a big screen TV (or multiple TVs), beer coasters and chip bowls on a coffee table, a dartboard, neon signs (a team logo or brand of beer), a poker table (with stacks of poker chips, cards, a card shuffler, chairs, a smoke haze from cheap cigars, highball glasses or beer bottles at players' elbows), a dimmer switch to control the lighting, leather couches to hold a crowd on game day, a minibar, a popcorn machine, "man-centric" wall signs (*Man Cave Ahead, Leafs Fans Welcome, Home is Where Your Harley is*), trophies on a shelf, animal heads mounted on the walls, a locked gun cabinet, framed pictures of the host engaged in various activities (fishing, hunting, camping with friends, crossing a finish line), freestanding table games (foosball, hockey, table tennis, pool)

SOUNDS
The doorbell ringing, the door opening and closing as guests come in, a sports announcer commentating on the TV, noisy applause at a play call, men cheering or criticizing a referee's decision, poker chips clinking as they're tossed on the pile, the shuffle of cards, laughter, swearing, lighthearted arguments, ice hitting the side of a highball glass, the hiss of a beer can opening, the groan of an old recliner opening up, the squeak of leather upholstery, burping, chip bags rustling, the buzz of a neon sign, the light slam of the minibar door being closed, noisemakers, cell phones going off, just-emptied shot glasses being slammed down on a coffee table

SMELLS
Yeasty beer, sweat, fried foods, chips, leather, gas

TASTES
Alcohol, beer, pop, energy drinks, pretzels, pepperoni, pulled pork sandwiches, popcorn, deep-fried snacks like corn dogs and chicken wings, pizza, chips and dip, chewing tobacco, cigars

TEXTURES AND SENSATIONS
The cushioned give of a well-padded reclining chair, the felt edge of a poker table against one's forearms, balancing on a stool, fighting with a tight screw-off bottle cap, stinging eyes from a haze of cigar smoke, spicy food burning one's throat, a cold glass against the palm, the ribbed edge of a poker chip, slick cards, the bumpy buttons on a TV remote, the weight of a plate laden with food, sharp darts, sticky fingers from eating finger foods, brushing shoulders on a crowded couch, stepping on spilled popcorn or chips

POSSIBLE SOURCES OF CONFLICT
Team rivalry getting out of hand
People drinking too much
Darts that go astray and damage the wall or furniture
Grousing or complaining about one's personal life and being overheard by family members

Messes or stains resulting from food or drinks
A friend voicing something that changes one's opinion of him
Having an uninvited friend show up at a gathering and feeling obligated to include them
Arguments over politics or other issues
A cigar being knocked out of someone's hand and burning a hole in the carpet
A discussion about infidelity and resulting internal conflict at a discovery

PEOPLE COMMONLY FOUND HERE
Family members, men and their friends

RELATED SETTINGS THAT MAY TIE IN WITH THIS ONE
Bathroom (40), living room (68)

SETTING NOTES AND TIPS
Man caves can be found in many different places in a home: in the basement, the attic, an unused bedroom, in a converted garage, or in a shed in the backyard. They may be big and sprawling or cramped and cozy, depending on the allotted space. It's also important to remember that man caves don't have to be sports-centric but instead will reflect the hobbies of the owner: hunting, fishing, cars, motorcycles, planes, etc. Like a bedroom, a man cave is more likely to reflect a mixture of interests.

SETTING DESCRIPTION EXAMPLE
Anna carried the tray of nachos to the coffee table where her husband and his friend watched the hockey game. They mumbled a thank you and started shoveling the gooey mess into their cavernous mouths. She was about to head upstairs when, as if by unwritten signal, the two started to rise from the couch in slow increments. On the screen, an Islanders' forward was skating toward Minnesota's goal. Bob and Mike froze, half-sitting, half-standing, chips midway to their mouths. The puck blasted between the goalie's legs. The buzzer sounded and the boys jumped up, cheering and slapping each other on the back, chip crumbs raining down on the carpet. Anna grimaced and went back upstairs. *Men.*
    Techniques and Devices Used: Multisensory descriptions
    Resulting Effects: Characterization

MANSION

SIGHTS

A perimeter fence or wall, a large lawn, manicured hedges and shrubs, a gated entrance, a security station, lots of lights, leafy trees, a long driveway that widens out or circles to the front entry, **a swimming pool** and spa, a gazebo, **tennis courts**, **a putting green**, **a multi-car garage** filled with expensive vehicles, **outdoor living spaces** for entertaining guests (comfortable outdoor lounging furniture, a gas-lit fire, a bar area, throw pillows, ambient lighting), **a flower garden**, **a conservatory or greenhouse**, **a guest house**, **staff quarters**, rooftop sitting areas, patios and balconies, statuary and fountains, **a large main building** partly covered in creeping ivy, an expansive entryway with double doors, high ceilings that are often painted or decorated, crown molding, curving stairways, chandeliers, expensive flooring (marble, stone, granite, slate, imported hardwood), spacious rooms, papered and textured wall accents, high windows, heavy curtains, expensive area rugs, high-end décor (stained glass windows, valuable paintings and artwork, custom lighting and window treatments, antiques), upholstered furniture made of heavy woods (walnut or oak) or metals (wrought iron), long hallways, large walk-in closets, multiple fireplaces, a bowling alley, a home theater, expensive electronics (televisions, a sound system, a security system), many bedrooms, a billiards room, a library, a home gym with top-of-the-line equipment, a dining hall, a wine cellar, a kitchen and well-stocked pantry, dumbwaiters or an elevator to transport food and equipment between floors, an indoor pool, a panic room

SOUNDS

Heavy gates swinging open, music and voices from the pool, the buzz and snip of landscaping tools, birds chirping, the splash of fountains, people noises (talking, laughing, walking, chatting on the phone), wind rustling the trees, cars driving in, doors opening and closing, the tapping of heels on walkways, televisions, phones ringing, dishes clattering, children running, the murmur of servers and staff, party noises, generic home noises

SMELLS

Fresh air smelling of the outdoors, cut grass, flowering plants, leather, firewood smoke, furniture polish, floor wax, fabric softener, potpourri and other artificial fragrances, food cooking in the kitchen, fresh-cut flowers, old books

TASTES

Food and drink, both average fare and more expensive offerings (caviar, lobster, prime rib, scotch, bourbon, port, champagne, fine wines)

TEXTURES AND SENSATIONS

Lush grass underfoot, warm pool water sliding over one's skin, working up a sweat in the gym or on the tennis court, climate-controlled air, plush carpets, slippery and cool silk or satin sheets, polished-smooth banisters, the textured fabric or leather cover of an old book, delicate crystal and china, linen napkins, cool marble and granite countertops, soft leather furniture, cushioned seats, textured upholstery, the weight of a crystal highball glass in one's hand, the smoothness of a pool cue sliding over one's hand, the plush quality of expensive towels and bathrobes

POSSIBLE SOURCES OF CONFLICT

Staff members jockeying for position or selling gossip to the press

Violence or sabotage from jealous family members

A sudden change of ownership after a death in the family

A structural weakness that threatens the entire mansion

Being sued by a guest who was injured on the grounds

Getting caught decorating with stolen goods

Discovery of an affair that causes a family rift

A family member dying under strange circumstances and being subject to the rumor mill

Sightings of a ghost or other paranormal activity on the older parts of the grounds

Finding a hidden passage or room and discovering old family secrets

Stress and financial strain from having to cover up a family member's indiscretions

Threats against the family over past business dealings

Covering up the owner's mental decline (due to Alzheimer's or dementia) to ward off financial instability in a family-run company

PEOPLE COMMONLY FOUND HERE

Butlers, caterers, chauffeurs, contractors, cooks, delivery men and women, family members, guests, interior designers, landscapers and maintenance workers, maids, nannies, private tutors, security guards

RELATED SETTINGS THAT MAY TIE IN WITH THIS ONE

Rural Volume: Boarding school (106), wine cellar (100)

Urban Volume: Ballroom (194), black-tie event (196), limousine (262), penthouse suite (104), yacht (286)

SETTING NOTES AND TIPS

While mansions are commonly associated with the rich and famous, many other people frequent them. Staff, friends, delivery people, contractors, and others will also make appearances in your story. Be sure to keep them in mind to provide contrast and a different perspective.

SETTING DESCRIPTION EXAMPLE

The driveway was so long and well lit, I was afraid an airplane might try and land on us. And once I saw my destination, I was kind of hoping one would. The white stucco walls of the mansion loomed six stories high, the many floodlights surrounding it casting a cold gleam over its surface. Turrets rose from its corners to puncture the night. I could imagine guards with military-grade gear standing at the windows, just waiting for the chance to take out anyone who posed a threat. I shifted in my seat and tried to look insignificant. With that monstrosity looming ever nearer, it wasn't that hard.

Techniques and Devices Used: Contrast, metaphor, simile

Resulting Effects: Establishing mood, reinforcing emotion

MOTOR HOME

SIGHTS
The driver's area with swivel driver and passenger seats, **a lounge area** (a couch, comfy chairs, pillows, end tables that pull out from the wall, a TV), **a dining area** (a permanent or a pullout table, chairs or bench seating), **a kitchenette** (cabinetry, cooktop, dishwasher, sink, microwave, refrigerator and mini freezer), windows with curtains or pull-down shades, mosquito screens, overhead storage, **a bathroom** with a standing shower, **a bedroom** (a fixed bed or bunks that fold down, linens, pillows, a closet, storage drawers) that is divided from the rest of the motor home by a curtain or pocket door, a stacking washer and dryer, tile floors, skylights, toys on the floor, a laptop on the dining table, dishes in the sink, damp towels hanging over seat backs to dry, rumpled bed linens, meals being prepped in the kitchenette, scenic views out the windows, crumbs on the floor, water droplets on the tabletop, clothes piled in laundry baskets, a map of hiking trails spread out on a table, wet swimsuits hanging in the shower

SOUNDS
Music playing on the radio, TV noises, the wheels thumping over bumps or ruts in the road, the hum of the engine, traffic noises (horns honking, cars speeding by, sirens), hydraulics groaning as outside awnings are extended, items falling over in cabinets or toppling to the floor, shades being pulled down, windows creaking open, drawers sliding shut, dishes rattling in cabinets, beverages being poured, ice tinkling in glasses, people chatting and playing cards on rainy days, kids laughing or crying, a fly buzzing, curtains sliding along a rod, electronic sounds from a game being played on a tablet or phone, phones ringing, toilets flushing, the shower running, wind whooshing through the windows and hatch, rural sounds coming through the open windows at night (insects chirping, birds singing, the wind in the trees), adults arguing over which way to go

SMELLS
Leather, food cooking, fresh air, coffee, rain, exhaust, sweaty kids, stinky shoes, garbage, campfire smoke wafting in open windows

TASTES
Fast food, meals prepared in the motor home kitchen, snacks, food cooked over a campfire outside (hot dogs, s'mores, popcorn)

TEXTURES AND SENSATIONS
Swaying with the motor home's motion, catching items as they slide or jump on the tabletop, carsickness, a soft couch or bed, feeling claustrophobic in a cluttered motor home where there isn't enough space, the breeze from an open window tousling one's hair, excitement over one's trip or vacation, carefully pouring a drink in the moving vehicle, tripping over toys on the floor, squeezing into a small bed, the nip of mosquitoes, banging one's head on an open cabinet door, bumping one's hip into a counter, swiveling in a bucket seat, a warm shower, sun hot on one's arm as it streams through the window

POSSIBLE SOURCES OF CONFLICT

Breaking down on a long trip

A toilet that stops working or backs up

Too many people in a too-small space

Noises or activities that distract the driver

Difficulty finding a parking space

Spills, breakage, or items falling out of a cabinet and hitting passengers

Someone hogging all the hot water

Getting into an accident

Discovering problems with one's rental after the trip has started (a broken awning, a shower that doesn't function)

Picking up a hitchhiker and being car-jacked

Items falling out or being stolen from an unsecured outer storage space

Assuming one's teen is sleeping when they've actually snuck out to meet friends

Unpleasant smells in the small space

Kids or teens that do nothing but complain about the trip

Struggling with a lack of privacy

Driving under a low bridge with height restrictions that one's motor home does not meet

PEOPLE COMMONLY FOUND HERE

Families, retirees

RELATED SETTINGS THAT MAY TIE IN WITH THIS ONE

Rural Volume: Campsite (152), country road (156)

Urban Volume: Truck stop (284)

SETTING NOTES AND TIPS

Motor homes come in many sizes and may be anything from ultra-luxury to a squalid box on wheels. The larger vehicles are quite spacious with clearly delineated rooms, full-sized beds, complete kitchens, and ample storage space. Older models will have fewer bells and whistles and a worn look. Smaller motorhomes can be very compact with fewer amenities. Because the level of comfort will depend on the purchase or rental price, you have a lot of options when it comes to choosing this vehicle for your hero. A motorhome's mobility also allows authors to incorporate a variety of settings into the story that might not be otherwise possible.

SETTING DESCRIPTION EXAMPLE

The keys jingled in Sarah's hand as she dodged the raindrops and ran up the steps to see her new home. There was the little table where she'd be eating. Next to it, the tiny kitchenette didn't exactly gleam but it was functional, and she breathed in the imagined smells of the meals she'd cook there: chili, homemade pizza, grilled cheese. Outside, rain thrummed against the roof and drenched the windows, but here, it was dry and cozy as a rabbit's den. A smile quirked Sarah's lips. It was small, but it was hers, and without a mortgage, she'd be able to pay off her medical bills in no time.

Techniques and Devices Used: Multisensory descriptions, simile, weather

Resulting Effects: Characterization, hinting at backstory, reinforcing emotion

NURSERY

SIGHTS
Light streaming through a window, dim light shining from a lamp, a crib with a colorful mobile hanging overhead, a dresser, a diaper pail, a changing table with supplies (diapers, wipes, baby powder, diaper rash ointment, hand sanitizer), a clothes hamper, a nightlight casting a soft glow, a rocking chair, a baby swing, the baby's name on a plaque or spelled out in decorative letters on the wall, stuffed animals, a music player or white noise machine, walls painted in soft colors and hung with artwork, picture frames with family photos, knickknacks, a baby monitor, burp cloths, safety nail clippers, a comb and brush set, blankets and quilts, pacifiers, rattles, teething rings, board or cloth books, a toy box, baby clothes (onesies, rompers, dresses, overalls), baby shoes, stray socks, a baby lying or kneeling in the crib, toys strewn across the floor, drawers standing open and clothes pulled out, glowing stars on the ceiling, decorations hanging from the ceiling (butterflies, birds, airplanes), a closet (filled with blankets, boxes of diapers, outerwear, and assorted clothing the baby will eventually grow into)

SOUNDS
The crank of a wind-up swing, music from a mobile, soft static from a white noise machine, the rustling of the plastic-encased crib mattress, toys rattling or squeaking, the click of a diaper pail opening and closing, the ripping sound of diaper tabs being pulled, rustling diapers, snaps being fastened, lamps being clicked on or off, a creaking rocking chair, a baby cooing or crying, caregivers humming and singing, siblings playing on the floor while the baby is being changed or sung to sleep, sounds from outside the window (rain pattering, wind blowing, trees swaying, crickets, birds singing, cars passing, neighbors talking, lawn mowers), the air conditioning unit or heat turning on, the hum of a humidifier, the muffled voices of people in another room, drawers sliding open and shut as one puts clothing away, blinds zipping up and down, the baby sucking a thumb or slurping at fingers, sleep sounds (snoring, wheezing, breathing deeply)

SMELLS
Baby powder, baby lotion, the medicinal smell of diaper rash ointment, urine, poop, spit-up, sour milk, air fresheners, disinfectant

TASTES
Formula, milk

TEXTURES AND SENSATIONS
Fuzzy blankets, cuddly stuffed animals, a baby's sweaty or silky hair, the warmth from a sleeping baby's body, smooth skin, slobbery baby kisses, damp or soaked diapers and clothes, a plush changing pad cover, cold wipes, heated wipes from a warming machine, warm sun beaming through a window, heat from a lamp or nightlight, a warm plastic baby bottle, the tugging pull of a baby sucking on a bottle, squishy diapers, drool, viscous spit-up, baby powder dusting one's hands, greasy lotion, squirming babies, cold metal snaps, soft clothing, the soothing slide of the glider or rocking chair, the gradual ceasing of motion as a baby falls asleep in one's arms

POSSIBLE SOURCES OF CONFLICT
A colicky or temperamental baby
A sick baby with symptoms that baffle caregivers and doctors
A diaper explosion when time is of the essence
SIDS (Sudden Infant Death Syndrome)
Safety issues (blind cords, electrical outlets, choking hazards)
Stepping on toys in the dark
Someone snatching a sleeping baby from its room
Untrustworthy babysitters that injure or neglect
First-time parenting insecurities
Sleep deprivation
Postpartum depression or psychosis
Arguments over differing parenting styles—especially generational ones
Jealous or resentful siblings seeking negative attention or to even harm the baby
A single parent passing away suddenly with no one else at home to care for the child
Noisy neighbors that wake the baby by holding boisterous parties or engaging in loud arguments

PEOPLE COMMONLY FOUND HERE
Babies, babysitters, cleaning staff, family members, guests, nannies

RELATED SETTINGS THAT MAY TIE IN WITH THIS ONE
Playground (122), preschool (124)

SETTING NOTES AND TIPS
Nurseries are as varied as the families who fill them. The nursery in a wealthy home might have its own suite. Twins or triplets may occupy one room. Decorations can be lush or scarce depending on the family's financial resources and motivation. An over-eager parent determined to stimulate brain growth may follow careful routines, purchase toys and books meant to stimulate brain activity, and adapt patterns and shapes into the décor to adhere with the latest expert advice. A family who embraces co-sleeping might see the nursery as simply a place to store the baby's things. Overall, a nursery is a very personal space that more represents the parents than the baby, so keep this in mind when designing a nursery setting for a story.

SETTING DESCRIPTION EXAMPLE
Sunlight filtered through the sheer window curtains, lighting up the finished nursery. Framed prints of cartoon dump trucks and tractors hung on the cornflower-blue walls. Soothing rainforest sounds whispered from the white noise machine. Margaret pushed the wooden train on the dresser, rolling it back and forth. She breathed in the smells of fresh paint and new furniture and sighed, rubbing her bulging belly. *Whenever you're ready, little man.*

   Techniques and Devices Used: Light and shadow, multisensory descriptions
   Resulting Effects: Establishing mood, reinforcing emotion

OUTHOUSE

SIGHTS
Rough plywood walls, light shining through a sickle-shaped cut in the door, a peaked roof, a hole or toilet seat on a closed wooden bench, a roll of toilet paper on a wire hanger, dirt clumps and dead grass fragments on the rough floor, dead flies, cobwebs and spiders, a mosquito trying to find its way out, a door with a hook latch, a mound of toilet paper and feces far below in the hole

SOUNDS
The wind trying to sneak into cracks and edges, creaking wood, feet tapping against the plywood as the occupant does his business, wind sliding through the tall grass that butts up against the outhouse, people walking across packed earth outside, the sound of farm equipment (tractors, trucks, backhoes, combines) starting up, ranchers calling to one another or farm animals going about their day, the patter of urine falling through the hole, someone banging on the door, the whine of a mosquito near one's ear

SMELLS
An overpowering ammonia-like smell of urine and feces

TASTES
Some settings have no specific tastes associated with them beyond what the character might bring into the scene (chewing gum, mints, cigarettes, etc.). For scenes like these, where specific tastes are sparse, it would be best to stick to descriptors from the other four senses.

TEXTURES AND SENSATIONS
Rough boards pinching one's skin, the painful prick of splinters, the softness of toilet paper, a draft causing gooseflesh, sliding home a cold metal bolt or hook on the door, sitting stiffly so one will touch as little as possible

POSSIBLE SOURCES OF CONFLICT
Animals burrowing under the outhouse and weakening the foundation
Friends who think it might be funny to tip the outhouse over while one is in it
Being caught inside when animals are prowling around
A sinkhole effect happening while one is inside
Pranks that involve one being locked inside the outhouse
Hearing scratches and scuffs as something tries to chew through the wood frame
Having to hide in or under the outhouse because one's life is in danger
A door that leaves a gap when it closes
People impatient with waiting their turn
Running out of toilet paper

PEOPLE COMMONLY FOUND HERE
Family members, people living off the grid or in remote locations (such as farmers or ranchers without running water or electricity), property owners

RELATED SETTINGS THAT MAY TIE IN WITH THIS ONE
Backyard (36)

SETTING NOTES AND TIPS
Outhouses are most commonly found on farms or in hunting camps in remote areas where there is no running water. This setting also has crossover with chemical toilets found on construction sites and at outdoor events, as well as the non-flush toilet facilities at small roadside stops and remote parks.

While this may seem like an odd choice for a setting, characters, while inside, are rather vulnerable. Their imaginations tend to run wild when they're in an enclosed space that is not only unpleasant, but also usually located in a remote area. Their thoughts may quickly jump to the worst case scenario should they hear someone (or something) rustling around just beyond the door, leaving them with the choice to either remain inside and wait or face whatever is happening on the other side of the latch. This makes an outhouse a very unique setting for tension and conflict.

SETTING DESCRIPTION EXAMPLE
Micah stepped into the dusty yard, preferring to explore Auntie Lo and Uncle Jim's farm instead of being stuck inside in the boiling heat. Buildings crouched in the wild grass and giant trees juggling millions of coin-shaped leaves caught the sunlight, sending flickering shadows over her shoes. She spotted a tiny building with a crescent hole cut in the narrow door. The outhouse! Micah pulled on the handle, wondering what it would be like to go to the bathroom outside. A dented roll of paper sat next to a yellowing toilet seat with a dead fly on it. Above, a strip of flypaper held a dozen more corpses. Foul air wafted out of the tiny hut and she slammed a hand over her mouth and nose. *Gross!* It smelled like the time her little brother got the flu during their two-day drive to the coast.

    Techniques and Devices Used: Contrast, light and shadow, weather
    Resulting Effects: Reinforcing emotion

PATIO DECK

SIGHTS
A ground-level stonework area or raised wooden space with a view of the backyard, a hot tub, a table and chairs, flower boxes, planters and hanging baskets providing bursts of color, a trellis or pergola with climbing vines, an awning or umbrella covering part of the area, a mix of sun and shadow as sunlight filters down through the trees around the patio, doors leading to the inside of the house, a grill, a fireplace or fire pit, a pile of firewood, an outdoor seating area (sofas, cushioned chairs, a coffee table, decorative pillows), a box to store seat cushions and pillows, scattered toys on the lawn, an outdoor clock on the wall, a thermometer, tiki torches and citronella candles, deck lighting, glasses and a jug of mojito mix beaded with condensation, a porch swing or bench seat, wind chimes, spiderwebs in the corners, ants and flies, wasp nests under the stairs, scattered dust, pollen and pine needles in need of sweeping up, homeowners sitting outside in the sun and enjoying a cold beer or morning coffee, a pet cat or dog meandering around the furniture and investigating the corners of the yard

SOUNDS
Birds chirping in the trees, insects buzzing, frogs croaking, doors opening and closing, people talking, voices coming from inside or from a neighbor's yard, house noises (the TV, music playing, the garage door going up) filtering through an open window, kids playing in the yard, dogs barking, a chittering squirrel or chipmunk, traffic noise, running feet, laughter, boards creaking, the gurgle of a hot tub or fountain, chairs scraping across the patio, the splashing sound of plants being watered, the sputtering of food on the grill, wood snapping in the fire pit, logs being tossed on the fire, the wind sliding through the leaves, the rumble and whine of lawn maintenance machinery (mowers, leaf blowers, edgers, chainsaws), chimes ringing in the wind, ice tinkling into a glass at the bar, a creaking swing or deck chair, tall trees creaking in the wind, the flutter of a flag as the breeze catches it, dog claws clicking across the patio

SMELLS
Wood smoke, food cooking on the grill, insect repellant, flowering plants, coffee, rain, musty cushions, citronella candles, tiki torch fuel

TASTES
Drinks (coffee, tea, hot chocolate, beer, soda), snacks, s'mores, grilled meat and vegetables, dinner eaten outside to enjoy the evening with family or friends

TEXTURES AND SENSATIONS
A mosquito's sting, a cool mist of insect repellant being applied to the skin, warm wooden boards on the soles of one's feet, a rough wooden railing, uneven stone pavers that cause one to trip, warm water from the hot tub, the press of heat from a fire in the pit, stinging eyes from smoke as the wind veers, cushioned seats, hard wooden benches, the sway of a swing or hammock, heat or chill from the outside air, the cozy warmth of a blanket in the evenings, wind ruffling one's hair, the powdery feel of a tabletop dusted with pollen, a smooth glass tabletop, wrought iron furniture warmed by the sun, being blinded by the sun at certain points during the day

POSSIBLE SOURCES OF CONFLICT
Nosy neighbors who stare out their windows into one's patio
A police chase through the neighborhood
Falling through the railing
Accidentally setting the deck on fire with a mishandled torch or moveable fire pit
A collapsing deck from rotten supports
Being caught in a compromising situation in the hot tub
Falling trees or branches after a storm
People disturbing someone's "alone time" on the deck
Seasonal allergies that steal one's enjoyment of the yard
Arguments among family members
Tempers flaring due to weather that is too hot or too cold
A deck party invaded by mosquitoes
Lonely neighbors who come over to visit as soon as they spot activity in the yard or on the patio
Guests who spill food and drinks, bringing in a swarm of ants
A hidden wasp nest with occupants that sting people who draw near
Sunbathing on the patio and feeling watched
Overhearing neighbors gossiping about one's family on the other side of the fence

PEOPLE COMMONLY FOUND HERE
Friends and relatives, guests, homeowners, neighbors and their kids

RELATED SETTINGS THAT MAY TIE IN WITH THIS ONE
Backyard (36), flower garden (52), house party (64), kitchen (66), tool shed (88)

SETTING NOTES AND TIPS
As legitimate living spaces outside the home, patio decks can be the setting for much conflict within a story in the form of family dramas, pensive thoughts, reflective moments, and emotional outbursts. They offer a little more scenery than an interior room, and the organic activity that takes place in nature can give an inactive scene a sense of motion and forward momentum. Also, for those living in the suburbs where a neighboring house is just a few steps away, there are the hidden dangers of being overheard, being seen, and most important of all, being caught.

SETTING DESCRIPTION EXAMPLE
Tiki torches glowed orange, casting a faint light that left much of the deck in shadow. I lit a few more and sparked up some candles, too. People were huddled in groups, their voices pitched low and solemn as we all waited for Rick to show up—all except his mom, who was pushing her untouched sandwiches and brownies on everyone. I rolled my eyes. Leave it to Margaret to bring snacks to an intervention.

Techniques and Devices Used: Light and shadow
Resulting Effects: Characterization, establishing mood, tension and conflict

ROOT CELLAR

SIGHTS
A hatch-type door that slants into a grassy hillside and leads down into the ground, exposed pipes with mesh to allow for drainage and airflow ventilation, cement casing walls and steps leading down into the earth, a secondary door at the bottom of the stairs, a floor made of bricks or concrete with a drain, or made of dirt with cement brick walls, wood shelving holding glass jars (cherries, peaches, jams, pickles, tomatoes, pears), bins or crates holding root vegetables and fruit (potatoes, carrots, beets, parsnips, radishes, cabbages, squash, onions, apples, pears), buckets of dry beans, loops of curing sausages and other meats, dusty canning jars with dates scrawled on the lid, canning supplies, a temperature and moisture gauge, clumps of dried dirt on the floor

SOUNDS
Voices echoing in a small space, boots scraping on the rough floor, hollow wails as the wind catches the edge of an air vent, the thump of a dropped potato on the floor, the papery crinkle of a dried onion skin, glass jars clinking as they are lined up on a shelf, the scrape of a basket or crate as it's pulled from a shelf and set on the floor, the thump of a heavy bucket of beans as it's set down, a flashlight snapping on or off (if there's no electrical lighting), the sound of one's breath in an enclosed space, squeaky door hinges, the thump of boots on the steps, the splintering crash of a dropped jar of fruit, a mouse or small critter trying to pry back the grate on an air vent to gain access, the echoing snuffling sounds of animals smelling at the exposed ground-level airflow pipe, the open door creaking as the wind catches it

SMELLS
Moist earth, cold concrete, ripening apples, musty air, a rotten potato at the bottom of a crate, fruit that's starting to ferment, mold, vinegar and dill from a broken jar of pickles, smoky flavoring and spices (if meat is also curing)

TASTES
Air that tastes heavy and earthy, the crisp bite of an apple, the mealy taste of an under ripe pear, sweet syrup from a can of peaches or cherries

TEXTURES AND SENSATIONS
The chill on one's skin as one descends from outdoor warmth into the cool of a root cellar, a packed dirt floor underfoot, rough baskets, cold glass jars, a breeze from the open door giving one goose bumps, slippery-smooth onions, a heavy bushel of apples, the scabby skin of an old potato, the heaviness of a cold glass jar, knobby potato sprouts, bumpy cabbages, the wrinkled skin of aging fruits and vegetables, dusty vegetables, slightly soft fruits that are beginning to turn, crumbling dead greenery (carrot tops, leaves, stems), gripping a flashlight to scan jar labels for the correct one, feeling a moth bump against one's skin as it's drawn to the light one holds, gingerly plucking a rotten potato or squishy apple out of the pile and tossing it into a bag for disposal

POSSIBLE SOURCES OF CONFLICT

A large animal forcing its way into the root cellar

Running out of food and being unable to get more (in a remote area with a harsh climate)

Unseasonable weather (a heat wave, a cold snap) that causes food to freeze or spoil

Flooding that gets inside the root cellar and ruins one's stores or fills it with mud

Small animals (squirrels, raccoons, etc.) gaining access through loose mesh on airflow pipes

Being accidentally locked inside one's root cellar

Canning jars that aren't sealed properly, making the contents go bad or explode

Slipping and falling on a rotten piece of produce and losing consciousness

Finding something hidden in one's root cellar that one did not put there

Realizing someone has been stealing items from one's stores

Mold growing on one's food or improperly cured meats that makes it dangerous to eat

Ants that smell something rotting and follow the smell through an airflow pipe, taking over the space

PEOPLE COMMONLY FOUND HERE

The homeowner and family members

RELATED SETTINGS THAT MAY TIE IN WITH THIS ONE

Basement (38), farm (160), vegetable patch (96)

SETTING NOTES AND TIPS

Root cellars can be simple holes dug in the ground, storage rooms set into the side of a hill, or part of one's existing basement. They may be made of dirt and rock or framed with wood and cement. To successfully keep food from spoiling, a balance of moisture, temperature and airflow is needed. Some people use their root cellars as emergency shelters during poor weather. While root cellars are not as common as they once were, they're necessary in some areas—where power is not consistent or available, for instance—to keep meat and other perishables from spoiling.

SETTING DESCRIPTION EXAMPLE

The door leading down to the root cellar was so warped it scraped across the top stair like a zombie's dragging step. I flicked on the light and one bare bulb sputtered to life, too dim to reach the corners. I hurried to the shelves, looking for the peaches. Of course, it never failed; whatever Nana sent me down here to fetch, it was always somewhere in the back. I steeled myself against the thought of spiders and rats and reached past the preserves. In the half-light, the jars could have been as easily filled with eyeballs and vital organs as with jam. Something skittered against my hand and I shrieked, jerking back. Fluttery cobwebs stuck to my fingers. I wiped them on my jeans, grabbed a jar of apricots, and fled. If Nana wanted peaches, she could come get them herself.

    Techniques and Devices Used: Light and shadow, multisensory descriptions, simile

    Resulting Effects: Tension and conflict

SECRET PASSAGEWAY

SIGHTS
A hidden entrance (behind a bookcase, beneath a rug, a hatch in the ground, in the back of a pantry or closet, past the back panel of a cupboard or wardrobe, a wall seam hidden by a wallpaper pattern), rough walls (made of brick, stone, dirt, mud, or wooden boards), stairs leading below the floor level, an uneven floor covered in dirt, a narrow path that snakes between rooms and hallways or is deliberately straight and purposeful, walls coated with dust and dirt, a storage area for emergency supplies (food, water, blankets, candles, flashlights, extra clothing), a door leading to a hidden room, alcoves and passageways opening off the main path, tree roots poking through the walls (if below ground), water dripping from the tunnel roof, a flashlight beam trained on a floor littered with fallen bricks or stones, old pipes and dangling wires overhead, support beams at intervals, spiders and spiderwebs, rats, evidence of squatters or former residents (food wrappers, crumpled cups, moldy sheets and blankets, cardboard pieces laid over the dirt floor), a small lit radius from one's candle or flashlight, dust motes floating in the air, historical artifacts (forgotten tools, broken weapons, rusted lanterns, dates scratched in the walls) dating the passage to when it was first built

SOUNDS
Water dripping, footsteps scuffling in the dirt or scraping over stone, feet splashing through puddles, echoes, heavy breathing, wind blowing through the passage, muffled voices, critters scurrying, sounds coming from whatever lies at the other end of the passage

SMELLS
Damp earth, dirt, wet stone, dust, rot, sweat, sulfur from a lit match, a burning candle

TASTES
Some settings have no specific tastes associated with them beyond what the character might bring into the scene (chewing gum, mints, etc.). For scenes like these, where specific tastes are sparse, it would be best to stick to descriptors from the other four senses.

TEXTURES AND SENSATIONS
Running a hand along a dusty wall or grabbing onto rough-hewn tunnel supports for balance or navigation, dust filtering from the bricks where one has touched them, a cobweb sticking to one's skin, stale air, wet stones, rocks and tree roots underfoot, a rough brick wall, stumbling over debris on the floor, feeling one's way through complete darkness, shoulders scraping the walls in tight spots, pressing against the wall while climbing down treacherous stairs, air blowing from a side passage or air vent, water dripping onto one's head or hand, dust or dirt settling onto one's skin, crouching to walk in a low-ceilinged passage, squeezing through tight spots, claustrophobia, feeling something skitter across one's skin in the dark and stifling a scream

POSSIBLE SOURCES OF CONFLICT
Finding a passageway in an unsettling place (in one's closet, under one's house, in the basement) Discovering evidence that someone or something has been living in the passage

Getting lost while one explores the passage

Having a door to the passageway shut and finding oneself locked in

Being attacked by another in the passage

Finding spyholes in the passageway that look into personal rooms (a bedroom, a bathroom)

Being trapped in a cave-in and suffering an injury

Finding something unpleasant at the end of the passage

Discovering housemates knew about the passage and didn't share the information

Being chased into the passage and having no idea where to go or hide

Having no light source and having to navigate the dark

A victim getting away from their bonds and trying to escape

Sinkholes, rotten railings or stairs and other hazards that make the passageway dangerous to use

Discovering a room at the end of the passageway filled with voodoo or devil worship materials

Blocked memories returning when the passage leads to the room where one experienced a traumatic event

PEOPLE COMMONLY FOUND HERE

Anyone aware of the passage's existence (the builder, the owner, trusted family and friends), owners using them to transport victims to hidden torture chambers, people fleeing danger or simply wishing to move from one place to another unseen, squatters using an entrance for a variety of reasons (safety, sleeping, storage of special possessions)

RELATED SETTINGS THAT MAY TIE IN WITH THIS ONE

Rural Volume: Abandoned mine (142), ancient ruins (144), basement (38), mansion (72), mausoleum (172), wine cellar (100)

Urban Volume: Sewers (118), subway tunnel (276)

SETTING NOTES AND TIPS

Some secret passageways can be civilized, finished spaces that have been painted, decorated, and well maintained. These passages, be they opulent or simple, usually lead to a regular room one might find in any house, a private space for the passageway's owner to relax or work in private. Passageways can also be the result of a violent mind, and lead to hidden subbasements for keeping a person imprisoned, a soundproof room for torture, or a room specifically designed to dispose of bodies after the fact. But, because of the dramatic and uncertain nature of rough secret passageways underground, we have decided to devote this entry mostly to them.

SETTING DESCRIPTION EXAMPLE

I ran along the passageway, one hand trailing the dirt wall while the tree roots and stones grabbed at my feet, tripping me. My panicked breathing was loud in my ears, but I could still hear the snarls behind me, getting louder with every second. My candle flame flickered just as the draft of clammy air washed over me. I jerked to a stop, choking back a sob as I cupped my hand around the spitting and sputtering flame. It died, and the dark rushed in to fill its void.

Techniques and Devices Used: Multisensory descriptions, personification

Resulting Effects: Establishing mood, foreshadowing, tension and conflict

TEENAGER'S BEDROOM

SIGHTS
Typical bedroom staples (a narrow or often too-small bed, a desk, a chest of drawers, a mirror, a chair and nightstand), clothing covering the floor, an unmade bed, posters that reflect beliefs and interests (celebrity or music idols, models, political statements and world views), a dresser (holding a hodge-podge of loose change, makeup, nail polish bottles, jewelry, picture frames, deodorant, aftershave, a wallet, receipts, a pocket knife), a laptop open on the desk, a phone and phone charger, music listening devices, a clock radio, a desk lamp, a rug on the floor, a pile of study notes, old marked tests and quizzes in a pile on the desk or shoved in a drawer, balled-up or orphaned socks, a closet (shoes lined up or thrown together in a jumble, shelving, coats, clothing on hangers, old books and board games, a box of childhood keepsakes), sports trophies and medals on a shelf, stuffed animals, a bathrobe on a hook, a mirror on the back of the door, sports equipment (a tennis racket, a football and pads, sports shoes, swim goggles, a basketball, a volleyball), a duffel bag, a backpack, a television and gaming console, hidden alcohol, a drug or cigarette stash, a garbage can that is almost overflowing, empty water bottles, pop cans and energy drinks on the desk or nightstand, stacks of dirty plates and bowls needing to be returned to the kitchen, stains on the carpet, incense sticks or candles in holders

SOUNDS
Music, TV or video streaming, an alarm going off, squeaky door hinges, shoes being kicked against the wall, drawers opening and closing, the clink of hangers sliding on a metal bar, talking and laughing on the phone or video calling, the ding of a new text, binder rings being pulled open or forced shut, typing, paper rustling, swearing, creaking bedsprings, sounds filtering in through an open window (neighbors in their yard, wind, lawn mowers, street traffic, the thud of a basketball as local kids play a game of pick-up, a fan blowing, the crackle of a computer shutting off, a low-level hum of running electronics, the door slamming

SMELLS
Perfume, body spray, deodorant, nail polish and remover, makeup, hairspray, rotting orange peels or other organics, sweat, aftershave, freshly washed hair, moldy leftover food, chips, microwaved pizza, pot, cigarettes, beer, dirty laundry, wet towels, smelly shoes and gym clothes, body odor funk

TASTES
Energy drinks, pop, water, food, mints, gum

TEXTURES AND SENSATIONS
Different cloth textures (wool, polyester, cotton, silk, chenille, denim, leather) from one's clothing, bedding, and furniture, the pull and stretch of struggling into tight jeans, holding a phone to the ear while chatting, the weight of a backpack strap pulling on one's shoulder, metal zippers and cold snaps, flopping into bed, the welcome sag of a comfy beanbag chair, slapping at an alarm clock to turn it off, sprawling on the bed or floor to read, a warm comforter, a fuzzy

teddy bear, sorting through fun bling or refined jewelry pieces for the right look, the slide of a scarf around one's neck, pulling clothing on and off, trying on hats and tugging them into place before checking a mirror, sliding a hard through one's hair to smooth, digging a hand into a bag of salty chips while watching a movie in bed, the soft give of a pillow at bedtime

POSSIBLE SOURCES OF CONFLICT
Waking up to a strange noise
Realizing someone has been snooping in one's room
Having something of value go missing
Hearing someone in the next room crying
Waking up and knowing someone else is in the room
Discovering one's laptop has been hacked (email, private diary files, control of the video camera)
Parents who discover a drug or condom stash
Not feeling safe in one's room (family violence and abuse)
Parental snooping that leads to the discovery of pornography on one's computer
Sharing the room with a sibling or a friend who was kicked out and so having no privacy
Secrets swapped during a friend's sleepover that cause internal conflict over when it is okay to tell an adult something worrying
Being assaulted or abducted from one's room

PEOPLE COMMONLY FOUND HERE
The owner of the room and his or her friends, parents, siblings

RELATED SETTINGS THAT MAY TIE IN WITH THIS ONE
Bathroom (40), child's bedroom (50)

SETTING NOTES AND TIPS
The bedroom is one's personal space and is a great way to reflect a character's personality, emotions, and interests. Keep in mind that not everyone may respect a teen's privacy, so if parents or siblings have access to the room, the room's owner may only show what is "parent approved." Writers can have fun with the idea of secrets and hidden spaces where a teen might hide important things that he or she would like to remain hidden, or show other signs of a dual personality, one that parents expect to see, and one that reflects who the character really is.

SETTING DESCRIPTION EXAMPLE
Leslie closed her laptop and snuggled deeper under the covers. The room was still and black, with only the tick of her wall clock breaking the quiet. As her eyes adjusted, she could see the shape of her desk, the posters on her wall, and the whiteness of her closet door. Her breath hitched. A thin black line ran up one side, about an inch wide. An inch was pretty insignificant—unless the movie you'd just finished watching was based on a Stephen King novel. Leslie threw off the covers and ran to shut the door.

    Techniques and Devices Used: Contrast, light and shadow
    Resulting Effects: Characterization, establishing mood, foreshadowing, reinforcing emotion

TOOL SHED

SIGHTS
Dust motes floating in the air, shafts of light filtering through dirty windows or cracks between the siding and roof beams, a work table, lawn tools leaning in the corner (rakes, shovels, hoes, sledge hammers, post diggers, brooms, axes, hedge clippers), stacked paint cans, painting supplies (brushes of various sizes, metal pans, paint stirrers, drop cloths, masking tape), a lawn mower, tool boxes and stray tools (hammers, saws, a file, a level, measuring tapes, wrenches, screwdrivers, ratchets, a socket set), old bikes, folded-up lawn chairs, a chainsaw, garden tools (a spade, gloves, a ratty sunhat, a claw), dirty flower pots, garden hoses, rolled up twine and extension cords, winter car chains and spare tires, bags of lawn fertilizer and potting soil, coffee cans or mason jars filled with odds and ends (nails, nuts, bolts, screws, hooks, magnets, washers), oil and gas cans, power tools (sanders, a miter saw, a table saw, drills), sawhorses, projects in various degrees of completion, broken items waiting to be fixed, sandpaper, safety goggles and gloves, wood glue, vices, bags of birdseed, rolls of chicken wire, a yardstick, degreasers, paper towels, shelves stacked with boxes and cans, pencils, an oscillating fan, dirty or cracked windows, cobwebs and spiders, mouse droppings, mice or chipmunks, dead flies on the windowsill, an overflowing garbage bin, a floor littered with fine debris (dirt, sawdust, wood shavings, blown leaves, grass clippings)

SOUNDS
Clumping footsteps over a wooden floor, a sack of fertilizer being dragged across creaky floorboards, a bee or fly buzzing against the window, the scrape of boxes being moved, the metallic clatter of screws and nails being sorted, a nail clinking to the floor, swearing or muttering in frustration at trying to find something, a grunt of exertion when moving something heavy, scuffs and scrapes from bumping into things in a small space, coughing on dust, the pitter-patter of rodent feet, overhanging tree branches scraping at the roof, wind sighing under the eaves, banging hammers, the cutting sound of hand saws, the squeal of a tight bolt coming loose, the roar of a chainsaw starting up, dirt pouring into a flower pot, items clattering to the floor when a pile is disturbed, falling pine cones and pine needles clattering against the metal roof, the drum of rain and booms of thunder during summer storms

SMELLS
Dust, mulched grass from the lawn mower blades, fertilizer, rusted tools and nails, sunbaked metal, oil, grease, gasoline, paint, dirt

TASTES
Some settings have no specific tastes associated with them beyond what the character might bring into the scene (chewing gum, mints, lipstick, cigarettes, etc.). For scenes like these, where specific tastes are sparse, it would be best to stick to descriptors from the other four senses.

TEXTURES AND SENSATIONS
Hefting a bag of fertilizer or bird seed by the corners, getting poked as one reaches into a can or container of nails, stiff work gloves, sweat trickling into one's eyes, stumbling over something

left out, dirt on the hands, dust in one's throat, wind drifting through open windows, smooth tool handles, trying to get what one wants without toppling a precarious pile of boxes or cans, cobwebs brushing one's face, grease on one's fingers, the vibration of a power tool starting up, exerting pressure to open a can that's stuck tight

POSSIBLE SOURCES OF CONFLICT
Having to clean out a hoarder's shed when an elderly relative passes away
Discovering mice have gotten in, ruining fabric items and tearing holes into seed bags
A cut or jab on something rusty requiring stitches and a tetanus shot
A leaky roof that ruins expensive or customized equipment
Not being able to find what one is looking for
Having to do yard work when one would rather be doing something else
Running into someone dangerous who has taken refuge in one's shed
Wasting time looking for a tool before remembering a neighbor borrowed it but never returned it
Going to retrieve a tool and finding dried blood on it

PEOPLE COMMONLY FOUND HERE
Homeowners, kids

RELATED SETTINGS THAT MAY TIE IN WITH THIS ONE
Backyard (36), basement (38), garage (54), workshop (102)

SETTING NOTES AND TIPS
Tool sheds are often small structures where people keep their tools and lawn equipment. Sometimes it's spacious enough to include bigger equipment or a workspace (for building projects, gardening, or a hobby such as making stained glass). The odds and ends inside a tool shed can be a great way to show a family member's unique interest, provide a place to hide evidence of a crime, stash away something secret one doesn't want family members to find, or to have privacy while indulging in taboo or illegal activities. Since sheds appear to be a chaotic mess to the casual observer, they make a great dumping ground for items one wishes to keep close, but away from prying eyes.

SETTING DESCRIPTION EXAMPLE
Pa said the train set was in the back of the shed next to my old bike, and I figured it would be the perfect thing to set up for my little cousin. But my smile faded in the doorway. I'd been in this shed a thousand times, sent in to grab the broom, or an Allen wrench, or a bag of birdseed. Now, with night coming on, gloom clung to the walls and shelves and hung over the barrels of feed, darkening everything. Each breath I took was thick with dust, and when a gust of wind sent tree branches screeching across the tin roof, I spun around and high-tailed it back to the house. Davy would have to make do with a puzzle.
  Techniques and Devices Used: Contrast, light and shadow, weather
  Resulting Effects: Establishing mood, tension and conflict

TRAILER PARK

SIGHTS
Trailers and mobile homes in close proximity to one another, homes laid out in a logical fashion or sprawling haphazardly across the park, narrow dirt roads, tiny lawns with spotty grass, stepping stones across the grass, outdoor living areas (porches that have been added to a trailer, portable canopies, awnings), tool sheds, flags flying, lawn décor (flamingoes, pinwheels, garden gnomes, planters with flowers, wind chimes hanging off a porch light), plastic chairs on the porch, a ladder leaning against the side of a trailer, piles of debris (broken furniture, paint buckets, old coolers, bicycle wheels, empty crates), garbage cans, metal antennae or satellite dishes on top of the trailers, people sitting on the porch, power lines connecting the trailers to power poles, cement block supports under the trailers, window air conditioning units, cars covered with tarps, community mailboxes and recycling bins, charcoal grills, potted plant boxes, weedy fringes and dandelions growing along wooden trailer skirting, clotheslines drooping with hanging laundry, gravel driveways with potholes, cars parked along the roadside, broken washing machines and dryers on the porch, propane tanks, mildew and grass stains on the trailer siding, rusty trailer hookups, torn window screens, bicycles leaning against trailers or trees, neighborhood watch signs, a management office, trees and hedges, fallen leaves scattered across the lawn and road, birds and squirrels, mosquitoes and flies, ants, mud puddles

SOUNDS
Screen doors screeching and slamming, wheels crunching over dirt and gravel, flags flapping, wind chimes tinkling, the clang of an air conditioning unit turning on, footsteps in gravel, bicycles rattling over unpaved roads, sounds from TVs and radios, people's voices wafting through open windows or propped-open doors, kids playing, traffic from a nearby road, the hum of lights and power lines, someone sweeping off a front porch, buzzing mosquitoes, crickets chirping, cars firing up, loud music playing from a party, drink cans being popped open, the chain of a dog's lead dragging across the ground

SMELLS
Food cooking, a charcoal grill, bug spray, rust, mildew, garbage, dirt and mud, car exhaust

TASTES
Some settings have no specific tastes associated with them beyond what the character might bring into the scene (chewing gum, mints, lipstick, cigarettes, etc.). For scenes like these, where specific tastes are sparse, it would be best to stick to descriptors from the other four senses.

TEXTURES AND SENSATIONS
Loose gravel underfoot, long grass tickling one's ankles, the sting of mosquitoes, flies buzzing around one's head, the cool air under an awning or porch roof, a smooth concrete slab, the hot metal of a garbage can sitting in the sun, a wobbly plastic chair, gingerly sinking into a lawn chair with missing slats, dirt dusting one's bare feet, the warmth of a grill that's warming up, wet laundry dripping on one's skin as it gets hung on the line, car wheels bouncing over the dirt road,

the vibrating grip of handlebars as one's bike crosses uneven ground, the sun beating down as one walks along the narrow road, trickling sweat in the summer heat

POSSIBLE SOURCES OF CONFLICT
People living in close proximity who don't get along
Messy or loud neighbors
Living without heat or air conditioning
Being teased or looked down on for living in a trailer
Not having a private space of one's own
Frequent power outages, leaks and plumbing issues
Roach or ant infestations
Thefts and break-ins
Dogs wandering off leash that are violent or unpredictable around children
Having to evacuate when a hurricane is approaching
Having no safe place to go in the event of a tornado
Falling tree branches during a storm that take down power lines
Worrying about the health or welfare of a neighbor whose family never visits
A city road expansion forcing residents out of their park

PEOPLE COMMONLY FOUND HERE
Garbage collectors, mail carriers, management, repair people, trailer park residents, visitors

SETTING NOTES AND TIPS
Trailer parks can be permanent residences where people move in and out of existing trailers on the property or temporary residencies, with people hauling their trailers from one location to another. They tend to be populated with an eclectic mix of people, including those who can't afford the suburbs but still want their own dwelling, people who are only around seasonally (working part of the year out of the country or in oilfield camps) and those down on their luck. Still others may be living with conditions and illnesses that restrict their ability to make a living, they may have a shady past and wish to be off the grid as much as possible, or they are working to support a family on a reduced income and so choose this affordable housing alternative.

Similar to a trailer park is a site dedicated to RV parking, where people with motor homes temporarily park their RVs while on vacation, or even pay for a yearly rental spot. Higher-end RV parks may have regulations that control the appearance of the trailers in their park. They may also have amenities, like a swimming pool, laundromat, exercise room, or a clubhouse.

SETTING DESCRIPTION EXAMPLE
I sat on the porch, waiting for the next blast of the fan's cool air to swivel my way. Sweat soaked the back of my shirt and my legs stuck to the lawn chair's slats. Luke's music blasted out the kitchen window loud enough for Mrs. McDonald to yell about. I should tell him to turn it down, but like our broken air conditioning unit, in August, I just didn't have the juice.
    Techniques and Devices Used: Multisensory descriptions, simile, weather
    Resulting Effects: Characterization, establishing mood

TREE HOUSE

SIGHTS
A rope ladder or boards nailed to the tree trunk to form a ladder, a trapdoor, wooden planks, a cut-out window, cloth nailed over the window to make curtains, ratty furniture, carpet remnants, *Keep Out* or club name signs, a pocket knife, flashlights, a secret stash of treasures or forbidden items, toys, collections (stones, stickers, action figures, coins), paper items stashed in plastic bags to protect them from the rain, chipped and mismatched dishes, junk food wrappers, empty soda cans and water bottles, crumbs, books and magazines, old cushions or pillows, posters nailed to the wall, names written on or carved into the wood, playing cards, board games with missing pieces, spiderwebs, legs dangling from the sides or through the trapdoor, leaves shaking in the breeze and causing dappled shade and sunlight patches, a rope with a bucket tied to it to lift heavier items into the fort, leaves and branches surrounding the house, dangling moss, squirrels, birds, insects, lizards, a view of the backyard

SOUNDS
The squeak of boards, the rope ladder scraping against the tree trunk, wind in the leaves, branches creaking and scraping against the roof, curtains flapping, soda cans popping open, the rustle of candy wrappers, the crunch of potato chips, birds singing, lizards scrabbling on wood, insects buzzing, squirrels chattering, laughter, conversation, pages turning, muffled sounds from a music player, rain on the roof, the click of someone texting or gaming on a device, distant voices from the house or neighborhood, the drone of cars on the road, dogs barking, doors slamming, the rhythmic patter of sprinklers, whispering, giggling

SMELLS
Flowers, fresh-mown grass, new wooden planks, sawdust, rain, clean air, tree sap, sweat, food cooking on a grill in the backyard, chimney smoke, musty cushions or carpet

TASTES
Water, soda, juice, chocolate, candy, chips, sandwiches, cookies, rain, sweat, stolen cigarettes or beer

TEXTURES AND SENSATIONS
Rough wooden planks, nail heads sticking out of boards, cool air slipping through gaps in the floorboards, the tree house swaying in a strong wind, a breeze blowing through the window, curtains brushing one's skin, scratchy rope, nappy carpet, soft cushions or pillows, the padded softness of a sleeping bag, the glossy feel of magazines or papery book pages, rough tree bark, the bite of a mosquito, raindrops landing on one's skin when one holds an arm out the window, splinters caught under the skin, fingers getting pinched between boards, roughhousing with friends, the hard floor beneath one's back, running one's fingers over a cherished item (a collectible baseball card, the skull of an animal that was found, a metal box with personal items in it), a knife carving through wooden planks

POSSIBLE SOURCES OF CONFLICT

The tree house falling apart due to poor workmanship

Being found by someone one is trying to avoid

Falling out of the tree house and being injured

Wasps building a nest inside the tree house

Rain ruining a favorite toy or keepsake

Getting caught with forbidden items (cigarettes, adult magazines)

Playing with matches or candles and lighting the tree house on fire

Bedbugs from moldy furniture

Peer pressure to take risks one isn't comfortable with

Friends bullying to get their way

Spying into a neighbor's bedroom window from the high vantage point and being caught

Secrets told in confidence to a friend being spread around to others

Overhearing one's parents in the backyard talking about getting a divorce

A rival getting into the tree house and tearing it up

Friendships that break up over something silly

Having an older sibling take one's tree house over

Seeing something while in the tree house that places one in danger (witnessing a murder or other crime)

PEOPLE COMMONLY FOUND HERE

Kids, neighbors, parents, siblings

RELATED SETTINGS THAT MAY TIE IN WITH THIS ONE

Backyard (36)

SETTING NOTES AND TIPS

Tree houses are a kind of rite of passage among many youngsters. While the traditional tree house is constructed of rough materials, today's hideout can also be bought prefabricated, complete with glass windows, decks, awnings, slides, and many other features. Regardless, it is a tree house's interior that truly reflects the personality of its inhabitant. Is it cobwebby or swept clean? Decorated with scrounged items or matching furniture bought at a second hand store? Is it the private haven for an isolated child or the noisy gathering place for neighborhood kids? As always, the devil is in the details; keep this in mind and use your tree house to say something about your character.

SETTING DESCRIPTION EXAMPLE

I looked up to see what everyone was doing. Nora was polishing the rocks she'd collected at the creek and lining them up on the narrow shelf above the window. Melissa and Bree were painting the far wall—a jumble of images that I couldn't identify yet. I grinned and turned a page of my magazine. This is what summer was all about: hanging with the girls, no guys, no parents . . . and most importantly, no schoolwork to worry about.

Techniques and Devices Used: Seasons

Resulting Effects: Establishing mood

UNDERGROUND STORM SHELTER

SIGHTS
A square or rectangular hole with a hinged or sliding door, a locking mechanism on the inside, narrow steps leading underground, strong walls (cement blocks, steel, reinforced fiberglass), a domed or flat ceiling, benches where people can wait out the storm, a fan for ventilation, a first aid kit, blankets, small toys and games, lanterns, flashlights and glow sticks, candles and matches, bottled water, a Swiss army knife, a whistle, a portable toilet, toilet paper, emergency food, plasticware and paper towels, dry pet food, extra clothing, copies of important papers, cash, cobwebs and spiders, leaves and debris on the floor, dim lighting from a candle or glow stick, frightened faces, quivering lights from candles held in shaking hands

SOUNDS
The door sliding or falling shut, high wind, a rumbling sound like a train going by, scrapes and screeches as large debris shifts outside, tree branches and heavy debris falling overhead, people speaking in low voices, echoes, children crying and sniffling, people shifting and trying to get comfortable, static sounds from a portable radio, the whir of a fan, matches being struck, the crumple of food wrappers, shoes scraping on the floor, the crack of a glow stick being lit, quiet singing or whispering in an attempt to soothe a frightened child, a whistle being blown to make rescuers aware of one's position should the door be blocked by debris, packaging being ripped off bandages and gauze to attend to someone who is injured, heavy breathing, a grunt of pain

SMELLS
Dust, sweat, unwashed bodies, sulphur from a lit match, burning candles, musty blankets, toilet smells, antiseptic wipes

TASTES
Emergency stores (granola bars, crackers, cereal, peanut butter, dried fruits, nuts), water

TEXTURES AND SENSATIONS
Hard benches and walls, scratchy blankets, extreme cold or heat from being crammed up against other bodies, air from the ventilation system wafting across one's skin, straining one's eyes to see in the dark, the warmth of a lantern or candle, huddling close to a light source, humid air, an itchy scalp from not washing one's hair, limp clothing, dry mouth from conserving one's water supply, gnawing hunger, boredom, lethargy from sitting for so long in the dark, claustrophobia, a child burrowing into one's lap, the trembling of a pet leaning against one's leg, flipping the pages of a book, fiddling with the radio knob in hopes of finding a broadcast, pushing and ramming a shoulder at a stuck door once the storm has passed

POSSIBLE SOURCES OF CONFLICT
Getting trapped in a shelter for a long period of time
Running out of supplies
Sustaining a serious injury on the way to the shelter and needing medical attention

Taking refuge in a shelter that has no supplies

Discovering that one's supplies have expired or gone bad

Having too many people in one shelter

Sharing a shelter with an irritating or volatile person

Arguments over the distribution of supplies

Sustaining damage to one's ventilation system that cuts down on the fresh air available

Discovering a structural problem with the shelter

Not being able to close the door during a storm

A pet that poops in the shelter

The door ripping off mid-storm

Hearing screams for help outside and being torn as to whether to risk everyone's safety to let them in

Getting into the shelter only to discover someone in one's family is not there

Being unable to fit anyone else in the shelter and having to shut the door on those outside

Having someone need medication and not being able to access it (insulin, for example)

Someone having a panic attack when the storm is over, but the exit is blocked

Hearing someone cry for help outside in the aftermath but being trapped within the shelter

PEOPLE COMMONLY FOUND HERE
Families, neighbors

RELATED SETTINGS THAT MAY TIE IN WITH THIS ONE
Backyard (36), basement (38), bomb shelter (46)

SETTING NOTES AND TIPS
Storm shelters can be found both above- and underground. Some are separate features, built away from a residence while others are existing basements or cellars that have been reinforced to withstand storms. The most common shelters these days are prefabricated, but shelters have been created out of many materials, including septic tanks, broken-down buses, and shipping containers. Typical spaces may comfortably house ten to twelve people for a few hours, and often have the barest of supplies. Others may plan for the worst, filling their shelters with emergency supplies to get them through many days of being stuck in a shelter.

SETTING DESCRIPTION EXAMPLE
The door to the shelter slid shut with the finality of a coffin lid closing. Eli screamed and clawed his way into my lap. I held him, whispering comfort while trying to quell my own terror, but to a three-year-old, darkness would always trump words. He clung to me while I felt my way across the shelter—over the musty blankets, under the rough wooden bench to the plastic container of supplies. I found the latch, ripped the lid off, and rummaged through matchboxes, granola bars, and paper towel rolls until my hand closed over a long metal cylinder. The flashlight beam lit the small room, softening Eli's cries to hiccups and slowing my own panicked breathing.

Techniques and Devices Used: Light and shadow, metaphor

Resulting Effects: Establishing mood, reinforcing emotion, tension and conflict

VEGETABLE PATCH

SIGHTS
A fence enclosure to keep deer and rabbits out, a gate for easy access, carefully tilled rows of healthy plants in various sizes and shades of green, weeds in need of pulling, tomato plants held up by metal cages, pea vines curling through chicken wire and around wooden posts, frilly carrot tops, hilled potatoes, tall corn stalks shuddering when a breeze comes along, bright lettuce greens, spiky onion tops, tall and thorny raspberry bushes loaded with red berries, strawberry plants dotted with delicate white flowers and green runners, bees pollinating flowers, slugs leaving shiny trails on the cement walking paths, caterpillars chewing holes into lettuce leaves, fluttering butterflies and moths, earthworms churning through wet soil, leaves decaying under bushes, discolored leaves, mulch and bark scattered around each plant's base, a black compost bin, sunbaked and cracked soil in need of watering, wilted stalks and limp leaves, vegetables or roots with nibble marks from small animals, a coil of green hose, watering cans, seed markers at the end of each row, an old scuffed wheelbarrow

SOUNDS
Wind sliding through the leaves (rustling, soughing, howling), the crackle of lighting from a summer storm, hail smacking the eaves of a nearby shed, rain pattering against wet leaves, dead leaves ticking along the path, water dripping off the leaves, crickets, frogs, the laughter of nearby children, dogs barking, the chuck sound of a shovel or hoe being thrust into the dirt, a rototiller's motor firing up, the spray of water from a hose hitting thick leaves, the squeak of a half-open gate caught by a gust of wind, bees droning, the tearing sound of a vegetable being pulled free of the earth, the snap of a pea or bean from the vine

SMELLS
Pungent tomato vines, mint leaves, fresh-mown grass, damp earth, the tang of ozone before or after a storm, homegrown herbs, exhaust from a mower or rototiller, onions, ripe fruit or berries, warm earth, dust, moldering compost or mulch, rotting vegetables, charcoal and smoke from a nearby burning barrel, clean rain, crisp frost, the chemical smell of fertilizer, fruit trees laden with ripe fruit, blooming flowers, fragrant honeysuckle or lilac bushes in full bloom

TASTES
Fresh vegetables, sweet and juicy fruit and berries, not-quite-ripe fruit or tart berries, woody or mealy apples, sugary honeysuckle flowers, the freshness of a plucked mint or basil leaf, rain or snow on the tongue, crunchy sweet apples, pungent chives or onions, dirt from an unwashed carrot pulled straight from the ground, fresh herbs, spicy radishes

TEXTURES AND SENSATIONS
Saw-edged or felt-soft leaves, squeezing a tomato or melon for ripeness, the slight give of ripe fruit, dirt under the nails, the stickiness of muddy hands, cold and damp soil, a puff of dirt hitting one's face when a weed pulls free, chalky or crumbly fertilizer, the sharp pinch of a bee sting, prickly sunburn on the neck while one is weeding, the weight of heavy root vegetables

(carrots, parsnips, beets) dangling in one's grip, the give of a weed as it releases its hold on the ground, slimy mulch, the coolness of a breeze in the shade, sweat gathering on one's brow, the frilliness of carrot leaves brushing one's wrist when fumbling for a good handhold to uproot it, the smoothness of a shovel or hoe handle, painful blisters forming on one's palms from a long day of gardening, thick gloves that decrease dexterity and make one's hands hot

POSSIBLE SOURCES OF CONFLICT
Small creatures getting in and eating the plants (rabbits, mice)
Drought, disease, slugs or aphids ruining the harvest
An enemy or rival tearing up the plants for fun or revenge
A poor harvest that will not be enough to feed one's family
Theft of one's vegetables in lean years
A fungus that spreads through the soil, rotting produce
An underground wasp's nest that makes it impossible to garden
Planting too early or too late
Being new to gardening and planting seeds that are not suitable for growing in one's location
Being judged by one's neighbors by the robustness (or lack thereof) of one's garden

PEOPLE COMMONLY FOUND HERE
Children and other family members, neighbors or visitors, the vegetable grower

RELATED SETTINGS THAT MAY TIE IN WITH THIS ONE
Backyard (36), farm (160), farmer's market (162), flower garden (52), patio deck (80), root cellar (82), tool shed (88)

SETTING NOTES AND TIPS
A vegetable garden can be both functional and recreational; people all over enjoy cultivating their own food, either out of desire or necessity. However, just because they wish to grow vegetables doesn't mean they'll be good at it. Think about how the state of a vegetable patch might characterize the owner—and don't forget to carefully research the climate and culture where this gardener lives. What plants are staples in this area because of climate? Which seeds grow well, but the owner refuses to sow them because she doesn't enjoy eating them? What does the owner plant that fails to grow well, but it doesn't stop her from trying? There are many ways to make your vegetable patch stand out as unique and provide opportunities to characterize.

SETTING DESCRIPTION EXAMPLE
The sun had already set, but Sandra couldn't resist crossing the field to the vegetable patch she'd played in as a kid. She unlatched the gate and stepped inside. The air was cool, and moonlight glistened on the dew-soaked leaves of Mother's bean vines and beet plants. As her eyes adjusted to the dark, she spotted the pine tree they'd planted together at the edge, all those years ago. Her vision blurred as she took it in; no longer a skinny stick, it rose up tall and regal at the center of the garden, the way Mother had always looked through her childish eyes.

Techniques and Devices Used: Symbolism, weather
Resulting Effects: Establishing mood, reinforcing emotion

WAKE

SIGHTS

Drawn curtains, mourners in black, tables laden with food (casseroles, sandwiches, tarts, banana loaves, pasta salad, fruit and veggie platters, crackers and meat trays, olives), plates and cutlery, a pile of condolence cards in envelopes on a sideboard table, the kitchen bustling with friendly women (bringing out trays of food, making coffee and tea, washing dishes), grieving family members clutching tissue wads as they thank guests for coming, pictures of the deceased prominently displayed, a guest book, folding chairs crowding the living room to provide more seating, a pile of shoes by the door, coats tossed in a pile on a chair or overtaking a row of coat hooks, children sent to the backyard to play or visit with cousins, smokers on the back porch discussing the funeral and catching up with relatives, flower arrangements displayed on coffee tables and end tables

SOUNDS

People talking quietly, the clink of cutlery, a busy kitchen full of scraping and chopping sounds, dishes rattling as they're loaded into the dishwasher or stacked in clean piles, mothers calling out instructions to children, a teacup being placed on a saucer between sips, noses being blown, subdued laughter as family and friends recall fond memories of the deceased, the gurgle of wine glasses being topped off, ice hitting the edge of a glass, thick pages turning in family albums, doors opening and closing, the doorbell ringing

SMELLS

Casseroles, fresh-brewed coffee, spices (garlic, oregano, cinnamon), tea leaves, strong perfume or cologne, coffee breath, tobacco smell wafting off a smoker's clothing

TASTES

A selection of food provided by the family and those who are paying their respects (meat and cheese trays, macaroni salads, potato salad, lasagna, casseroles, pie, coleslaw, brownies, pies, cookies), coffee, tea, alcohol, some of the deceased's favorite foods and drinks

TEXTURES AND SENSATIONS

A thick wad of a tissue in one's grip, starched clothing rubbing at the skin, shoes that are too tight, swiping a finger under the eyes to catch tears, stiffness in the face from trying to maintain a fake smile or refrain from crying, clutching one's hands tightly to keep them from shaking, warm steam from a cup of coffee or tea, smoothing down the fabric of a skirt or tugging a tie straight, the pinch of a tight waistband, worrying at a hem or button, scratchy eyelids from crying and lack of sleep, a throat that feels thick with tears, a light-headed and disconnected sensation

POSSIBLE SOURCES OF CONFLICT

Family feuds cropping up as alcohol loosens tongues
Arguments over the will or distribution of assets
Being unable to find a will yet knowing there was one
Discovering something surprising or unsettling through discussions with far-reaching relatives

Worry over the deceased's debt

Old family secrets being shared at last

A shocking discovery while going through a photo album

Someone showing up that no one wants there (a lover from a past affair, a critic of the deceased)

A relative playing martyr who feels she took on the biggest burden of care over the years

Extended family laying on guilt regarding their hardship in hopes of getting something

A family member having a heart attack or stroke over the stress of the deceased's passing

Items of the deceased going missing as relatives take what they believe they should be given (as eldest of the family, as the baby, because of a shared interest)

Having someone pass who was not well liked, and no one shows up at the wake

A wake following the tradition of the deceased being present, leading to mixed feelings among attendees and frightening smaller children

A fake mourner at the wake stealing items while everyone is distracted by grief

A second family showing up to the wake to the surprise of the deceased's original family

PEOPLE COMMONLY FOUND HERE

Close neighbors, co-workers, family, friends, members from groups or organizations the deceased was involved with, members of one's church

RELATED SETTINGS THAT MAY TIE IN WITH THIS ONE

Rural Volume: Church (154), graveyard (164), kitchen (66), living room (68), mausoleum (172), patio deck (80)

Urban Volume: Funeral home (68)

SETTING NOTES AND TIPS

Most wakes take place in the home of the deceased or the home of a family member, providing close family and friends the opportunity to break bread and socialize by remembering the one who has passed. Wakes may be held in a larger public location, such as a church or funeral home, if the deceased was a much-loved community fixture or had a large family and circle of close friends. It's important to note that some cultures have special traditions surrounding a wake, including body viewings. If your character belonged to a specific religion or culture, make sure that any customs belonging to that culture are observed for authenticity.

SETTING DESCRIPTION EXAMPLE

I stepped into Aunt Edith's house and was immediately transported back in time. Doilies crowded the tabletops and spider plants hung in the windows, where sunlight strained to get through the lacy drapes. Her giant curio cabinet stood in the corner, filled with the teacup collection I'd spent many a childhood hour staring at and wishing Auntie would let me touch. I squeezed through the narrow archway into the living room and a smile overtook my face. Auntie might be gone, but she was still here, too. Despite the house being packed with mourners and there not being enough seats, no one dared to sit on Auntie's plastic-covered couch.

Techniques and Devices Used: Personification

Resulting Effects: Characterization

WINE CELLAR

SIGHTS
Smooth racks (of redwood, mahogany, cherry or oak) or single rack beds on the walls, a case for wine and port glasses, a polished marble or granite-topped tasting table with a glass decanter, glasses and an aerator, horizontal boxes to display labels, recessed pot lighting dimmed for ambiance, display lighting, a refrigerator, stone or tile flooring, a tempered glass door, a temperature gauge for climate control, wine bottles, decorative facings on walls, a wine barrel for displaying a special bottle of wine, block wooden counters, carved cabinetry, hidden music speakers, a tray of cheeses, dried fruit and nuts for tastings and pairings, napkins

SOUNDS
The soft purr of a split cooling system, the slight echo of voices and footsteps in a smaller air-controlled space, soft music, laughter, the clink of wine glasses, the gurgle of wine running through a diffuser or aerator, the splash as it pours from a decanter, cabinets or drawers opening and closing, the crack of a screw cap's seal breaking, the pop of a cork coming loose, the scrape as one pushes a glass toward someone across the granite tabletop, the papery scrape of a thumb running across a bottle's label

SMELLS
Wood, stone, oak, grapes, scents associated with different kinds of wine (earthy, acidic, spicy or smoky), old cork

TASTES
Wine (tart or sweet, fruity, vinegary, dry, peppery, earthy and flavorful), carefully selected foods to compliment the tasting (water, cheese, nuts, dried fruit, chocolate), the rancid skunky taste of an old wine gone bad

TEXTURES AND SENSATIONS
The weight of a wine bottle in one's hands, dust or fingerprints on an older bottle, fingertips pinching a hard glass stem, twisting or pulling to gently work an older cork from a bottle, the patterned swirl of red wine in a glass to release flavor, the give of a soft cheese or bumpiness of a nut, the burst of flavor on one's tongue at the first sip, licking tartness from one's lips, patting at the mouth with a napkin, accidentally dropping a full glass or bottle and feeling the spray of liquid against one's legs

POSSIBLE SOURCES OF CONFLICT
The cooling system breaking down when one has sensitive older wines in storage
An earthquake that weakens shelving or breaks bottles
Theft of a rare bottle or a large quantity of wine
Discovering a broken seal that spoils an expensive bottle of wine
Dry corks from bottles left upright that causes air to get in and ruin the wine
A clumsy guest who drops a bottle

A friend who cannot hold his alcohol and embarrasses the host
A friend who does not share a wine passion and makes fun of those who do

PEOPLE COMMONLY FOUND HERE
A restaurateur, a sommelier (in a hotel, a special club, or high-end restaurant), friends and family (if it's a private wine cellar), homeowners, waiting staff

RELATED SETTINGS THAT MAY TIE IN WITH THIS ONE
Rural Volume: Basement (38), kitchen (66), mansion (72), winery (194)
Urban Volume: Art gallery (190), ballroom (194), black-tie event (196)

SETTING NOTES AND TIPS
A wine cellar is no longer an indication of snootiness and wealth as it was in days gone past. The popularity of wine has grown over the years, and with the inception of wine bars, has become a popular pastime of many individuals. Your character may have a custom designed, climate-controlled wine cellar with a tasting area, high-end crystal ware and range of expensive wines, or he may have simply converted a room in the basement to dedicate to this pastime. Regardless of the décor, it's really about what's housed within the cellar: the wine.

SETTING DESCRIPTION EXAMPLE
Linden was rushing me up the stairs to see whatever he was so excited about. I was trying to be supportive but was still reeling from the three economy flights and the brutal layovers it had taken to get here. When Mom had said he was in a bad place after his breakup and that he needed me—though he'd never admit it—I'd dropped everything and come, like always. But as we passed through an oak archway with a laurel-leaf pattern that must have cost more than my rent, I was rethinking that decision. Linden pushed open a glass door and the temperature dropped ever so slightly. Floor-to-ceiling slate facings and hundreds of diamond shelves, each holding a wine bottle, framed a circular granite tasting table. Like a magician eager to wow his audience, Linden waved his remote with a flourish. The lights dimmed and an aria slid out of hidden speakers. I forced a smile. Doing poorly? If a fully stocked wine cellar was my spoiled brother doing poorly, I'd hate to see what rock bottom looked like.
Techniques and Devices Used: Contrast, simile
Resulting Effects: Characterization

WORKSHOP

SIGHTS

A long wooden table holding the latest project, a stack of lumber piled on the floor or leaning against the wall, workbenches (with tools, glue, measuring tape, pencils, levels, a T-square) a chair on coasters, pegboards with hooks for tools, larger equipment such as a table saw and drill press, a metal cabinet for power tools (drill, sander, circular saw), a beat-up looking shop vac, old coffee tins full of screws and nails, red standing chests with drawers full of tools (a hammer, a screwdriver set, a socket set, drill bits, pliers, files, clips, a soldering kit), table clamps, a milk crate filled with spray paint and sealants, cordless tools and batteries, fillers, a garbage can, sawdust on the floor, a fan, a radio, bright lighting, pencils in a jar, twists of metal shavings, labeled storage bins on dusty shelves, sticky notes stuck to the wall, grease stains on the floor, dry paint splatters, tape rolls on a peg (electrical tape, duct tape, painting tape), safety goggles and gloves, welding equipment, a smudge-covered cloth, a broom and dustpan, a tall plastic bucket filled with dowel rods, discarded coffee cups and water bottles, a stool, oil-stained boxes stacked in a pile, jugs of fluid lined up on a shelf, oil cans and grease bottles, a red gas can on the floor

SOUNDS

Running machinery (the stutter of a drill press motor, the whine of a sander sliding along wood, the high-pitched grind of a circular saw cutting through a 2 x 4), the scuff of shoes across a gritty floor, a vacuum sucking up floor debris, hammering, someone blowing sawdust off a piece of wood, music from a radio, humming, the scrape of sandpaper against wood or a file screeching against metal, swearing when a hammer misses its mark, the creak of boards and rattle of paper, rollers as a chair is pushed back, the scrape of broom bristles against the floor, paint hissing from an aerosol can, oil and other liquids sloshing in jugs or bottles, wood pieces clattering to the floor when a board has been cut, the squeal of metal joints that need oiling, drawers opening and closing, the clink of metal as one sorts through a toolbox for the correct tool, a paper towel being ripped from a roll, banging a dustpan against the inside of a trashcan to dislodge dust

SMELLS

Glue, varnish, freshly cut wood, paint fumes, overheated motors, oils, lubricants, acetone, burning wood, grease, metal, wood shavings

TASTES

Some settings have no specific tastes associated with them beyond what the character might bring into the scene (chewing gum, mints, lipstick, cigarettes, etc.). For scenes like these, where specific tastes are sparse, it would be best to stick to descriptors from the other four senses.

TEXTURES AND SENSATIONS

Gritty sawdust on a worktable, cuts and smashed fingers, blobs of paint, sticky glue and caulking, the vibration of power tools, a hot welding mask or restrictive breathing mask, a spark landing on the skin, safety glasses slipping down one's nose, sweat building on one's brow and making hands hot inside thick gloves, the sting of a splinter piercing the skin, a rough surface slowly becoming smooth with the help of sandpaper, peering through smudged safety goggles, muscle fatigue from repeated motions (plying a hammer, filing a surface, swinging an axe), a tickle in the nose that heralds a dust-induced sneeze, sawdust coating the hair on one's arms

POSSIBLE SOURCES OF CONFLICT

A fire caused by overheating power tools or an electrical short
Growing light-headed due to chemicals in the air and a lack of proper ventilation
A clumsy visitor who accidentally knocks a table support, resulting in breakage
A power tool mishap that sends one to the emergency room
Taking on a job that is beyond one's skills
A nagging spouse to complete projects before starting new ones
Trying to work with a child who wants to "help"
Being electrocuted by faulty wiring and having no one around to help
Having another family member's project taking over one's workshop space

PEOPLE COMMONLY FOUND HERE

Customers (if the workshop is part of one's business), family members, friends and neighbors, the workshop owner

RELATED SETTINGS THAT MAY TIE IN WITH THIS ONE

Basement (38), garage (54), tool shed (88)

SETTING NOTES AND TIPS

Workshops will contain the tools, supplies, and equipment that are related to the interest of its owner, so understand what your character uses his shop for—small home-based projects, building model planes, woodworking, knife making, or a host of other things. Consider as well that the shop's organization level will say a lot about the person using it. Is everything organized with all tools housed in their appropriate places, or are shelves a hodge-podge of items that leads to frustration when something can't be found? Are tools well maintained or barely functional? Is the area swept up or a black hole of coffee mugs, beer cans, and food wrappers? Choose details that highlight aspects of your character's personality to describe both the workshop and the person who owns it.

SETTING DESCRIPTION EXAMPLE

Late morning light filtered through the tiny window—sufficient to see the million dust motes in the air but not enough to count Eddie's nail supply. Still, I could tell by rattling the can that I'd be making a trip to the hardware store. I glowered at the minefield of wood chips coating the floor, rusted garden implements crowding the corners, and machinery bits piled all over. Why was it Eddie kept his workshop packed to the rafters with useless junk but couldn't keep enough nails on hand to build a gate with?

    Techniques and Devices Used: Light and shadow, metaphor
    Resulting Effects: Characterization, reinforcing emotion

At School

BOARDING SCHOOL

SIGHTS
A grassy quad crisscrossed with sidewalks and surrounded by buildings, a campus chapel with a bell tower, an administrative building containing a headmaster's office and infirmary, an atrium, a library, lecture halls, a performing arts theater, buildings with many classrooms inside, laundry facilities, commons areas and lounges, a cafeteria, dormitories with many floors and shared bathrooms, staff quarters, a fitness center, sports fields, an outdoor tennis or basketball court, a maintenance or custodial shed, a dining hall, a pond or lake, leafy trees, resting benches and picnic tables, parking lots, banners and posters decorated with the school colors and symbols, students in uniform (lounging on the quad, hanging out in commons areas, studying in the library, gathering in the dining hall)

SOUNDS
Students (talking and laughing, collaborating on school projects, whispering during lectures, running to class), footsteps on wooden or tile floors, footsteps banging up and down stairs, heavy doors clanging shut, teachers instructing their classes, music and gaming sounds from dorm rooms, blow dryers humming, showers running, singing, coaches yelling during practices and blowing their whistles, echoes and voices bouncing off cinderblock stairwells, intercom announcements, printers spitting out pages, a heavy book slapping shut, the tap of keys on a laptop, people talking on cell phones or streaming funny videos, cutlery and glassware clinking in the cafeteria, bicycles squeaking, nature noises on the quad (wind causing tall trees to creak, dry leaves scraping along the ground, birds chirping, small animals scampering up and down tree bark or across the grass), cell phones dinging or vibrating, maintenance staff (mowing lawns, cleaning windows, trimming hedges, watering the lawns, blowing sidewalks clear of debris)

SMELLS
Food cooking in the cafeteria, strawberry licorice from a candy stash in a dorm room, shampoos, perfumes, deodorant, aftershave, body spray, sweat, wet towels and dirty clothes, chemicals and sour gasses in the science wing, sun-warmed earth and new leaves on the quad, roses blooming, freshly cut grass, pine trees, laundry soap, bleach and dryer sheets in the laundry

TASTES
Comfort food from home (pasta, meat loaf, ham, steamed vegetables, sandwiches, cereal, French toast, roast beef, fish and chips, barbeque ribs and steak, fruit, breads, cookies), coffee, tea, milk, vitamin water, sports drinks, energy drinks, care packages from home containing candy and chocolate, smuggled-in alcohol and tobacco

TEXTURES AND SENSATIONS
The weight of a backpack pulling on one's shoulder, holding books to one's chest while walking to class, sleeping on a thin mattress, a stiff neck or back from focused studying at one's desk or in the study hall, soft napkins and cold cutlery in the dining hall, stiff chairs, the smoothness of paper, clutching a phone to one's ear with the shoulder to be hands-free, the stubble of grass

against one's legs, warm sun on one's face and shoulders, the kiss of a breeze, changing from hot to cold as one enters or leaves buildings, fatigue from partying or studying too late

POSSIBLE SOURCES OF CONFLICT

Exclusive and hurtful cliques
Thefts from one's room
Being caught with liquor or drugs and facing expulsion
Financial difficulties at home that threaten one's enrollment
Getting caught breaking curfew
Peer pressure that leads to eating disorders
Bullying that worsens anxiety and creates situational depression
Being sent to boarding school against one's will
Being cut from a team or club because of one's grades
Abusive situations that students are too afraid to talk about
Teachers who play favorites
Feeling that one doesn't fit in (due to financial differences)
Missing younger siblings and friends back home
Being stuck at school over breaks and holidays because one's parents are never home
Struggling to keep up grades because of a learning disability
Being the scapegoat for a more popular and influential student's antics and not being believed

PEOPLE COMMONLY FOUND HERE

A headmaster and administrative staff, a school nurse and counselor, cafeteria and janitorial staff, coaches, dorm parents, repair personnel, students, teachers, visiting parents, visiting speakers

RELATED SETTINGS THAT MAY TIE IN WITH THIS ONE

Dorm room (110), gymnasium (114), high school cafeteria (116), university quad (138)

SETTING NOTES AND TIPS

Boarding schools vary from country to country and may have different facilities and programming depending on their focus and financing. While all boarding schools focus on academics, some may also have a particular specialization, such as specific sport training, unique arts and music programming, a foreign language focus, or other areas of interest. Boarding schools may also cater to a certain type of student, such as the visual or hearing impaired.

SETTING DESCRIPTION EXAMPLE

Hannah sipped her strawberry tea, trying to read while Lisa pawed through the drawers of her desk, ranting that someone must be stealing her things. Notebooks, her laptop charger, a half-eaten bag of potato chips, and a pink bra all landed on Lisa's bed, adding to the pile of items that were not her cell phone. Hannah sighed. Her American roommate's side of the room was a disaster, and it was only the second week of term.

    Techniques and Devices Used: Contrast
    Resulting Effects: Characterization

CUSTODIAL SUPPLY ROOM

SIGHTS
Shelving units filled with different-colored chemicals (glass cleaner, floor wax, stainless steel cleaner, antibacterial sanitizer), dust brooms of various sizes clipped to the wall, boxes of fresh trash bags, bathroom supplies (toilet paper, paper towel rolls, soap dispenser refills), a stocked supply cart or two (holding a garbage bin, cleaners in spray bottles, a handheld brush and dustpan, rubber gloves, sponges and scrapers, cleaning cloths, toilet brushes, dusters), a vacuum cleaner, mops in buckets, boxes and totes with labels, a fold-up chair or two, looped power cords hanging on the wall, safety and best practice posters, a bin for dirty cloths, brooms standing in the corner, ladders tucked against the wall, a toolbox, folding step stools, garbage bins on wheels, a utility sink with a hose, a floor drain, a cramped office desk area (paperwork, requisition forms, a computer, walkie-talkies or cell phones), a bulletin board with notices or drawings from a younger student pinned to it, a clipboard holding checklists and forms hanging from a nail on the wall, pegs for clothing (back support belts, jackets, winter gloves, other outerwear)

SOUNDS
The door opening and closing, the jingle of a large key ring, squeaking cart wheels, the glug of liquid in a bucket, the click of a broom being pulled from a wall clip, footsteps racing past outside the door, hallways filled with voices, the buzzing or ring of a phone, water rushing from a tap, the crinkle of trash bags being lifted and knotted, a cardboard box flap being pulled back, a box cutter slicing through tape, a gurgling drain, a dripping water faucet, the tick of a wall clock, paper crumpling, the scratch of a pen against paper, a heavy box or tote scraping across the floor, the thunk of a heavy toolbox being set down, tools clinking, a rolling bucket *ka-thunk*-ing over cracks in the tile, paperwork being shifted or stacked

SMELLS
Chemicals, dust, glue, plastic, musty mops, stagnant water

TASTES
Some settings have no specific tastes associated with them beyond what the character might bring into the scene (chewing gum, mints, cigarettes, etc.). For scenes like these, where specific tastes are sparse, it would be best to stick to descriptors from the other four senses.

TEXTURES AND SENSATIONS
A slippery trash bag, eyes watering when a chemical spills, cold water splashing one's hands, stiff work gloves, rough callouses on one's hands, the weight of dragging a heavy box into place or pulling a jug from a shelf, paper crumpling, a gritty floor under one's shoes, foamy soap lather, damp cloths, the sharp poke of keys in one's pocket, work-related cuts and scrapes, water dampening one's sleeves or pant cuffs, a smooth mop handle in one's hand, the smoothness of cardboard, warm invoice sheets from the fax machine, the cling of rubber or latex gloves, the burn of a chemical on sensitive skin

POSSIBLE SOURCES OF CONFLICT
Slipping on a spill
A strain or sprain from lifting something too heavy
Discovering contraband hidden in the shelves and not knowing whose it is
Discovering a suicide or a student who has been beaten and tossed inside by classmates
Finding traces of vermin in the school or building one maintains
Overhearing a conversation outside the door that suggests someone is in danger but not knowing who it is
Health risks associated with chemicals that have been breathed in or absorbed through the skin
Students who create deliberate messes
Hazing or traditions that go too far, causing a custodian's violent outburst
A fire starting because of lax safety protocols
Resentment toward the people in one's building for the lack of respect for one's job and position
Impossible expectations from administrators when one's department is understaffed and underfunded

PEOPLE COMMONLY FOUND HERE
Building management, custodians, delivery people, inspectors, maintenance workers, staff

RELATED SETTINGS THAT MAY TIE IN WITH THIS ONE
Elementary school classroom (112), gymnasium (114), high school hallway (118), locker room (120), science lab (132)

SETTING NOTES AND TIPS
Custodial storage spaces may range from the size of a tiny closet to a large area housing several supply rooms, an office, a break area, and an adjacent boiler room. The state of the room and supplies will vary. Some buildings' custodial areas are strictly regulated and inspected (such as in a hospital) while others may be cluttered, disorganized, and full of equipment that is in disrepair (such as in an understaffed and underfunded school). Custodial work is often a thankless job and custodians themselves are so integrated into the routine that they can be invisible to others; as a result, the supply closet can make for an unusual setting where all sorts of private meetings and rendezvous could take place.

SETTING DESCRIPTION EXAMPLE
Kent slipped into the closet and shut the door behind him, cutting off the noise, the mess, and the millions of germs carried by the 2,579 students that moved through the halls every day at Roosevelt High School. Breathing deeply through his nose, he inhaled the bleach-scented air before feeling settled enough to open his eyes. Gleaming chrome shelves lined the walls. The bottles—ammonia, floor polish, glass cleaner—stood in orderly rows, their labels facing due north. Mops hung on a rack, safely away from the dust and dirt that kept trying to collect in the corners. Feeling better, he sank into his chair and straightened the pencil holder on the desk. Father had always said that someone like Kent would make a terrible custodian. But who could do a better job of keeping things clean, he wanted to know?

Techniques and Devices Used: Multisensory descriptions, symbolism
Resulting Effects: Characterization, establishing mood

DORM ROOM

SIGHTS
Posters (motivational, humorous, ironic, celebrity or sport icons, edgy rock bands) on the walls, a small window with empty energy drink cans lining the ledge, a set of narrow beds with linen choices that say something about the owner's personality (frilly, plain, sports-themed, geometric patterns, homey, dramatic, colorful, threadbare), a shared desk area (with laptops, phone chargers, a music docking station, textbooks, a printer, notebooks, a box of tissues, a mini-fan, pens and pencils), a closet that is well organized to maximize space (clothing on hangers, shoes on a rack, a milk crate holding snacks and drinks, a few cleaning products, extra personal care items, towels), a small microwave and mini fridge (holding fruit, yogurt, salsa, cheese, fruit cups, drinks, takeout containers), a dish full of takeout condiments, a baggie holding hot chocolate packets and teabags, a corkboard collage (of pictures, cards from home, class schedules, motivational quotes, mementos from nights out, concert tickets), a night table with an alarm clock and lamp, a foldable chair for guests, a trash can, a case of water bottles or favorite pop, a chest of drawers, door hooks (holding a selection of scarves, coats, or hoodies), storage bins that double as an ottoman or coffee table, a coffee maker and mugs, a mirror on the wall, a small shared bathroom, a duffle bag full of sports equipment, laundry sacks, textbooks and binders

SOUNDS
Music, audio from streamed content or video games, roommates talking or laughing, singing in the shower, the hair dryer blowing, the clatter of dishes, the crunch of a foil or plastic snack bag, the whir of a fan, cell phone ringtones and text dings, the chirp of bedsprings, pillows being fluffed, water running, noise from outside coming in through an open window, someone knocking on the door, drawers being opened and shut in a frantic search for something, the gurgle of a brewing coffee pot, the hum of a running microwave or fridge, a ticking clock, arguments in the hallway, popcorn clattering in the microwave, a breeze ruffling papers on the desk

SMELLS
Sweat, dirty laundry, air freshener, stale bread, moldy fruit peels in the garbage can, smelly shoes and socks, perfume, body spray, hand creams, hairspray, food being heated in the microwave, coffee, freshly popped popcorn, peanut butter, paper, markers, stale cigarette smoke

TASTES
Coffee, tea, hot chocolate, alcohol, pop, water, energy drinks, crackers, cereal, yogurt, fruit, protein bars, chips and other snack food, fast food from local restaurants

TEXTURES AND SENSATIONS
The springy give of one's bed after a long day, smooth keyboard keys, a warm coffee cup pressed to the lips, the glossy feel of textbook pages, the spongy softness of a freshly laundered bath towel, air from a portable fan wafting over one's skin, cramming one's feet into comfortable shoes and rushing out the door, the slap of a hand against the alarm clock, a cold doorknob, a backpack

balanced over both shoulders, tripping over debris on the floor, a breeze drifting in through the open window

POSSIBLE SOURCES OF CONFLICT
Incompatible roommates
Arguments over personal space or cleanliness
Personal items going missing
The room being broken into and items stolen
A roommate having frequent guests over when one needs to study
A roommate who borrows one's things because her own items are lost or used up
A roommate who uses illegal drugs and keeps them in the dorm room
A nosy and power-hungry resident assistant (RA)
Strict rules that cause anxiety and frustration
Getting caught breaking dorm rules
A roommate who goes through one's stuff, reads one's email, or engages in other privacy violations
Having a roommate who seems suicidal and not knowing what to do
Walking in on a roommate who is self-harming
A roommate who needs help but is in denial

PEOPLE COMMONLY FOUND HERE
A dorm RA, friends, roommates, students, visiting parents

RELATED SETTINGS THAT MAY TIE IN WITH THIS ONE
Rural Volume: Boarding school (106), university lecture hall (136), university quad (138)
Urban Volume: Coffeehouse (142), laundromat (82), library (84), sporting event stands (240)

SETTING NOTES AND TIPS
A dorm room should match the personality of the owner, and a male's dorm will likely look much different than a female's. In the case of a shared room, the two sides may be vastly different and suggest many possible clashes in the making. All furniture will be economical to fit the space. Some dorms will have a shared bathroom while others may have a more communal bathroom space. Organization is a must, even for people who are traditionally disorganized, in order to create space for all of their things.

SETTING DESCRIPTION EXAMPLE
A slice of light cut the darkness, waking me. Then the door slammed shut. I gauged Rick's drunken path by the noise he made—the oath as he smacked the corner of the desk, the muffled kick of his shoes bouncing off our trash bin. Finally he dropped onto his bed, springs screeching painfully at his six-foot-three frame. Two seconds later, snores rattled the room, filling the air with the smell of stale beer. I glared up at the ceiling and prayed to the university gods that he would flunk out quickly and be replaced by a better roommate.
Techniques and Devices Used: Light and shadow, multisensory descriptions
Resulting Effects: Tension and conflict

ELEMENTARY SCHOOL CLASSROOM

SIGHTS
Whiteboards stretching across the front of the room, a ledge running along the bottom with a colorful collection of markers and erasers, the teacher's desk (a computer and printer, a garbage can, grade and attendance folders, a coffee mug, knickknack gifts from previous students, a wall calendar, a stapler, a chair), a tiled or carpeted floor (dotted with orphaned pencil stubs, erasers, and sparkly hair bands), decorated bulletin boards with art displays or special projects stapled to them, foam cups holding flower seedlings on the windowsill, books crammed on a bookshelf, rows of student desks (each with books, paper, and notebooks stacked on their scratched surfaces), desks filled with books and school supplies, painted foam planets and constellations hanging by strings from the ceiling, labeled hooks at the back of the room for backpacks and coats, a sink with soap and a stack of brown paper towels, a cupboard (filled with art supplies, puzzles, math games, visual aids), a sharpener attached to the wall that bleeds pencil dust onto the floor, a pair of computers at the back of the room, a box for lost and found items, a wall clock, a treasure chest or reward bin (containing stickers, individually wrapped candies, tattoos, and dollar store trinkets), a fish tank or class pet cage, an alphabet stretched across one wall, an intercom, a teacher instructing the class at the board or offering one-on-one help to a student, a teaching aide or parent volunteer helping with projects, students goofing around or passing notes

SOUNDS
Students (talking, laughing, whispering, shouting, singing, moving around the classroom), the drone of the teacher's voice, the shrill ringing of a fire alarm, squealing or muffled feedback from an old intercom as the principal addresses the school, doors slamming, sneakers squeaking, voices echoing in the hallway, chairs scraping, backpacks unzipping, the chewing sound of the pencil sharpener, a student repeatedly clicking the button on a pen, the clang of items dropping into metal garbage cans, students whispering in the back of the room, papers shuffling and crumpling, the spring of a binder being opened, paper being torn from a notebook, the clack of fingers against a computer keyboard, the *chunk* sound of a stapler, the snick of scissors, a ticking wall clock, timers ringing, the wind blowing outside or rain pattering against the classroom windows, voices from the playground drifting in through an open window, the snap and whir of the heat or air conditioning coming on, a book thumping to the floor

SMELLS
Greasy cooking smells from the cafeteria, fresh air drifting through an open window, waxy crayons, scented markets, sweaty bodies, smelly feet, glue, rubber erasers, the sharp odor of hand sanitizer or cleaning supplies, paint, clay, old carpeting, rotten fruit forgotten on a shelf or in a backpack, scents associated with science projects (chemicals, soil, water, vinegar, metal, plastic, rubber, heat lamps), snack foods (crackers, cookies, chips), the clean smell of rain

TASTES
A wooden pencil, fruity chewing gum, mints, cupcakes or doughnuts on a classmate's birthday, snacks, water, juice, sweat licked off a lip

TEXTURES AND SENSATIONS
A smooth desktop, the ridges of a pencil, felt-like carpet under the hands when one is sitting on the floor, the slight squish of an eraser, the grinding vibration of a pencil sharpener, a hard seat that just isn't comfortable, bashing one's knees against the bottom of a too-small desk, a backpack sliding off one's shoulder to the floor, floppy shoelaces, being poked in the back by the person behind one's desk, smooth sheets of paper, the ticklish bristles on a dry paintbrush, slick paint, sticky glue, the teeter of a chair as one leans back, dried gobs of glue stuck to a desk, eraser bits from the desktop sticking to one's forearm, the weight of a book in one's hands, the slats of a chair pressing into one's back, being bumped or tripped when waiting in line

POSSIBLE SOURCES OF CONFLICT
Bullying among classmates or rivalries between students
Hurt feelings and friendship breakups
Doing poorly on a test or reading at a low level and feeling stupid
Not being chosen for a team
Crushes that are exposed to the class
Items that go missing or are stolen
Pranks played on the teacher or another student
Intolerance (toward an obviously poor child, a transgender child, children embracing a certain religion, etc.)

PEOPLE COMMONLY FOUND HERE
A school nurse, parent volunteers, resource aides, special guests (visiting entertainers or authors), students, teachers, the principal

RELATED SETTINGS THAT MAY TIE IN WITH THIS ONE
Child's bedroom (50), custodial supply room (108), gymnasium (114), playground (122), principal's office (126), school bus (130)

SETTING NOTES AND TIPS
Elementary classrooms will vary greatly depending on what kind of school they're in, where the school is located, and its funding. But even more influential to a classroom's look and feel is the teacher. Is she organized or messy? Traditional or forward thinking? Warm and fuzzy or down-to-business? If the classroom scene in your story is a small one where the setting is incidental, a brief description will do. But if this setting plays an important part, it will help to know the teacher well and design her room accordingly, and in turn, shed light on possible classroom conflicts.

SETTING DESCRIPTION EXAMPLE
The door slammed shut as my last student escaped, and I surveyed the damage. Glitter twinkled in the air. The whiteboard displayed a pungent rainbow of jelly, apple juice, and strawberry yogurt. Water dripped from the overflowing sink, making my shoes squish as I crossed the carpet to turn off the faucet. Not bad for my first day.

    Techniques and Devices Used: Hyperbole, multisensory descriptions
    Resulting Effects: Characterization

GYMNASIUM

SIGHTS
A ticket counter, a foyer filled with trophy cases, a concession area where snacks are sold, cinder block walls and shiny wood floors, pads on the bottom portion of the walls, hanging banners that celebrate a winning season, the school name and mascot painted on the floor, handwritten posters for upcoming school events, advertisements along the walls, bleachers that retract into the walls, basketball hoops (stationary fixtures or ones that can be raised, lowered or folded back), a scoreboard, speakers, marks painted on the floor, a small glassed-in booth for announcers and scorekeepers, a curtained stage set into one wall for when the gym serves as an auditorium, audio and stage equipment set up for a program, a floor polisher, multiple sets of double doors, hanging flags, sporting equipment for a physical education class (racks of balls, wrestling mats, tennis rackets, weight equipment, balance beams, jump ropes, small trampolines, beanbags, a parachute, balance beams and other gymnastics equipment), loose balls, plastic cones to mark off certain areas, attached locker rooms for boys and girls, restrooms, water fountains, children engaging in athletic activities during physical education class, sports teams practicing or competing, coaches interacting with their students and blowing whistles, maintenance workers changing lightbulbs and waxing the floors, spectators in the stands during a game

SOUNDS
Echoes, an announcer's voice coming over a sound system, squeaking sneakers, the thunder of many running feet, a referee's whistle, buzzers going off to indicate the end of a time period, coaches yelling to their teams, spectators clapping and shouting, teammates calling to one another, balls bouncing, volleyballs being smacked, players sliding along the floor, basketballs swishing through nets and banging against backboards, heavy doors banging shut, kids laughing, students chatting, a tumult of shrieks and applause when someone wins, teams slapping hands at the end of a game, parents yelling out encouragement or criticism, cheerleaders cheering

SMELLS
Sweat, hot concession food, coffee, smelly shoes, fabric softener from a newly laundered uniform, floor wax and cleaners

TASTES
A plastic mouth guard, a metal whistle, concession food (nachos, slices of pizza, hot dogs, burgers, chips, candy, popcorn), water, soda, coffee

TEXTURES AND SENSATIONS
A hard metal or wooden bleacher, an ache in the back from sitting with no support, balancing snacks on one's lap, sweat dripping along one's skin, a flopping shoelace, hair coming loose from a ponytail and getting into one's face, a rough and bumpy basketball, a smooth volleyball, pounding a volleyball over the net, jostling and bumping into other players, hitting the floor, slamming into the padded portion of a wall, jarring a knee or twisting an ankle, a foot being stepped on, aching muscles from heavy exertion, breaths tearing in and out of the chest, playing through injuries, dry mouth, extreme thirst, guzzling water during a break, a sweaty uniform

stuck to one's skin, sweaty hair plastered to one's forehead, nervous jitters as one prepares to start a game, a child's exhilaration at being able to run and play during recess or PE, a too-loud sound system that hurts one's ears, being high-fived by a teammate

POSSIBLE SOURCES OF CONFLICT
Parents yelling at coaches, upset with how they're managing the team
Students, coaches, or parents being ejected from games for bad behavior
Injuries (accidental or intentional)
Internal conflict about one's abilities
Making a crucial mistake during a game
A sound system or a broken scoreboard that's on the fritz
Pressure at knowing that scouts are in attendance
Ball hogs during physical education class
Biased coaches who pander to their favorite players
Players being offered bribes and kickbacks at upper levels
Gambling rings betting on high school sports
Extreme rivalries between teams and schools
A physical assault after hours
Parents who are always too busy to make games

PEOPLE COMMONLY FOUND HERE
Coaches, college scouts, parents, physical education students, referees, reporters, spectators, sports teams and athletes, teachers

RELATED SETTINGS THAT MAY TIE IN WITH THIS ONE
Rural Volume: Boarding school (106), elementary school classroom (112), high school hallway (118), locker room (120), prom (128), university lecture hall (136), university quad (138)
Urban Volume: Sporting event stands (240)

SETTING NOTES AND TIPS
While school gymnasiums are primarily for athletic events, their large space and seating accommodations make them optimal for other gatherings, too. Depending on size and resources, the gym may be used for awards ceremonies, dances (including prom), as a community voting station, an entertainment venue (hosting hypnotists or magic shows), or for graduation.

SETTING DESCRIPTION EXAMPLE
Coach Turner blew his whistle but nothing happened. Hula-hoops still rattled to the floor. Balls flew every which way. Kindergarteners writhed on the gym floor like puppies, showing utter disrespect to the school mascot as they rolled back and forth over his majestically painted face. The coach ran a hand over his buzzed head and second-guessed his decision to make a few extra bucks teaching primary PE.
   Techniques and Devices Used: Simile
   Resulting Effects: Characterization, tension and conflict

HIGH SCHOOL CAFETERIA

SIGHTS
Bright florescent light strips running across the ceiling, double swinging doors, handmade posters on the walls advertising school events, murals, rows of long tables with uncomfortable plastic chairs spaced along them, stained trash cans with piles of used trays on top, a line full of jostling teens, colored plastic or metal trays, grumpy lunch staff wearing white aprons and hairnets, a cash register, paper plates and plastic cutlery, a menu board listing items and prices, stainless steel counters, hot plates keeping food trays warm for serving, soup tureens and ladles, steam rising off meat or pasta drenched in sauce or grease, a salad bar, scratched-up sneeze guards covering the food selections, heat lamps, small coolers holding desserts or drinks, students (sitting, lounging, grouping into cliques, pushing and shoving, goofing off, reading, eating), water bottles or pop cans on the tables, juice and milk containers, condiment dispensers on a separate counter, wet spills, pudding blobs and stepped-on fries on the floor, crumpled napkins, teens with bag lunches, scrunched-up balls of plastic wrap on the floor, crumbs on the tables, ketchup or gravy spills, mushy food left on trays, sandwich crusts on seats

SOUNDS
Laughter, talking, squealing, shouting, trays slamming down on tables, chairs scraping the floor, chewing, the hiss of a pop can opening, the ding of the cash register, dishes clattering and clanging in the kitchen, a ladle full of lasagna slopping onto a plate, the bubbling of oil as a basket of fries is lowered into a vat, trays sliding along the counter, the clink of change in one's pocket, glass sliding doors being pulled open on coolers, the suction sound of a sealed fridge door opening, the whir of a microwave heating up burritos, popcorn popping in a microwave, crinkly chip bags being torn open, shoes squeaking against the floor, a voice over the intercom calling a student to the office, bells chiming or buzzing as the period ends

SMELLS
Menu items of the day (hot dogs, chili, chicken fingers and fries, corn dogs, burritos, tacos, hamburgers, pizza), grease, pop, sweet ketchup, astringent mustard, burned smells from spillovers or over-cooked food, butter, spices (chili powder, cinnamon, garlic), onions, bad breath

TASTES
Whatever's being served that day (soups, salads, hot dogs, burritos, corn dogs, fries, hamburgers, pizza, stews, chili, chicken strips, tacos, subs, bagels, muffins, chips, cookies, candy bars, veggies and dip, wraps, pasta), food brought from home (squished sandwiches, slightly bruised bananas or apples, a bag of grapes, pasta salad, leftovers), energy drinks, milk, pop, juice or iced tea

TEXTURES AND SENSATIONS
Hard plastic trays, cold metal counters, greasy fries leaving fingers slick, hard benches or plastic seats, a tabletop covered in salt granules, the press of people in crowded lines, bumping elbows with other people at the table, warmth from a hot cup of coffee, rough paper napkins, balling up a wrapper and tossing it in the trash, shaking a pop can to see if anything's left inside, a cold

mayonnaise blob on the corner of one's mouth, the slight give of ripe fruit, poking a nail into the top of a banana to peel it, accidentally brushing someone's foot beneath the table, dusting crumbs off a seat before sitting, licking a blob of ketchup off a finger, stepping in something soft, slipping on a liquid spill

POSSIBLE SOURCES OF CONFLICT
School cliques that exclude others
Bullies who mess with one's food or who are into school-wide humiliation
Trying to pay and discovering that one's wallet was left at home
Discovering that one's lunch account is empty
Going hungry because one cannot afford to eat
Having an allergic response to one's lunch
Getting food poisoning
Having no one to sit with and feeling like everyone is staring
Eating disorders or body issues that make one afraid to eat in public

PEOPLE COMMONLY FOUND HERE
Custodians, delivery people, health and safety inspectors, lunchroom staff, students, teachers

RELATED SETTINGS THAT MAY TIE IN WITH THIS ONE
Rural Volume: Boarding school (106), gymnasium (114), high school hallway (118), school bus (130), science lab (132), teacher's lounge (134), teenager's bedroom (86)
Urban Volume: Sporting event stands (240)

SETTING NOTES AND TIPS
School cafeterias may be set up differently depending on location. Some work on card systems, where food charges are paid for at the start of the year and students scan an ID card to pay, while others are cash only. Some schools have financial assistance programs or a teacher who is known for supplying bagels and muffins to those needing something to eat. Larger schools will often have several lunch periods to control cafeteria numbers. Cafeterias are also located in hospitals, universities, and select big box stores, so this description can be tweaked to these locations as well.

SETTING DESCRIPTION EXAMPLE
I stood in the doorway, my gaze darting from one line to the next. The drool-worthy smell of greasy pizza wafted from the lengthiest row, while in the middle, stick figures picked at the salad bar. The right-hand line was the shortest, identifiable by the siren-call of rustling plastic: snack cakes, chips, and candy bars. I shifted from one foot to the other, trying to make up my mind. My bathroom scale said *salad* but my stomach said *snack cakes*. One glance at the clock sealed the deal. I headed to the right, secure in the knowledge that my eating habits were really the fault of the powers-that-be; if they wanted us to eat well, they should give us more than twenty-three minutes for lunch.
Techniques and Devices Used: Multisensory descriptions
Resulting Effects: Characterization, tension and conflict

HIGH SCHOOL HALLWAY

SIGHTS
Walls of dented or scraped lockers, scuffed floors, a trophy case, student-painted murals, colorful handmade posters for school events (an upcoming prom, a chess club tournament, drama tryouts, pep rally reminders), fire extinguishers, classroom doors, a display case of student sculptures, class pictures, a framed school jacket or school banner, garbage cans, a floor dotted with debris (discarded gum wrappers, broken pencils, pencil-top erasers, crumpled papers), janitors pushing wide brooms, teachers making for their classes or stopping to chat with students, a school police officer wandering the halls, students (rushing to class, digging in backpacks, slamming locker doors, sitting with their backs against lockers, hanging out in groups, chatting with friends, cramming for a test with a pile of books or a backpack resting on the floor next to them, texting on phones), restrooms, small graffiti carved into door frames or written in marker on the walls, shiny silver locks on lockers, papers and shoelaces sticking out of locker door vents, stairs leading to another level

SOUNDS
Shoes squeaking on the floor, echoes, students (talking, laughing, shouting greetings to friends), the clink of locks being opened, the thump of books being set on shelves or shoes tossed into a locker, doors slamming, people being jostled against lockers, teachers ordering kids to settle down or get to class, a bell or buzzer signaling a period change, announcements on the intercom, muffled music leaking out of someone's headphones, phones dinging and being quickly silenced, coughing, sneezing, the drone of a lesson

SMELLS
Perfume, deodorant, aftershave, hairspray, nasty-stuff-in-a-locker smell, minty breath, cleaning supplies, sweaty gym clothes, food odors from the cafeteria or student kitchen, marker smells from newly hung posters, paint, the smell of photocopy ink from just-printed fliers, pot or stale cigarette smells wafting off smokers, alcohol on someone's breath, cleaning supplies, floor wax, newly painted lockers

TASTES
Food grabbed on the go (bagels, granola bars, fruit), sweets (candy, chocolate, gum, mints), fizzy pop or energy drinks, bitter or sweet coffee, water, mouthwash, food caught in one's braces, dust, the sour taste in one's mouth after falling asleep in class, cigarettes or vapor, alcohol from a flask

TEXTURES AND SENSATIONS
A cold metal locker, the weight of a lock in one's hand, smooth paper, plastic binders, sweaty hands, the woody taste of a pencil one has been chewing, the pull of a backpack on the shoulder, long hair getting stuck to newly applied lip gloss, being slammed into a locker by a well-placed nudge or shove by a friend, the welcome anonymity of losing oneself in a tide of students between classes, gooey gum stuck to one's shoe, trying to write on a piece of paper held against the bumpy cinder block wall, shaking a pen that has run out of ink

POSSIBLE SOURCES OF CONFLICT
Bullying or peer pressure
Drug deals
Fights, body checks, and other physical harassment
Being yelled at or humiliated by a teacher in front of other students
Someone pulling the fire alarm
Dropping one's purse and having something embarrassing fall out (tampons, condoms, a crack pipe) Telling a friend something private and being overheard
Worrying when a friend jokes about killing himself
Having one's locker messed with (lube squirted in the vents, a condom placed on the lock, etc.)
A punctual friend who doesn't show up as promised and is not answering texts
Noticing a friend with bruises or cuts and them not wanting to talk about what happened
A nasty breakup in full view of everyone
Pranks (throwing a watermelon down a hallway and watching it explode, emptying a huge bag of jellybeans down a stairwell)
Smoke filling the hallway from a fire in the culinary arts kitchen or chemistry lab
Theft from the lockers
Random locker checks leading to a drug seizure
A spur-of-the-moment silly string battle turning the hall into a foamy mess
A lockdown that empties the halls

PEOPLE COMMONLY FOUND HERE
Administrative staff, custodial staff, guest speakers, police officers, school therapists and aides, students, teachers, the principal and vice principal

RELATED SETTINGS THAT MAY TIE IN WITH THIS ONE
Custodial supply room (108), gymnasium (114), high school cafeteria (116), locker room (120), principal's office (126), school bus (130), science lab (132), teenager's bedroom (86)

SETTING NOTES AND TIPS
Some schools have a police officer or constable whose duties are to break up altercations, conduct locker sweeps, and ensure that all visitors have identification and a legitimate reason for being on campus. Their goal is not to keep students on the straight and narrow through fear, but to ensure the school is a safe place for everyone while forging good relationships with students who may need help or advice later on.

SETTING DESCRIPTION EXAMPLE
I strode out of my office into the hall, inhaling the telltale smells of bleach and lemon-scented cleaner. Sun streamed through the windows, gleaming off the freshly buffed floors. Rows of lockers lined the walls—sturdy sentinels proudly displaying their uniforms of fresh paint. I smiled. Everything was as it should be. Soon, summer would end. Soon, the halls would again be filled with young minds eager to learn.
    Techniques and Devices Used: Metaphor, multisensory descriptions
    Resulting Effects: Characterization, establishing mood

LOCKER ROOM

SIGHTS
Narrow metal lockers with horizontal slits, bright florescent lighting, benches, a plain tile floor with mildew-darkened grout, showers with thin cloth or plastic privacy curtains, gouts of steam circling the roof above the showers, a bin for dirty towels, clothes and shoelaces poking out of closed lockers, a wall of mirrors and sinks, toilet stalls and urinals, a pool of gummy pink liquid below the soap dispensers, stringy hair caught in shower drains, a floor littered with small debris (clumps of dirt, used tissues, hair, power bar wrappers), empty lockers with doors ajar, scuffed gym equipment and dirty sports paraphernalia (padding, jerseys, jock straps, shoes), a forgotten comb on the counter, stray clothes tossed on the benches, floor drains, graffiti and garbage inside empty lockers, an orphaned sock

SOUNDS
Echoing shouts, laughter, teammates gossiping or teasing one another, complaints about the coach or opposing team, the clink of locks bumping against metal, the clang of metal doors opening and slamming shut, the thump of duffel bags and equipment being dropped on the benches or floor, shoes scuffing and squeaking against the floor, curtains being drawn back, the hiss of hot water, gurgling floor drains, the farting squirt of an almost-empty shampoo bottle, someone singing in the shower, flip-flops snapping across the tile, the hiss of aerosol cans (body spray, deodorant, hairspray), the crinkle of potato chip bags, the snap of a wet towel and a cry of pain, zippers opening and closing, bodies banging into lockers, cell phones going off, tinny music issuing from earphones, items from a locker hitting the floor, showers blasting spray, blow dryers blowing hot air

SMELLS
Sweat, body odor, body spray or perfume, deodorant, shampoo-scented steam coming from the adjoining showers, grass and mud on football uniforms or soccer jerseys, wet towels, bleach or pine cleaners, dirty clothes, air fresheners, hairspray or other hair products

TASTES
Sweat, water, sports drinks, quick snacks from a locker (energy bars, chips, granola bars, candy) eaten after practice or gym class

TEXTURES AND SENSATIONS
Soft cotton towels, cold locker doors, the cold ridges of a lock dial, yanking on a zipper pull, the splash of water on the face at the sink, the hot spray of a shower on tired muscles after practice, sweat trickling over one's face and body, the sweaty cling of uniforms, the dig of tight padding, fingers gently probing a bruise or other injury, the stretch or ache of tight muscles, the heaviness of exhaustion, a fresh cotton towel pressed against the face, cool air hitting a sweaty body after pulling a uniform off, the slap and sting of a snapped towel on the skin, lighthearted touches after a game (shoving, slapping, high fives, hugging), the relief of pulling hot feet out of cleated shoes, slumping on a hard bench, the cool feel of water on a parched throat, a throat that's raw

from yelling, slamming a fist into a locker, the bulky feeling of being dressed in full gear, a cool concrete wall

POSSIBLE SOURCES OF CONFLICT
Anger over a loss
Playing the blame game with teammates
Being yelled at by the coach
Having one's locker rifled through as a joke
Being the target of bullying or peer pressure
Personal insecurities over one's abilities
Envy over a teammate's success or popularity
A referee's bad calls causing tempers to flare at halftime
Inappropriate teasing that gets out of hand
Players with body issues struggling to feel okay about undressing around others
Witnessing scars or cuts that suggest long-term abuse or self-harm and not knowing what to do
Someone taking videos or pictures with a phone
Witnessing body shaming or other abuse but being too scared to say something
Finding something disgusting in the locker room (used sanitary pads, feces on the floor)
New team members being threatened with hazing
Friendship friction (a teammate who is going out with one's ex, for example)
Gender and sexuality differences that make the student or other students uncomfortable in the locker room

PEOPLE COMMONLY FOUND HERE
Coaches, custodial staff, players, students changing for gym class

RELATED SETTINGS THAT MAY TIE IN WITH THIS ONE
Rural Volume: Gymnasium (114), high school cafeteria (116), high school hallway (118), school bus (130), teenager's bedroom (86)
Urban Volume: Sporting event stands (240)

SETTING NOTES AND TIPS
Locker rooms are usually situated in fitness gyms and school gymnasiums—places where people are feeling either very confident or very insecure. Add to this the vulnerability of changing clothes in public, and you've got a setting that's naturally ripe for conflict.

SETTING DESCRIPTION EXAMPLE
I sagged onto the cold metal bench, sweat skating down my back and sides. The stink of my grungy pads and soaked uniform was almost enough to knock me out cold. My gaze stayed on the worn blue tiles at my feet as the others filed in. No one spoke; the dragging scuffle of shoes and lockers being opened with muted creaks spelled out our crippling loss just fine on their own.
Techniques and Devices Used: Multisensory descriptions
Resulting Effects: Establishing mood, reinforcing emotion

PLAYGROUND

SIGHTS
A pad of black rubber mats, wood chips, artificial turf or pea gravel with playground equipment on it (swing sets, slides, jungle gyms, a tube maze, tire swings, monkey bars, a low climbing wall), a sandbox with half-buried toy cars and digging tools, small shade trees and bushes, benches or picnic tables, shiny or rusty metal pieces (a pole, ladders), dirt hollows under the swings, bugs and grass in the sandbox, sun glinting off the slide, kids running around playing tag or pretending the ground is lava, babies in strollers kicking their legs or trying to squirm free, moms and dads sitting on benches, juice boxes and baggies with snacks in them sitting out on a picnic table, groups of teenagers hanging out on a nearby grassy hill, squirrels collecting acorns, dragonflies and butterflies skimming the grass, ladybugs crawling over the foliage, ants swarming a juice spill on the concrete, birds diving for fallen crackers and bread crusts, trash barrels surrounded by litter, bikes on kickstands with helmets hanging from handle bars, scooters and bikes lying on the ground, a chain link perimeter fence, houses and streets nearby

SOUNDS
Kids laughing and shouting, parents talking on cell phones or to each other, chains from the swing set creaking, the rhythmic whoosh of swings going back and forth, rubber shoes on the slide, the swish of sand pouring back and forth in the box, wind blowing, feet scraping the wood chips, a child crying after a fall, lawn mowers roaring, kids calling to parents to watch them, pounding footsteps, insect sounds, birds chirping, shoes filled with pea gravel being dumped down the slide in a pinging rain, kids shrieking when it's time to leave, noises from a nearby soccer field or baseball diamond, cars driving by, dogs barking, the *chuck-chuck-chuck* sound of scooter wheels rolling over the cracks in a cement slab pathway

SMELLS
Fresh-mown grass, sticky-sweet spilled juice, a garbage can that needs emptying, pine trees, tree blossoms, wildflowers, mud, wet dirt, dusty gravel, cigarette smoke, sweat, warm rubber, car exhaust from the parking lot, hot metal, sunscreen, bug repellant, dog poop hidden in the grass

TASTES
Dirt, juice, water, coffee, popsicles, snacks for children (crackers, grapes, cheese, fruit gummies, sandwiches, apple slices, cookies), the chalky taste of stirred-up gravel or dust, mints, gum, pop, iced tea, sand in the mouth

TEXTURES AND SENSATIONS
Gravel poking through the shoes or against one's hands, cold metal, sun-warmed rubber tire swings, cool grass underfoot, the jab of a pine cone or pine needle, the smooth chain links of a swing, sticky or gritty hands, sweaty hands and faces, smooth plastic seats, gritty sand, the slats from a park bench pressing into one's back, cedar chips sliding underfoot, mulch caught in a shoe, getting sand in one's eye, a burning hot metal slide, the rise and thump of the swing set poles when someone swings too high, bumping into other kids inside the tube maze when

someone is going the wrong way, feeling nauseous from twisting the swing chains around and them letting them un-twirl, the bright sun and loud children causing a headache

POSSIBLE SOURCES OF CONFLICT

Falling off the equipment or injuring oneself (getting splinters, becoming stuck, cutting oneself)

Bullies or fair-weather friends

Questionable characters lingering around the playground

A child being abducted or wandering off

Finding a drug needle or used condom

A child freaking out in the tube maze and having to be rescued

Bumping into parents or other children that one would rather avoid

Parents who don't monitor their children

Becoming overheated on a playground with no shade

Adults who parent other people's children (when the adult is right there)

Play dates that turn out to be bad matches, either for the kids or the parents

Parents who judge other parents by the snacks they provide or their child's rowdiness of play

PEOPLE COMMONLY FOUND HERE

Babies, children, dog walkers and joggers, nannies and babysitters, older siblings, parents and grandparents, teenagers

RELATED SETTINGS THAT MAY TIE IN WITH THIS ONE

Rural Volume: Child's bedroom (50), elementary school classroom (112), preschool (124)

Urban Volume: Park (98), public restroom (112), rec center (230)

SETTING NOTES AND TIPS

Playgrounds have changed dramatically over the years. Some equipment perceived to be injurious has become scarce, like seesaws and merry-go-rounds. Concrete flooring has been replaced with mulch, rubber, dirt, or artificial turf in an effort to reduce injuries from falls—except in some urban settings, where space is limited. Authors tend to pull details about certain settings from their pasts, and this will work well when an older playground is needed for one's story. But if this isn't the case, it's safer to visit a modern playground to make sure the information included is up to date.

SETTING DESCRIPTION EXAMPLE

My steps slowed as we approached the playground. Bright, rusty scabs crawled up the slide's ladder and the slide itself looked like it'd gone a few rounds with Rocky Balboa—dented and scuffed and warped by the elements. The seesaw only had one painted seat, the blue color washed out by the sun. Its mate lay a few feet away, half-digested by gravel. When the wind turned the swings into a shrieking quartet of banshees, Amy's hand tightened in mine. Maybe we'd check out the YMCA instead.

Techniques and Devices Used: Hyperbole, personification, weather

Resulting Effects: Establishing mood

PRESCHOOL

SIGHTS

Walls covered with artwork, tiled or thinly carpeted floors, cubbies for shoes, labeled hooks for backpacks and coats, colorful lunchboxes, tables with child-sized chairs, pencil sharpeners, rectangular and kidney-shaped tables covered with newsprint for painting, children wearing adult-sized shirts as paint smocks, baskets holding school supplies (crayons, pencils, glue sticks, safety scissors, pipe cleaners for art projects), a bulletin board with "child of the week" pictures pinned to it, a music corner with soft mats and easy-to–use musical instruments (xylophones, tambourines, bells, maracas, recorders), a play area (with ride-on cars, playhouses, dress-up clothes, blocks and toys), a book corner with shelves full of books and beanbag chairs or pillows to sit on, garbage cans surrounded by balled-up pieces of paper and cracker crumbs, a colorful rug for group activities, windows partially covered by seasonal appliqués and children's artwork, paper projects hanging from the ceiling, glitter sparkling in the rug, a private exit that leads to a fenced-in playground (containing slides, swings, playhouses built over sand pits or rubber mats), bathrooms, children running about or playing games, teachers supervising, parents picking up and dropping off children

SOUNDS

Children (laughing, telling make-believe stories, yelling, arguing, crying, or singing), children fighting make-believe battles with action figures and dinosaurs, doors slamming, the snick of scissors through paper, fun music and songs, squeaky swings, the rattle of leaves along the chain link fence on windy days, the teacher reading a story before naptime, crinkling snack bags, lunch boxes snapping open and closed, the slurp of the last bit of liquid being sucked from a juice box, chairs scraping against the floor or tipping over, block towers crashing down, toy cars smashing into walls, the quiet rustle of pages as children read, water splashing in the sink during cleanup time, toilets flushing, the playground gates creaking open, jacket zippers going up and down, musical instruments screeching and chiming, noses being blown, the noises of sickness (sneezing, coughing, sniffling)

SMELLS

Snacks (crackers, granola bars, cookies, chips, fruit), juice, milk, coffee, glue, paint, disinfectant, sweat, urine, air fresheners, scented markers, paper, vomit

TASTES

Snacks or lunches brought from home, juice, water, milk, sand, paint, dirt

TEXTURES AND SENSATIONS

Hot air blowing from air vents, the cool kiss of a fan, the sudden tight squeeze as a child gives one a hug, sticky hands, sweaty hair that sticks to a child's forehead, soft tissues wiping at one's skin, the smooth pages of a picture book, cracker crumbs from a chair sticking to one's legs, fuzzy carpets and stuffed toys, a hard plastic chair, a backpack pulling on one's shoulders, gritty sand and dirt from the playground, dusty chalk on the fingertips, a burst of pain after jumping from a chair or ledge and landing wrong, air rushing into the face while one is swinging, raindrops landing on one's face and hair, a hot slide burning the backs of one's legs, being pushed too hard during a game of tag, the soft give of a beanbag chair or pillow, glitter pieces stuck to one's skin, gooey glue, squishy molding clay, cold water from the fountain running down one's chin, wet finger paint

POSSIBLE SOURCES OF CONFLICT
Parental disputes erupting at pickup or drop-off times
An outbreak of lice
Fights between kids that cause drama or injuries
A child's unexplained bruises or cuts
The fire alarm going off
Parents who are late picking children up or who appear impaired
Losing sight of a child on a field trip to a nearby playground
Hearing children discuss something that causes concern (abuse, drug use, sexual misconduct)
An intruder in the school
A person attempting to pick up a child who does not have permission to do so
Discovering that one of the attending children has not been vaccinated

PEOPLE COMMONLY FOUND HERE
Administrators, aids, caregivers, children, parents and grandparents, special guests (magicians, musicians, authors, puppeteers), teachers

RELATED SETTINGS THAT MAY TIE IN WITH THIS ONE
Child's bedroom (50), elementary school classroom (112), playground (122), school bus (130)

SETTING NOTES AND TIPS
Some preschools are operated out of the preschool owner's home (a dayhome) while others are located in their own buildings. When choosing a location, consider if the preschool needs to be in a residential area (usually where your characters live) or close to work (in which case, the preschool will likely be in a commercial building). Dayhomes will also have less children attending than a larger preschool center.

SETTING DESCRIPTION EXAMPLE
Sarah let the teacher push her kindly out the door, then hurried to the window to gaze back in. Most of the class sat in the reading corner, either whispering, giggling, or pulling at the rug's loose strands as they waited for story time to start. Molly, her little girl, shuffled to the circle of kids, the fan blowing her hair as she crossed its path. After the longest five seconds of Sarah's life, a little boy in the circle scooted over so Molly could sit next to him. He held out a baggie of cheese crackers. Molly took one and smiled at her new friend. Swallowing tears, Sarah pushed back from the windowsill and went to work, her shoes making a lonely clacking sound on the tile.

    Techniques and Devices Used: Multisensory descriptions
    Resulting Effects: Establishing mood, reinforcing emotion, tension and conflict

PRINCIPAL'S OFFICE

SIGHTS

A large desk with the usual office supplies (sticky notes, calculator, stapler, pens and paper pads, a pencil sharpener), a nameplate and business cards, a lamp, a phone, a drinking cup (filled with water, soda, coffee, or tea), a box of tissues, stacks of files and papers, an overflowing inbox, a rolling chair, framed diplomas, notes or artwork from students hanging on the wall, filing cabinets, a bookshelf with textbooks and binders, personal items (family photos, hats and banners bearing college insignia, knickknacks), sports paraphernalia, trophies and awards, a potted plant or cactus, a vase of flowers, a wall clock, chairs for guests to sit in, plaques with quotes embossed on them, a computer and printer, boxes stacked in the corners, an umbrella, hand lotion, hand sanitizer, a garbage bin, a music player, a window with an air conditioning unit, a banner or flag that represents the school, a jar of candy

SOUNDS

Phones ringing, footsteps in the hallways or outer office, students running off when the buzzer signals a new period, teachers and students arguing, papers being shuffled, file cabinet doors sliding open and banging closed, copy machines and printers running, the buzzing sound of the front door being opened for a visitor, voices making announcements over the intercom, school bells or buzzers signaling a change of class, the murmur of voices coming through a wall, the click of a computer keyboard, the grinding noise of a pencil sharpener, a fire alarm going off, a pen repeatedly being clicked on and off, the creak of a chair as parents or students shift nervously in their seats, an air conditioner or heater clicking on, outside noises coming through an open window (children on the playground, teenagers playing basketball, traffic, birds singing, lawns being mowed, a chain hitting the flagpole in the wind)

SMELLS

Coffee, carpet, dusty books, flowers, air fresheners, hand sanitizer, lotion, sweaty children, cologne or perfume, musty carpet

TASTES

Coffee, tea, water, candy

TEXTURES AND SENSATIONS

Students unable to sit still as they wait to see the principal (fidgeting, kicking the legs of the chair with their heels, pressing their knuckles into the padded fabric seat), the shifting motion of a rocking desk chair, a crick in the neck from cradling the phone while typing or writing, a smooth or scratchy pen, the abrupt snap of a pencil lead, paper cuts, flipping through files to find the right one, metal knobs and handles, a child's legs dangling and swinging as he sits in a big chair, cold hand sanitizer, a breeze flitting through the open window, rummaging in a bowl of candy to find the desired one, a small child's hug squeezing one's knees, the slap of a high-five

POSSIBLE SOURCES OF CONFLICT
Disgruntled parents and uncooperative students
Disagreements between teachers
Being accused of inappropriateness by a student or staff member
Hearing gunfire or screams in the school
Discovering that a beloved student is guilty of a crime
Having to physically restrain a student
Being fired or having to let a teacher go because of budget cuts
A bomb threat or pulled fire alarm
Following up on a case of suspected child abuse
Deciding on punishments for errant students
Dealing with parents who want preferential treatment for their child
Having to reprimand a teacher (for inappropriate language, being late too often, for telling off a parent)
A student found carrying a weapon
Fights between students that cause injury
A forced lockdown of the school due to a perceived threat

PEOPLE COMMONLY FOUND HERE
Delivery personnel, office staff, parents, people interviewing for positions at the school, PTA or PTO members, school board members, students, teachers, the principal

RELATED SETTINGS THAT MAY TIE IN WITH THIS ONE
Boarding school (106), elementary school classroom (112), gymnasium (114), high school cafeteria (116), high school hallway (118), locker room (120), teacher's lounge (134)

SETTING NOTES AND TIPS
Principals reside at different levels within the education system and their offices often will reflect this. The décor in an elementary principal's office might look more primary when compared to the academic flavor of a university principal's office. School expenses will also play a part, since a facility with only a small space for the principal will likely be cluttered and crowded. But as with any personal space, the biggest contributing factor to its look and feel will be personality, which will determine whether the area is orderly or chaotic, warm or sterile, over-decorated or Spartan.

SETTING DESCRIPTION EXAMPLE
Principal Penn leaned back in her chair and stretched. It was hard to believe how much work she could get done after hours, in the quiet. No phones ringing, no tear-wrecked girls begging for their cell phones back . . . A door slammed shut and she jerked up straight. That was the south exterior door, the one that slammed so hard it shook the trophies in their cases. But who would be coming in after 10:00 on a Friday? Heavy steps echoed through what should be empty halls. She bolted out of her chair and grabbed the phone. Dead. She whirled around, but her cell was gone—out on the reception desk where she'd been using it earlier. A shiver worked its way through her body as the sounds of someone in the building drew steadily closer.
   Techniques and Devices Used: Contrast, multisensory descriptions
   Resulting Effects: Establishing mood, foreshadowing

PROM

SIGHTS
A chosen themed décor (Paris at Night, a Black-and-Gold Evening, All Things Musical, Mardi Gras, etc.), a balloon archway, glittering strings of lights, tulle draping, loose balloons, a table with attendants collecting tickets, a portable gazebo for taking photos, a dance floor, many circular decorated tables (with tablecloths, centerpieces, flickering candles, confetti), a disco ball or special lighting effect that sends glimmers of light across the room, a movie screen with scrolling photos of students and school activities, a DJ's booth, an organizer keeping the night on course, confetti littering the floor, spotlights that change color, strobe lights during the dance, tables of drinks and refreshments, girls in gowns with corsages and clutch purses, boys in tuxes and boutonnieres, people dancing, people sitting and eating or drinking, people checking their cell phones and snapping pictures, teachers and parent volunteers monitoring the events, teenagers sneaking drinks from flasks or heading outside for a smoke

SOUNDS
Music that swells and diminishes as doors open and close, high heels on tiled floors, laughter and chatter, people shouting to be heard over the music, hoots and hollers, catcalls and whistles, a DJ's amplified voice, the student body president giving a speech, the principal or a teacher making announcements, heels echoing the hallways as a couple sneaks off, groups of girls heading to the restroom, cheers and applause as the prom king and queen are crowned

SMELLS
Fresh flowers, hairspray, cologne and perfume, mouthwash, refreshments

TASTES
Punch, water, soda, juice, fruit, pretzels, chips, peanuts, raw veggies with dip, cheese and crackers, sandwiches, stuffed mushrooms, kabobs, meatballs, cake, cookies, brownies, treats from a chocolate fountain (strawberries, marshmallows, pineapple squares, cheesecake bites, biscotti), mints, gum, lip gloss, alcohol

TEXTURES AND SENSATIONS
A tight-fitting dress or collar, a hot suit jacket, an unwieldy corsage on one's wrist, hair that has been pinned and sprayed into place, flowing dress material, rough sequins or lace, teetering on high heels, new shoes that pinch the feet, dancing closely with one's partner, resting one's cheek against a date's shoulder, holding a hand that is warm or sweaty, bumping into other dancers, grabbing a drink between dances, adjusting one's dress to make sure it stays in the right place, bass notes thumping in one's chest, sweat flowing as the room heats up with dancing, the transition from hot to cool when stepping outside to get some fresh air

POSSIBLE SOURCES OF CONFLICT
Overspending in an effort to impress one's friends or one's date
Getting dumped the day before prom

Spilling something on one's dress or suit

Being embarrassed by one's clothing or date

Being the only single person in a group of couples

Losing the prom king or queen campaign

Encountering an ex who is enjoying making one jealous

Being victimized by mean girls or bullies

A restroom being taken over after a breakup as supportive friends console the dumped girl

Attending prom with a date that one finds too needy or just plain annoying

Being pressured to do certain things during or after prom

Attending with a date who wasn't one's first choice

Discovering that one's date is a horrible or embarrassing dancer

Parents who insist on picking one up at an unreasonable curfew

Parents who are embarrassments, volunteering at prom to keep an eye on their children

Having one's drink drugged

Wanting to ask someone of the same sex to dance but fearing rejection and coming out publicly

Finding one's date making out with someone else in the hall

Struggling with body issues or being body-shamed

PEOPLE COMMONLY FOUND HERE

A DJ, a photographer, students, teachers and the principal, the prom king and queen, venue staff (waiters and waitresses, management), volunteers

RELATED SETTINGS THAT MAY TIE IN WITH THIS ONE

Rural Volume: Boarding school (106), gymnasium (114), high school hallway (118)

Urban Volume: Ballroom (194), black-tie event (196), casual dining restaurant (140), hair salon (72), limousine (262)

SETTING NOTES AND TIPS

Prom extravagance runs along a sliding scale from down-home simple to Hollywood red carpet. A school in a well-to-do area might host prom at a hotel where a large variety of delectable refreshments are served, the decorations are upscale and swag bags are handed out. At the other end of the spectrum, smaller proms may be held in the school gymnasium or at a local rotary club or church hall.

SETTING DESCRIPTION EXAMPLE

Hundreds of balloons hovered near the ceiling, blocking out the sports banners that usually decorated the gym. Lights twinkled and the basketball court was hidden by girls in glitzy dresses and hot guys in tuxes. It usually smelled like sweat and humiliation in here, but tonight the air was scented with perfume and hairspray. The door opened, letting in a draft that shivered my bare shoulders. I tugged up the bodice of my dress, patted my hair, and ventured on four-inch-heels into the most awesome night of my life.

Techniques and Devices Used: Contrast, multisensory descriptions

Resulting Effects: Establishing mood, reinforcing emotion

SCHOOL BUS

SIGHTS
A yellow vehicle with black detailing, the bus's number on a piece of paper taped to the window, flashing lights on the front of the bus, a stop sign and extendable gate that pop out and tell drivers to stop, smudged windows, faces pressed against the glass, a flashing fog light on top of the bus for use in bad weather, accordion doors and high steps, a narrow aisle going down the middle and separating rows of green or black seats, an emergency door at the back, a trash can, windows along the sides that slide up and down, a driver's area with rearview mirrors to see to the back of the bus, signs (emergency exits, rules, the bus driver's name), a small oscillating fan, steering wheel and pedals, a pull bar for operating the door, students sitting sideways with their legs in the aisles, backpacks on the floor, garbage (paper wads, candy wrappers, pencil nubs, snack crumbs), seat belts that may or may not be used, gum stuck to the floor or bottom of the seats, kids (talking to seatmates or those sitting across the aisle, reading or doing homework, staring out the windows, bouncing on the seats, hanging over seats, checking cell phones, listening to music, getting yelled at by the driver), bodies swaying with the motion of the bus, pencil holes in the seat backs, graffiti written on or scratched into the bus's walls, children filing on or off, cars and landscapes whizzing past the windows, kids in the back seats bouncing when the bus hits a bump

SOUNDS
The steady rumble of an idling bus, escalating noise as the bus picks up speed, screeching brakes, the driver greeting riders as they enter the bus, music playing on a radio, a dispatcher's voice coming over the dispatch radio, a bus monitor telling kids to settle down, kids laughing and talking over the bus's noise, backpacks hitting the floor, feet shuffling down the aisle, bodies dropping into seats, a pencil or crayon rolling back and forth, chip and snack bags being opened, increased traffic noise as a window is opened, the wind whooshing through an open window, abrupt silence as the driver calls for quiet while stopping at a railroad crossing, phones ringing, hands slapping seats as kids walk down the aisle, candy wrappers crinkling, juice boxes and water being slurped, the ripping sound of Velcro on lunch bags, backpack zippers opening

SMELLS
Feet, sweat, fruity or minty gum, perfume and body spray, fresh air from open windows, mildew and mud (on cold, wet days), exhaust

TASTES
Flavored lip balm, leftover lunch items (granola bars, fruit, sandwiches, chips, cookies, carrots, celery), pop, water, juice, gum, mints, candy, chocolate bars

TEXTURES AND SENSATIONS
Thinly padded seats, cold metal bus walls, the pull of a backpack on the shoulder, lifting a heavy backpack off the seat, shoes sticking to a spill on the floor, someone kicking the back of one's seat, the rush of cool air from the window, being tapped from behind, pokes and prods, hugging a backpack to one's chest, flipping through a book or comic, a cold drink in the hand, scraping

frost or fog off the window to see outside, drawing or playing a game of tic-tac-toe on a frosty window, breathing on the window and writing with one's finger, kicking the seat ahead, too-short legs swinging from the seat, pulling oneself up to see over a seat, rooting through a bag or pack, condensation on drinks making a hand slick, struggling to open or close a window, dropping into a seat, squishing three to a seat, being knocked about as the bus rolls over a speed bump, grabbing the seat in front when the bus driver hits the brakes

POSSIBLE SOURCES OF CONFLICT
Bullies and physical altercations on the bus
Spilling a forbidden snack or drink and making a big mess
Peer pressure to do something stupid to annoy the driver
Desperately needing to use the restroom
Missing one's stop
Unwelcome romantic advances by another student
Kids who bully the driver, threaten to spread lies, and cause damage on purpose
Having to ride the bus because one is grounded and not allowed to drive
Reckless drivers that don't stop when the stop sign pops out
A child being hit by a car

PEOPLE COMMONLY FOUND HERE
Bus monitors, drivers, students

RELATED SETTINGS THAT MAY TIE IN WITH THIS ONE
Rural Volume: Elementary school classroom (112), group foster home (58), gymnasium (114), high school cafeteria (116), high school hallway (118), preschool (124), principal's office (126), summer camp (188)
Urban Volume: Rec center (230)

SETTING NOTES AND TIPS
The atmosphere on a school bus will vary greatly depending on how many students are riding the bus and their age level. The noise and activity will be amplified at certain times of the year, like the day after Halloween, the day of an anticipated field trip, or right before Christmas vacation. The drivers (and monitors, if present) play a huge part in influencing their charges and dictating how easy or difficult the ride to and from school will be. Engaging, alert adults will have a much different ride to school than those who are apathetic, harried, or inattentive.

SETTING DESCRIPTION EXAMPLE
I walked down the aisle, holding my breath tight like that could somehow make me smaller, like it could keep my hips from brushing the seats on each side. The bus was silent, dozens of gazes on me. I eased into the first empty seat and for the first time in a long time, hope welled up that this school might be different. A smile pulled at my lips. Then I heard the too-loud whisper behind me: "Someone needs a wide load sticker!"

    Techniques and Devices Used: Metaphor
    Resulting Effects: Reinforcing emotion

SCIENCE LAB

SIGHTS

Long countertops with deep sinks and gas valves, cabinets filled with equipment (microscopes, Bunsen burners, ring stands, beakers, Erlenmeyer flasks, cylinders, petri dishes, test tubes in racks, and other glassware), desks and tables, an air exchanger, labeled totes holding smaller supplies (wipes, glass slides, plastic pipettes, wire gauze, crucible cups, evaporating dishes, watch glasses, spot plates, stirring rods), drawers holding equipment (test tube holders, beaker and crucible tongs, clamps, clay triangles, sparkers, burets, funnels, thermometers, hoses, scalpels), tissue paper, educational posters and safety practice notices on the walls, bright florescent lights, a fire extinguisher, electrical outlets, bins of safety goggles, an eye wash station, scales, trash cans, a locked cabinet or closet for chemicals and expensive equipment, squeeze bottles, a periodic table of elements, a fume hood for vaporous experiments, a whiteboard, boxes of disposable gloves, a first aid kit, jars of solid compounds, lab coats or aprons, lab experiments gone awry (a fire erupting in a beaker, chemical explosions, chemical vapor polluting the lab, spills and burns)

SOUNDS

Water rushing from faucets, liquids bubbling and foaming, the *whump* sound of the gas being lit, high power fans from the air exchangers, the hiss of gas, a dripping faucet, the crunch of a balled-up paper towel, the scratch of a pencil on paper, chairs and stools scraping the floor, hinges on cabinet doors squeaking open and closed, drawers slamming, glassware clinking together, a beaker dropping to the floor and shattering, the thump of a heavy microscope being set on a worktable, the click of a sparker, students discussing the experiment, teachers addressing the class or writing information on the whiteboard

SMELLS

Acrid chemicals and vapor, formaldehyde, vinegar, alcohol, a burning smell from unattended experiments, hand soap, cleaners, gas, bleach, hot rubber, latex gloves

TASTES

Some settings have no specific tastes associated with them beyond what the character might bring into the scene (chewing gum, mints, lipstick, cigarettes). For scenes like these, where specific tastes are sparse, it would be best to stick to descriptors from the other four senses.

TEXTURES AND SENSATIONS

Gripping a pencil to make notes, the cling of latex gloves, the resistance in a tension-spring sparker as one lights a burner, the fragility of a glass beaker or tube, a microscope's heavy weight, the pebbly feel of granular compounds beneath one's glove as they are swept up for disposal, a thin slide or watch glass pinched between one's fingers, warm metal tongs or clamps, cold water on one's face during an emergency eye wash, the tight strap of one's goggles digging into the skin, the itch and burn of an abrasive chemical on the skin, the warmth of a burner flame, stiffness in the back and neck from bending over one's experiment

POSSIBLE SOURCES OF CONFLICT

A chemical reaction that explodes or causes a noxious vapor to form

Tripping and splashing a classmate with a dangerous liquid

A fire extinguisher malfunction

Someone fainting at the sight of blood after a scalpel nick

Applying uneven heat to a tube and causing it to shatter

A classmate who is showing off and causes an accident

Inattentive teachers who don't monitor students closely enough

Expensive equipment that goes missing

After hours break-ins

A chemical splash that causes skin damage

A Bunsen burner catching a sleeve on fire

PEOPLE COMMONLY FOUND HERE

Custodial staff, students, teachers

RELATED SETTINGS THAT MAY TIE IN WITH THIS ONE

Boarding school (106), dorm room (110), high school hallway (118), school bus (130), university lecture hall (136)

SETTING NOTES AND TIPS

A school lab's look and feel will depend a lot on the level of funding the school receives as well as the age of the students using the lab. To authentically write a scene that takes place in this location, familiarize yourself with typical experiments that would occur for the age group you're writing about. Without getting overly technical, ensure that you understand the nature of the experiment and the type of equipment and best practices that are used so you can write the scene from a position of authority.

SETTING DESCRIPTION EXAMPLE

Kat fiddled with the dials on her Bunsen burner, eyes darting between the flames and the liquid simmering there. Lord, wasn't it supposed to be boiling by now? She reached out to adjust the dial, but her violinist's fingers were shaking so bad, she accidentally bumped the water flask. Grabbing at it, she knocked over the alcohol, soaking the paper towels she'd collected in case of a spill—and kept apparently too close to her burner, as she learned when they spontaneously combusted. The towels ignited her neighbor's loose-leaf notes, then chewed into *his* neighbor's notebook like a wood chipper mowing through timber. Kat tried to put out the fire with the water, but grabbed the alcohol instead. The flames roared. Glass exploded, sending shrieking kids diving under their desks. Kat shrank back against the wall as Mr. Gruber came running through the smoke to save the day. She'd told her advisor that chemistry was a bad idea. Why hadn't they let her take that second music elective like she'd wanted?

Techniques and Devices Used: Hyperbole, personification

Resulting Effects: Characterization, hinting at backstory

TEACHER'S LOUNGE

SIGHTS
Sturdy tables and chairs, older couches, a tray of goodies brought in by a parent or staff member, fake or real plants, a coffee machine, a kitchenette area (stove, microwave, fridge, sink, dish soap, counter, a paper towel dispenser), cutlery, coffee fixings (a coffee maker, cream, sugar, teabags), washrags and tea towels, upside-down coffee mugs left to dry on a towel, water bottles, papers laid out to grade on a table, a garbage can, a soda machine, teachers eating lunch, half-empty lunch trays, perspiring soda cans, a school event board with sign-up sheets, inspirational posters, a telephone, cupboards, fundraiser candies and snacks for sale, loose newspapers, mailbox cubbies, a copy machine and paper, a die-cut machine, a paper cutter, a television, an intercom box on the wall, office supplies (pens, tape, scissors, glue sticks, sticky notes, a stapler, white-out), rolls of bulletin board paper, empty mail bins, a bin for recycled papers

SOUNDS
Laughter, a beeping microwave, popcorn popping, the fridge door opening and closing, the rattle of cutlery in a drawer, water being turned on and off, a chuckling coffee pot, chairs scraping the floor, low whispers, food lids being popped off, the crackle and crinkle of food wrappers and paper bags, coffee or tea being sipped, the clink of a stirring spoon, air hissing out of a seat as someone sits down, cabinets opening and closing, grumbling and gossiping, dishes clattering together, the phone ringing or intercom buzzing, water hitting the metal sink, soda cans clattering out of a machine, the hiss of a soda can being opened, newspapers rustling, papers sliding out of a copy machine, a paper cutter slicing through paper as someone multitasks on a lunch break, a soap opera or news show on the television, coffee mugs being set down on a tabletop, an excited cheer going up as someone arrives with a pizza

SMELLS
Coffee, flavored creamers, food warmed for lunch, fast food brought in (hamburgers, pizza, subs), popcorn, tea, cologne or perfume, food gone bad in the fridge, burned food, cafeteria food, fresh baked goods

TASTES
Cafeteria food (soup, salads, sandwiches, pizza, hamburgers, chili, subs), snacks (chips, cookies, brownies, popcorn, candy), hot drinks (coffee, tea, hot chocolate), cold drinks (water, pop, juice, milk)

TEXTURES AND SENSATIONS
A blast of cold from the fridge, hot coffee splashing one's hand, irritating crumbs on the counter, plastic wrap peeling off a container and sticking to itself, a hard metal chair, a soft couch, the wobbling motion of a table with uneven legs, a warm plastic cafeteria tray, a steaming bag of popcorn, thin paper napkins, rough carpet on bare feet, newsprint on the fingers, wet hands from the sink, a pen scratching as papers are graded, warm paper from the copy machine

POSSIBLE SOURCES OF CONFLICT

Teachers who don't like one another

Conflicting political (or work-related) opinions

Jealous employees (because another teacher is more popular with students or was promoted, etc.)

Running out of coffee

One's lunch disappearing repeatedly from the community fridge

Forgetting one's lunch at home

One's break period being shortened or cancelled

Disgruntled teachers who are constantly complaining and bringing others down

Students using the staff kitchen and discovering an alcohol stash

Being afraid to voice certain things because a teacher present is known to gossip about everyone

Overhearing other teachers gossiping in an unkind way about a co-worker

Relationships between teachers being hidden from staff or the principal

A sloppy teacher who uses items in the kitchen but never cleans up

A teacher who brings leftovers from home that make the whole room stink

Catching a teacher making fun of a student's disability, dress, or intelligence

Frustration over factors that are beyond one's control (budget cuts, job uncertainty, difficult or absentee parents, apathetic students, unrealistic administrative expectations, testing pressures)

PEOPLE COMMONLY FOUND HERE

Administrators, aides, coaches, janitors, teachers

RELATED SETTINGS THAT MAY TIE IN WITH THIS ONE

Elementary school classroom (112), gymnasium (114), high school cafeteria (116), high school hallway (118), locker room (120), playground (122), principal's office (126)

SETTING NOTES AND TIPS

Teachers' lounges should be fairly standard from one school to the next, but the contents of each can vary depending upon funding. Higher income schools will have more money and teachers will have access to more and better supplies. Regardless of the school's status or location, perhaps the most influential variable upon the teacher's lounge is the overall mood. A lounge filled with disgruntled, bitter, or discouraged teachers will feel (and start to look) very different from one occupied by cooperative and energized employees. Mood is a huge factor in the setting, so this should be kept in mind, no matter where your story is taking place.

SETTING DESCRIPTION EXAMPLE

After two painful hours trying to teach algebra to the remedial math group, a hurricane-sized headache gnawed at my brain. I limped into the lounge and found a fresh pot of coffee on the burner and clean mugs on the wiped-down counter. The aroma of premium dark roast was more soothing than a bottle of aspirin.

Techniques and Devices Used: Hyperbole

Resulting Effects: Establishing mood

UNIVERSITY LECTURE HALL

SIGHTS
Double doors at the back of the classroom, tiered seating, fold-down seats with adjustable desktops, aisles that lead down to a teaching area with a podium and stool, a large whiteboard and chalkboard, a projector, posters on the walls, a bulletin board with announcements and ads near the exit, banners proclaiming the school name or mascot, a desk (holding the professor's laptop, a notepad, pens), visual aids to help with the subject matter, acoustical panels on the walls, students sitting in seats (taking notes, tapping on laptops, flipping through textbooks, sipping drinks, sleeping, asking questions), professors pacing the front of the room as they teach and call on students

SOUNDS
Professors giving lectures, audio sounds from a movie or video being shown, students (asking questions, whispering to each other, laughing in unison), laptop keys being clicked, loose papers rustling, textbook pages being turned, seats creaking as students shift around, doors slamming, footsteps, a pen or pencil scratching over paper, sneakers squeaking on tile, the scrape of the professor's stool over the platform floor, air conditioners or heaters clicking on, soda cans popping open, snack wrappers rustling, an announcement coming over the intercom, muffled voices from another room or the hallway outside, a cell phone ringing and quickly being silenced, backpacks zipping and unzipping, a pen being repeatedly clicked

SMELLS
Floor cleaner, air freshener, musty carpet, coffee, cologne and perfume

TASTES
Coffee, water, juices, pop, energy drinks, vending machine fare (candy bars, chips, cookies, snack cakes, trail mix), gum, mints

TEXTURES AND SENSATIONS
A hard plastic seat, a broken seat that tips too far forward or leans too far back, balancing many materials on a too-small desktop, rummaging through a backpack, heavy textbooks, air that is too cold or too warm, squinting to see the board from far away, a cramp in the hand from writing notes quickly, scratchy eyes from too little sleep, a hangover headache, perspiration from a cold can or bottle dampening one's notes

POSSIBLE SOURCES OF CONFLICT
Misconduct between students as rivalries flare up
A student suicide or hospitalization due to stress overload
Sexual harassment
Coming to class drunk or hungover
Sitting next to someone who is obviously very sick
Losing one's scholarship because one's grades slip

Taking a class that is much harder than one anticipated

One's laptop dying in the middle of a lecture

Arriving to class and realizing one doesn't have all the necessary materials

Being called on and not knowing the answer

A professor showing prejudice against a student with different religious or philosophical beliefs

PEOPLE COMMONLY FOUND HERE
Faculty members, grad students and interns, maintenance workers, students

RELATED SETTINGS THAT MAY TIE IN WITH THIS ONE
Dorm room (110), university quad (138)

SETTING NOTES AND TIPS
University lecture halls are ideal settings because of the inherent conflict that surrounds the people who frequent them. College students are just barely adults, and many of them are on their own for the first time. Weeks before, they were in charge of nothing, and now they're responsible for everything. Pressures to do well academically, appease friends and lovers, and make wise financial decisions can cause a great deal of anxiety for university students. Throw in too little sleep and easy access to alcohol, and you've got the right ingredients for potential decision-making catastrophes. These scenarios could easily play out in a lecture hall, or it might simply be the place where everything comes to a head.

SETTING DESCRIPTION EXAMPLE
Lucas silently opened the lecture hall door and slipped in like a ninja, dropping noiselessly into a seat in the last row. Professor Lonroy stood at the lectern going over a criminology case, his laser pointer drawing attention to specifics of the crime scene on the media screen. As he discussed the directional blood spatter, he gave his sleeve a shake to check his watch, then turned his disapproving gaze on Lucas. *Great.* Anyone else wouldn't have been noticed for being late, but when the professor was your dad, punctuality was expected and required.

    Techniques and Devices Used: Simile

    Resulting Effects: Hinting at backstory

UNIVERSITY QUAD

SIGHTS
A grassy lawn crisscrossed by sidewalks, benches spaced along the pathways, tall buildings around the perimeter (libraries, lecture halls, dorms, fraternity and sorority houses, dining halls, administrative offices, a security office, parking garages, an infirmary, a chapel, a bell tower or clock tower), a central courtyard (decorative pavers, a fountain, statuary, flags on poles, commemorative plaques), trees and bushes, flower beds, plants in large pots, garbage cans, decorative archways, navigational signs, bike racks, banners strung over the pathways or on buildings, students (lounging on the lawn, throwing a Frisbee or football, sitting in groups or alone, reading on benches, walking to and from class, handing out flyers, biking across campus, studying), security vehicles and pedestrian guards patrolling the campus, informational tables manned by members of various clubs and organizations, students milling about and signing up for events, a puppy program where stressed out students can take study breaks to pet and play with dogs in a special enclosure on the lawn

SOUNDS
Students talking and laughing, students calling to one another across the green, a bicycle rolling by, the wind in the trees, a breeze rustling papers, the crackle of snack wrappers being opened, running footsteps, birds chirping, traffic, an airplane flying overhead, the racket of lawn mowers and other maintenance machinery, doors opening and closing, cell phones ringing, backpacks dropping to a bench or the grass with a thump, water splashing in a nearby fountain, flags flapping and chains rattling against the poles, whining insects, the buzz of streetlights overhead

SMELLS
Fresh-mown grass, pine needles, wet earth warming in the sun, dew, flowers

TASTES
Coffee, water, juices, pop, beer, energy drinks, candy, chips, cookies, food eaten on the go, toothpaste, mouthwash

TEXTURES AND SENSATIONS
Cold air on the skin as one steps out of the dormitory to cross the quad, the warmth of the sun peeking out from behind a cloud, prickly grass against one's skin, the soft give of the grass as one steps on it, a warm metal bench against one's legs, the glare of sunlight glancing off a textbook page, a cold or warm metal door handle, hard cobblestones or bricks under one's feet, a breeze tangling one's hair, the bump of a bicycle over uneven ground, being jostled by other students, a heavy backpack strap pulling on one's shoulder, a bag bumping against the back as a student runs across campus

POSSIBLE SOURCES OF CONFLICT
Getting caught in the rain without proper clothing or an umbrella
Slipping and falling on the sidewalk

Pranks or hazing gone wrong

Being late and having to run across campus

Being mugged or sexually assaulted

Experiencing a public breakup

Misplacing one's backpack (including class notes, keys, and a wallet)

Performing the walk of shame across the quad as one hurries home to change before class

A student overdoing it the night before and passing out on the quad

Mismanagement of funds that results in money running out before the next scholarship check arrives

Struggling with an addiction and trying to hide it from concerned friends

A rival school playing a prank (toilet papering trees, releasing several goats in the quad, etc.)

A security guard trying to bully or use his or her authority in an inappropriate way

Eating lunch on the quad and witnessing a jumper take his own life

Witnessing an argument between a couple that turns violent

Going for a walk and finding a dead animal that clearly died by human hands

PEOPLE COMMONLY FOUND HERE

Campus security, faculty members, gardeners and janitorial staff, grad students and interns, maintenance workers, students, visiting parents

RELATED SETTINGS THAT MAY TIE IN WITH THIS ONE

Dorm room (110), university lecture hall (136)

SETTING NOTES AND TIPS

College or university campuses can vary depending on where they're located and what their focus is. Some are strictly academic, while others offer programs in the arts and technical fields. Also, consider the lineage of an institution, even if you are creating one from your imagination. How long has it been around? What traditions, ideals, and mottos does the institution promote and hold dear? Is enrollment open to all, is it based on academic standing, or does it only cater to the wealthy and well connected? If you choose to use a real institution in your story, be sure to research it well, ensuring that your details are correct.

SETTING DESCRIPTION EXAMPLE

Sasha dropped to the ground and sprawled, heaving a huge sigh. Finals were over! The chatter of passing students washed over her, the faint thump of their footsteps shuddering into her bones. The sun-warmed grass soaked into her skin and a breeze ruffled her hair. Behind her closed lids, the sun was bright and insistent, like it had made it through winter and spring, and come summer, it was gonna show you who was boss. She grinned. *Bring it on!*

    Techniques and Devices Used: Seasons, symbolism

    Resulting Effects: Establishing mood, reinforcing emotion

Rural Sights

ABANDONED MINE

SIGHT
Rough rock and dirt walls, thick beams supporting the sides and girding the roof, vertical shafts going nearly straight down, dust and dirt, debris blown in from outside (twigs, leaves, paper, garbage), broken pick handles, bits of chain, rusted nails and screws, old rails for carts, a rusted or broken handcart, a rotten wooden barrier, a broken lunch box, pools of standing water, flooded areas, water seeping from the walls, break-off rooms in case of a cave-in, low ceilings, drill marks in the rock, blackened blasting marks, bits of blasting wire, bats, insects, blocked-off shafts, rotted wood and plywood, uneven ground, narrow walkways, water dripping from the roof, stakes placed in drill holes to hold candles, wax drippings, a smashed lantern, a shaky railing weak with dry rot, piles of rocks from cave-ins and rockfalls, a flashlight beam or headlamp reflecting off puddles and slick walls, bones from small creatures (mice, lizards, bats) lying in the dirt, old rusted signs pitted with age, names carved in rock, graffiti

SOUNDS
Echoes, boots scuffing on rocks, the scatter of loose stones, creaking, shifting timber, dripping water, muffled sounds from outside (trucks driving by, construction noises), amplified breathing, the wind blowing down a shaft from a breach or exit, the rumble of a cave-in, voices, the flap of bat wings and squeaks, small animals skittering over the rock

SMELLS
Cold, stale air, rock and stone, must, mildew, dry rot, scummy standing water, sweat, dust, noxious gases

TASTES
Air tasting like ozone from the presence of rock and minerals, peaty moisture from standing water, grit in one's teeth from dust, dry mouth, saliva, a swig of water from a bottle or canteen

TEXTURES AND SENSATIONS
Rough rock, stiff work gloves rubbing against the fingers, back pain from bending over to maneuver through tight spaces, smacking one's head on a low ceiling, scraping one's knees while crawling through tunnels and over loose rock, perspiration slipping down the back of the neck, skinning one's knuckles on boulders and outcroppings, brushing up against other people in close quarters, slipping on shale and pebbles, dusty silt drifting through a crack and landing on one's face, the rubber grip of a flashlight, the smack of a flickering flashlight against one's palm as batteries begin to die, air that chills exposed skin, air that grows stuffy and hot, the chalky feel of dust on one's fingers, spiderwebs tickling the skin, a feeling of light-headedness as one passes through an area where oxygen has been depleted, the shakiness of a railing that is riddled with rot, running one's hands along the wall to navigate, the drop of one's gut when lights go out and one is in utter blackness, a feeling of being crushed or of not getting enough oxygen, panic flutters at not knowing which way is up or out, stepping in a puddle where fetid water oozes into one's boot, a shiver at the strange echoes and sound of one's breathing

POSSIBLE SOURCES OF CONFLICT

Falling down a vertical shaft and injuring oneself

Getting lost and running out of food or water

Being trapped by a cave-in

Running out of oxygen

Losing one's light source

Hearing noises that suggest movement when one is alone

Encountering pockets of toxic gases

Falling asleep and being bitten by rats

Scratching oneself on a rusty tool

Stepping on a nail or twisting an ankle in the dark

Becoming overheated or hypothermic

Experiencing a panic attack at being underground

Seeing a light approaching from a connected mineshaft

Hearing something breathing in the dark when one is alone

Finding odd markings on the walls or artifacts in the shafts that don't correspond with the history of the area

PEOPLE COMMONLY FOUND HERE

Drug-users, explorers, geologists, thrill-seeking teens

RELATED SETTINGS THAT MAY TIE IN WITH THIS ONE

Cave (206), quarry (178)

SETTING NOTES AND TIPS

One would think that an underground mine would be cold, but the temperature of a mine varies depending on its location and nearby geological formations. Some mines are cold, while others are unbearably hot; some get warmer the deeper you go, while others get cooler. Mines also vary in the type of gases they produce, which can be present even after years of disuse. Some gases, such as hydrogen sulfide, are harmless but have an unpleasant scent. Other highly toxic or flammable gases can't be smelled at all (carbon monoxide, radon gas, methane, etc.), making an abandoned mine a very dangerous place. Also, modern mines that have been shut down will have vastly different infrastructure than old ones (which we have described here), and stronger security measures to keep trespassers out.

SETTING DESCRIPTION EXAMPLE

Janet handed me her flashlight as she pulled back the rotting plywood that covered the shaft. The wood splintered as she chucked it into the dead scrub, leaving a yawning black hole. I swung the beam toward it but the light barely pierced the gloom. This had been my idea, but suddenly my brain filled with thoughts of homework and upcoming tests. Janet crossed her arms and gave me a knowing smirk. She wasn't going to let me get out of this one.

Techniques and Devices Used: Multisensory descriptions

Resulting Effects: Characterization, foreshadowing, tension and conflict

ANCIENT RUINS

SIGHTS
Weather-worn stone pillars surrounded by dead clumps of grass, half-crumbled buildings, cracked blocks and stones broken up by meandering tree roots, pitted steps and staircases, caved-in roofs weighed down by vines or other foliage, faceless marble or stone statues, inscriptions and carvings in stone, towering spires, dusty and cobwebbed corridors in the buildings, sculpted archways stained by mold or mildew (in humid climates), stones placed in deliberate patterns, uneven floors worn from the feet of many people, altars, rock walls, battlements with blast marks or bullet holes from old wars, ash scars on the stone from past fires, empty hearths or fire pits, shadows, curled dead leaves scattered on the ground, dappled sunlight filtering in through trees or overgrowth, small creatures (spiders, snakes, lizards, bugs, birds, bats) making the ruins their home, caves, carved animal totems important to the culture, ropy vines breaking down stone and encroaching through window holes or doorways, foliage native to the area (hardy grasses, ferns, scrub brush, trees), animal droppings, moss, abandoned nests, holes and crevices, rubble, dust, a hidden cache of items from the era (jewelry, pots, religious symbols, weapons, eating implements, tools), a shed snake skin, animal tracks in the dirt, animal scat

SOUNDS
Wind slipping through stone corridors and through window openings, grasses sliding against each other, birdcalls, the flutter of wings, crickets or other noise-making insects, the crunch of dead leaves underfoot, leaves rattling against stone, dead vines scraping the walls, trees creaking in the breeze, the clap of footsteps on cobbled stone

SMELLS
Chalky dust, mildew and cold stone, local flowers, grass and greenery, the earthy scents of moist dirt and dead leaves

TASTES
A dry mouth, water or a hydrating drink brought on the hike, backpacker-friendly foods (granola bars, nuts, seeds, beef jerky, dried fruits)

TEXTURES AND SENSATIONS
Broken rock underfoot, uneven ground, sweat clinging to the skin, rough stone on one's palms, cool stone against one's back, white dust clinging to one's hands, tall grasses brushing against the legs, squeezing into a tight space and scraping one's skin, cool or wet palm fronds or fern leaves sliding over one's arms, a breeze ruffling one's hair, the pull of one's backpack straps, condensation clinging to a water bottle, the smoothness of stone weathered by the elements, the give of moss or a carpet of leaves underfoot, spiderwebs sticking to one's skin, dangling vines brushing one's hair, the pinch of a mosquito or bug bite, not daring to move as a snake slides past or over one's foot, climbing a staircase or wall and sitting on a rocky ledge to take in the view

POSSIBLE SOURCES OF CONFLICT

Supernatural phenomena (seeing or hearing things)

Getting lost in a maze-like ruin

Having a wall or roof collapse and becoming injured or trapped

Being bitten by a venomous spider or snake

Superstitions surrounding the site that make guides reluctant to explore them

Stumbling into a secret room or chamber with traps that are still active

Needing help (due to injury, illness, or running out of food) but being far from civilization

Running out of batteries for one's flashlight

Bad storms or flash flooding weather that causes earth to soften and stones to shift

Hidden dangers such as sink holes and crumbling ledges

Hearing noises and realizing one is being hunted by an animal

Wanting to stay and explore but one's group wishes to leave

A bus showing up and flooding the site with tourists, ruining one's peace and quiet

A breakdown that forces one to stay overnight when there are nighttime dangers (animals, etc.)

PEOPLE COMMONLY FOUND HERE

Archeologists, hikers, history buffs, locals visiting the site to pay respect or pray to ancestors, tourists

RELATED SETTINGS THAT MAY TIE IN WITH THIS ONE

Cave (206), rainforest (234), secret passageway (84)

SETTING NOTES AND TIPS

Ruins come in all shapes and sizes. They may be aboveground or subterranean. Climate will greatly influence the ruins' appearance, determining what grows there, how quickly the ruins degrade, and the type of animals that might be present. If the ruins are part of a tourist destination, there will be tourists and tour guides, reclamation specialists, and usually roped-off areas where people are not allowed to go. If the ruins are far from cities or have not yet been discovered, natural debris will be common, and it will be difficult to find clear paths in the overgrown area surrounding it.

SETTING DESCRIPTION EXAMPLE

When the sun rose over Angkor Wat, a reverent gasp escaped Lauren's lips. The massive ruined city, with its hundreds of stone temples, passages, stairways, and statues, rose up like a hand praising God himself. Palm trees and rainforest pressed against each side, pulling at the stone in an attempt to reclaim it, and the massive moat surrounding the Wat shimmered orange and pink. Malaria-carrying mosquitoes buzzed around her, but in her long-sleeved jacket she paid no mind; in another hour the mosquitoes would be off seeking shade and she'd be crossing the cobblestone bridge, basking in the smiles of the Buddha statues surrounding her. It had taken twelve long years to get here, but despite all the obstacles, she'd finally arrived.

    Techniques and Devices Used: Contrast, multisensory descriptions, simile

    Resulting Effects: Characterization, hinting at backstory, reinforcing emotion

ARCHERY RANGE

SIGHTS
A large open field, green grass, a row of square targets lined up at specific distances, flags flying to show wind direction, bow racks and hangers, a tree line or a projectile barrier (a stack of hay bales, a natural hill, netting, etc.) to stop arrows, fences, an overhead roof or awning to block sunlight, a metal hoop to hold one's quiver, a small shop (for equipment rentals, targets, permits or memberships and gear), a parking lot, an information stand with rules of conduct for unmanned ranges (used by local archery club members only) and news flyers for upcoming archery events, concrete shooting pads behind a shooting line, picnic tables for spectators to sit at, warning signs, people with binoculars, a field marshal, archery enthusiasts tending to equipment and stretching in preparation for shooting

SOUNDS
A drawn out hiss or whoosh as the arrow flies through the air, the solid *chunk* of an arrow hitting the target, spectators going quiet as the participant draws back his or her string, a soft exhale before releasing the arrow, multiple *chunks* of arrows hitting targets in succession at a larger range, the scrape of a shoe against a concrete pad as the archer sets his footing, the soft ruffle of a finger through a feather fletching, birds chirping, grasshoppers whirring, the wind sliding through the trees and grass, the flap of a wind sock or flag

SMELLS
Grass, sweat, pine needles, dry earth, hay

TASTES
Some settings have no specific tastes associated with them beyond what the character might bring into the scene (chewing gum, mints, lipstick, cigarettes, etc.). For scenes like these, where specific tastes are sparse, it would be best to stick to descriptors from the other four senses.

TEXTURES AND SENSATIONS
Tension against fingers while drawing back the bowstring, one's hand brushing below the chin while aiming, a string pressing lightly into the chin as one draws back, the dragging weight of a bow slung over a shoulder, squeezing the grip, the sudden absence of tension as the arrow releases, the smoothness of the arrow shaft, the slide of a plastic or leather arm guard against the skin or sleeve and then a squeeze as it is secured, pinching the string with the pads of one's fingers, the weight of the bow as one aims, a soft breeze that presses against one's face or ruffles the hair that one must ignore to focus on the shot

POSSIBLE SOURCES OF CONFLICT
Competing in a tournament when one's emotions are high
Having one's equipment malfunction or break due to improper care or sabotage
Having a wayward hiker or inexperienced spectator cross the range as one is about to shoot
A difference of opinion between rivals as to whose shot is closer to the target's center

Forgetting to use an arm or chest guard and being injured when one shoots

Heat or a lack of water creating dehydration and affecting a competitor's concentration

Loud spectators or cars blasting music nearby and causing distractions during a tournament

An animal walking onto the field

Competing against a relative or sibling for a prize that both want

Working hard yet feeling one's skill has plateaued

Needing better equipment to excel and not being able to afford it

Forgetting something at the range and finding it gone when one returns

Being made nervous by a certain spectator (a crush, a parent with high expectations)

Competing against sore losers who will want payback for the loss

Weather conditions that make it hard to focus or may affect the shot (rain, wind, snowfall)

PEOPLE COMMONLY FOUND HERE

Archery enthusiasts, bow hunters, course marshals, instructors, maintenance people and property owners, medieval role play groups during festivals, spectators

RELATED SETTINGS THAT MAY TIE IN WITH THIS ONE

Rural Volume: Summer camp (188)

Urban Volume: Indoor shooting range (210)

SETTING NOTES AND TIPS

Some outdoor ranges are not simply paper targets in a field; some have a walking trail that spreads out over many acres with foam animal targets set up at intervals. These 3D archery ranges are often located in large, wooded areas and have strict walking paths between numbered stations to ensure there are no crossfire accidents. On these types of courses, there may be raised structures to shoot from along with stations at ground level, and they provide a bit of realism that some prefer, especially hunters and competitive archers. There are many different types of bows a character might use for hunting, recreational shooting, and competitive archery, so know which type your character should use so you can accurately describe each shot.

SETTING DESCRIPTION EXAMPLE

Nick rolled his shoulders and stepped onto the shooting pad, putting out of his mind his brother in the audience and the importance of this shot. The wind was stronger than he would have liked, pushing the field grass to the left. He stared at the target as he was taught, familiarizing himself with the blue and gold circles, letting his gaze travel inward. He lifted his bow, nocked his arrow, and slowly let out his breath. Locking onto the black center, he smiled as if recognizing an old friend. That was where his shot would land.

Techniques and Devices Used: Multisensory descriptions, simile

Resulting Effects: Characterization, establishing mood

BARN

SIGHTS

Tall double doors, rough wooden walls with hooks to hold tack (bridles, leads, curry combs, halters) and equipment (shovels, a hay grapple, rope, pitchforks, a broom), animal stalls or pens with simple latches or gates, animals in their enclosures (pigs, sheep, goats, cows, horses, or mules), straw scattered across the floor, water buckets, a feed trough, oat sacks, a salt lick block that has been worn into grooves, feed buckets, flies buzzing close to the animals, spiders spinning webs across posts and in the rafters, dust and chaff floating in the sunlit air, rusty nails, a few strands of horse hair caught on rough stall rails, manure, feathers, dirty clumps of straw, a hen's nest hidden in the hay, bales of clean yellow straw and hay, a wooden ladder leading up to a loft, a pull string dangling from a bare bulb light, mice skittering across floorboards and nesting in the hay, horse blankets draped over a sawhorse, windows with shutters, mud-splattered walls, grime, free-range chickens searching out dropped feed, cats stalking vermin or sleeping in the sun, dogs sniffing in corners, a tractor and grimy all-terrain vehicles parked outside

SOUNDS

The rustle of hay, creaking boards, stamping, animal-specific vocals (snorting, thumps, whinnies, squeaks, grunts, lows, barks, growls), huffing breaths, animals rubbing themselves on posts or rails, the clatter of grain spilling into a trough, the scrape of a shovel against the dirt floor, hay bales thumping to the floor, the crackle of dry straw being spread in a stall, the crunch of an apple treat, chewing noises, the swish of a tail, the squeak of a gate, a latch being set into place, the slosh of water, the clink of tack, the flutter of a horse blanket as it's shaken out, humans talking or clucking at the animals, the muffled thump of horse hooves crossing the floor

SMELLS

Nose-tickling straw, animal flesh, urine, manure, salt, sweet-smelling timothy hay, grain, wood, sawdust, mud, mouldering straw or hay

TASTES

The dry taste of chaff when straw or hay is stirred up, sweat on the upper lip

TEXTURES AND SENSATIONS

Prickly hay and straw, chaff sticking to the neck or getting into one's shirt, rough boards, sweat trickling down one's face, heat from a hat band, swiping dust and chaff from clothes and hair, heavy work gloves, the dry and hairy tickle of horse lips, the warmth of animal bodies, horsehide, rope burn from hoisting hay bales with no gloves, heavy boots thumping the floor, a square-headed shovel jolting over the floor as one collects soiled straw and manure, being kicked by an injured or frightened animal, splinters, a warm and dusty horse's flank, pulling a curry comb slowly over the curve of a horse's back, fighting against tangles in a horse's mane, dry horse hairs from a mane or tail, getting flicked by a tail, the sting of a horsefly bite, being butted by a goat, getting a splinter as one climbs a rough wooden ladder into the loft

POSSIBLE SOURCES OF CONFLICT

Disease among the animals

A batch of bad feed that makes the animals sick

A fire

Predators (wolves, coyotes, bears) getting into the barn

Discovering someone has been living in the loft

Rotten supports causing the roof to collapse

A weak spot in the barn that allows animals to escape

A difficult pregnancy and animal delivery

Having to deliver an animal without help

Struggling to care properly for one's animals (because one is sick, disabled, or alone)

Discovering a hidden hatch in the floor put there by previous owners

An animal (prone to injury or violent behavior) that needs to be kept away from the others

Animals (horses, cows, goats) that are escape artists and can unlatch the barn door

A horse getting spooked and accidentally trampling someone

A storm that damages the barn or causes a collapse, hurting one's animals

PEOPLE COMMONLY FOUND HERE

A veterinarian, farm workers, farmers or ranchers and their family members, farriers

RELATED SETTINGS THAT MAY TIE IN WITH THIS ONE

Rural Volume: Chicken coop (48), orchard (174), pasture (176), ranch (180), underground storm shelter (94), vegetable patch (96)

Urban Volume: Old pick-up truck (268)

SETTING NOTES AND TIPS

Barns often have a similar look but may house different animals depending on their size and the type of farm or ranch they're on. Some may house only one kind of animal, especially in large numbers, while others will have different animal residents that get along well enough to share quarters. Cleanliness will also vary depending on the owner. Some people will muck out the barn frequently to protect the animals from disease (especially if they are selling animal products commercially) and supply a comfortable place for them to bed down. Other owners may not take such care.

SETTING DESCRIPTION EXAMPLE

After a few inquisitive nuzzles at Andrea's pockets to make sure all the carrots were gone, Tango rested his chin on her shoulder. The bristles under his muzzle were prickly, an old broom sweeping at her skin. She leaned against him, breathing in the smell of horse and straw, relishing the sound of hooves scuffing the wood floor and the beauty of sunlight painting his coat honey-gold. As exciting as college would be, she'd miss this place.

Techniques and Devices Used: Light and shadow, metaphor, multisensory descriptions

Resulting Effects: Establishing mood, reinforcing emotion

BEACH PARTY

SIGHTS
A wide expanse of ocean lapping the shore, the beach strewn with seashells and seaweed, dunes with sea fauna (grass, cattails, sea grape, bearberry), a bonfire, driftwood logs for seats, scattered rocks and boulders, a nearby pier, beach chairs and umbrellas, blankets and towels spread on the sand, coolers, drinks and food, sticks for s'mores, a kite flying overhead, a covered pavilion with picnic tables, people playing various games (football, volleyball, horseshoes), people dancing, someone playing guitar, people lying on the sand or on blankets (tanning during the day, staring up at the stars at night), sandpipers running along the shore, a crooked row of surfboards stuck into the wet sand, seagulls landing to scrounge food, pelicans diving into the water

SOUNDS
Music from someone's music player and speaker system, live music, the twang of a guitar, waves crashing, the steady thrum of the surf, a bonfire's crackle, birds cawing, people laughing and talking, girls shrieking, a volleyball being smacked back and forth, horseshoes clanging, towels flapping in the breeze, the pop of a drink can being opened, the crackle of food wrappers, people splashing in the ocean, a lifeguard's whistle

SMELLS
Salt water, sunscreen and suntan oil, sweat, smoke, beer, chlorine from a nearby pool, the scent of fabric softener on freshly laundered towels

TASTES
Sweat, sandy grit in the teeth, beer, soda, water, ice, finger foods (sandwiches, fast food, chips, pretzels, nuts, fruit, roasted hot dogs, pizza picked up on the way, cold chicken, potato salad and coleslaw), s'mores browned over the fire

TEXTURES AND SENSATIONS
The wind whipping hair into one's face and pulling at one's clothes, wet sand sticking to the skin, hot sand burning the soles of one's feet, the drip of a wet swimsuit, a scratchy towel, sunglasses slipping down the nose, a slight headache from being in the sun too long, the tingle of sunburn, greasy sunblock, dried salt on the skin, the sharp pain of stepping on a rock or seashell, the bite of sand fleas, fatigue in the calves from dancing or running in loose sand, kicking off flip-flops, a cool drink on a hot day, rough driftwood, the itchy sensation of sand caught in one's clothing, bumping into others while dancing, the warmth of a bonfire, the sting of smoke in the eyes as the wind shifts, a burning spark or ember landing on the skin, chilled skin as the sun goes down, the warmth of a cover-up or sweatshirt at night, wiggling one's toes in the sand, being peppered with sand from a stray football or volleyball, the air cooling as the sun sets, surf running over one's feet during a moonlit walk

POSSIBLE SOURCES OF CONFLICT
Getting drunk and doing something stupid (and it being recorded and shared online)
Jellyfish and sharks

Bad sunburns

Cutting one's foot on a seashell or rock

Getting pulled under by a rip current

Losing one's swimsuit in the surf

Bad weather that ruins the fun

Conflict due to competitiveness while playing a game

Competition over gaining the attention of someone one is attracted to

Falling into the fire

Embarrassing oneself while dancing

A pavilion that collapses

A tyrannical lifeguard or beach patrol

People showing up who were not invited who ruin the vibe

Having family members show up when one wanted anonymity

Alcohol leading to impaired romantic judgment that one regrets the next day

Drugs being added to drinks without knowledge

Leaving the party to go for a walk with someone and being assaulted

The police showing up and discovering some of the people are minors

PEOPLE COMMONLY FOUND HERE

A DJ, beach patrol members, lifeguards, partiers, party crashers, sunbathers, surfers, swimmers

RELATED SETTINGS THAT MAY TIE IN WITH THIS ONE

Beach (202), lighthouse (170), ocean (230), tropical island (240)

SETTING NOTES AND TIPS

Beach parties have changed quite a bit over the years. It's illegal to drive on most public beaches now, and many of them either don't allow bonfires or require a permit for one. Some don't allow alcoholic beverages, while others have no such rules. Security patrols often cruise the sand at night to ensure the safety of beach-goers, which can put a crimp in the party. Private or remote beaches, on the other hand, are a lot less strict, so your character having access to one may be a boon to both you and your story.

SETTING DESCRIPTION EXAMPLE

The bonfire snapped, tossing sparks at me. One lodged in my sweatshirt and I smacked it off. Drew held up a beer, but I shook my head; no-see-ums were biting like crazy and someone had already puked, so the party was pretty much ruined. The wind whipped up the fire and groped at my clothes with its icy cold fingers, reminding me this would be the last party of the season. I rubbed my hands on my jeans and tried to avoid looking at my ex, which was hard since she sat straight across from me and was trying her best to crawl into Jake's lap. I gnawed my lip and glanced around for my ride. Yep, definitely time to go.

    Techniques and Devices Used: Multisensory descriptions, weather

    Resulting Effects: Hinting at backstory, reinforcing emotion, tension and conflict

CAMPSITE

SIGHTS

A gravelly patch of bare ground ringed by trees and bushes, a man-made fire pit, a pile of chopped firewood or scavenged deadfall, a picnic table holding a jug of water, a portable dish station, plastic or paper plates and cups, condiments, hot dog buns in a bag, puffy white marshmallows, a beverage chest (full of ice, beer, wine coolers, and pop), a food cooler (filled with meat, bread, cheese, eggs, fruit and other perishables), a portable grill, hot dog sticks, lawn chairs or wood stumps circling the fire, a bright blue tarp strung across the overhead trees in case of rain, colorful tents (containing sleeping bags, pillows, air mattresses, a duffle bag of clothing, extra shoes, flashlights or a battery-powered lantern), a recreation vehicle, a camper or tent trailer, an array of kids' toys and outdoor sports equipment (horseshoes, a badminton set, a kite, a football, boomerangs, balls, bats and mitts), a laundry line strung between trees with wet bathing suits and towels hanging over them, insulated coffee mugs or empty beer bottles sitting in cup holders, citronella candles and traps sending up foul-smelling smoke to ward off mosquitoes, bottles of bug spray and sunscreen, kids using pocket knives to carve sticks for roasting marshmallows, an axe or hatchet leaning by a pile of firewood, a propane-powered cooking stove, fishing poles and a net leaning against an open truck bed, the glow of the campfire in the darkness, flickering candles or a gas lantern on a picnic table during a game of cards

SOUNDS

Music from a car or portable radio, birdcalls, the burbling of a nearby brook, crackles from the fire as wood burns and sap pops, voices, loud parties coming from nearby campsites, coyotes howling at night, the hoot of an owl, tree branches snapping as someone wanders around in the brush, the creak of tall trees and leaves rustling in the wind, a marshmallow bag being torn open, the rapid pop of campfire popcorn, the quiet flare of a marshmallow catching fire, an axe chopping wood, beer bottles clinking together, a brother snapping a wet towel at his sister, cars driving past on gravel, the splash of dirty dishwater being thrown in the bushes, the chitter of squirrels, the hiss of a beer opening, tent zippers being opened and shut, something large walking around outside the tent and sniffing for food, crickets or frogs, the hiss of a deflating air mattress in the middle of the night, a mosquito whining somewhere in the tent, the patter of rain on canvas, a neighboring group of campers partying late into the night

SMELLS

Pine needles, fresh air, grass, smoke, charred meat, hot dogs cooking, coconut-scented sunscreen, acrid bug spray and citronella candles, fish cooked in butter, smoky bacon over the fire, sweat, oily hair, stale beer from a collection of empty bottles left in the sun, morning dew in the grass

TASTES

Charred hot dogs smothered in ketchup, beer, pop, chocolate-loaded s'mores, bacon, pan-fried hamburgers or fish, steaming hot chocolate, the crisp burned skin of a marshmallow, campfire popcorn, half-burned pancakes doused with syrup

TEXTURES AND SENSATIONS

Sticky marshmallow adhering to one's fingers, juice from a popsicle running down one's wrist, uneven rocky ground, splinters from a picnic bench, the sting of a bee or mosquito bite, greasy sunscreen on one's skin, the heat of sunburn, dripping hair from a splash in the lake, a towel that's been warmed in the sun, shifting campfire smoke burning one's eyes, the slight give of a lawn chair, cool condensation on a bottle of beer, aches from sleeping on hard ground, scratchy eyes when one hasn't had enough sleep, shivering and burrowing deeper into one's sleeping bag, tossing and turning to try and get comfortable, powdery soot on one's hands after making the fire, the cold shock of water when one jumps into a river or lake

POSSIBLE SOURCES OF CONFLICT

Being caught in a rainstorm (or having to pack up in one)
Having something go missing from the camp while one's at the lake or on a hike
Someone falling into the fire or being hurt in a remote area
Discovering that a fire ban is in effect that prohibits campfires
Loud neighbors in other campsites
Running out of important items (food, drinking water, sunscreen)
Noticing a flat tire right as one is about to leave
Bad weather ending a campout prematurely
A fire that gets out of hand
An animal prowling the site and getting into food that was not properly stored

PEOPLE COMMONLY FOUND HERE

Campers and their families, campground officials, wildlife officers

RELATED SETTINGS THAT MAY TIE IN WITH THIS ONE

Forest (212), hiking trail (216), lake (220), motor home (74), mountains (228)

SETTING NOTES AND TIPS

In designated camping areas, there are usually built-in fire pits, wood for sale, a small store nearby, a water pump, and bathroom facilities that sometimes contain showers. For your story, decide whether it's better for your characters to camp in a managed campsite or if they should rough it by choosing a more secluded spot where they will truly be on their own.

SETTING DESCRIPTION EXAMPLE

Uncle Ross nodded, agreeing to recount his story of the bear attack. We all grew silent; the wind in the poplar leaves and the crackle of the dying embers grew loud. Ross' lips tightened and pressed with the effort of starting the tale, but when the beer can in his grip crinkled, he forced his fingers to loosen and began. As he told us of cresting the ridge with his hunting rifle and finding himself face to face with a thousand-pound grizzly, my gaze followed the jagged scar that started at the corner of his left eye and ended at his jaw, a parting gift from the animal that had almost killed him.
   Techniques and Devices Used: Multisensory descriptions, weather
   Resulting Effects: Establishing mood, hinting at backstory, reinforcing emotion

CHURCH

SIGHTS

Polished wooden pews or folding chairs arranged in rows, a shelf on the back of each pew holding a Bible and song book, an altar, a pulpit, crucifixes and crosses on the walls, rosaries, arranged flowers, banners highlighting key scenes from the church's history or symbols of a specific religion, high windows, stained glass windows, statues of important religious figures, aisles separating the pews into sections, a baptistry where baptisms are held, a decorative lectern with a Bible on it, musical instruments (a piano or keyboard, an organ, guitars, a drum set) on the stage, decorative arches and moldings, a sound system, cordless microphones, a choir, offering baskets or plates, a communion table holding blessed wine and wafers, a padded bar for kneeling in the pews, shrines and statues, incense and burning candles, holy water fonts, priests and altar boys, confessional booths, thick doors separating the sanctuary from the entry area, complimentary pamphlets and religious books, a donation box, a church notice board, a nursery, classrooms for children's lessons and adult Bible studies, a youth area, a community hall (tables and folding chairs, serving tables, a kitchen), a nearby rectory where the pastor or rector lives

SOUNDS

The pastor or priest preaching or reading from scripture, children speaking in too-loud whispers, babies crying, children squirming against the benches, feet shuffling, musical instruments softly playing, a choir singing, voices mumbling agreement during a prayer, heavy breathing, coughing, sighing, the whisper of fabric as people shift in their seats, feedback from the mic, parishioners calling out affirmations (*Amen! Hallelujah!*), the assembly singing in unison and clapping during a song, a hymn book falling to the floor with a bang, doors opening and closing, feet whispering over thick carpet, the creak of a pew when one sits on it, kneeling benches banging down, the rustling sound of a congregation rising or sitting simultaneously

SMELLS

Incense and burning candles, cologne and perfume, hairspray, wood polish, cleaners, musty carpet

TASTES

Watered-down wine or fruit juice, tasteless wafers, gum, mints, cough drops

TEXTURES AND SENSATIONS

A wafer dissolving on the tongue, a child tugging on one's sleeve and asking when the service will be over, restless children shaking the pew, the hard benches numbing one's buttocks, shifting in one's seat to get comfortable, cushioned kneeler pads, making the sign of the cross, feeling constrained by tight collars or ill-fitting shoes, stifling a yawn, squeezing a loved one's hand, the firm pew back under one's hand as one stands, tapping a foot during hymns or when music is played, an opened book balanced on one's knee, a pen scratching over paper as one takes notes, a cooler spot on the forehead where holy water was placed

POSSIBLE SOURCES OF CONFLICT

Clashing religious beliefs, especially within a family

Personal conflicts and an inability to forgive

Cliques within the church that hold power over the congregation or isolated individuals

The church being unable to expand its basic tenets to adapt to changing ideals in society

Funding issues that threaten the church's future

Defacement of the church property

Abuse of power and authority

A style of sermons that is unpopular with certain members of the congregation

People judging one another

Arguments over silly things (what color to paint the hall, what time services should be held, etc.)

Confusion when a pastor leaves and there is no one to take his or her place

Trying to serve the community but being unable to meet all the demands

Needing to fundraise for special projects but knowing one's congregation is struggling financially

A flood that forces the church to close down an onsite soup kitchen or food bank

Criticism from the community when the church upholds an unpopular belief or ideal

Churchgoers who behave differently outside of church

PEOPLE COMMONLY FOUND HERE

Administrative staff, altar boys and girls, childcare, clergy members, musicians, parishioners either worshipping or volunteering in another area (with the choir, tech team, hospitality team), the worship band, visitors

RELATED SETTINGS THAT MAY TIE IN WITH THIS ONE

Graveyard (164), wake (98), wedding reception (192)

SETTING NOTES AND TIPS

The physical set-up of a church will vary largely depending upon its age, its funding, and the denomination with which it's aligned. Keep in mind, too, that while many churches own their own buildings and land, others choose to rent or lease existing facilities (such as a community center room). These church facilities are temporary and must be set up and broken down on days of worship in order to accommodate other users during the rest of the week. This makes for more of a minimalist layout and design.

SETTING DESCRIPTION EXAMPLE

Nyda sat ramrod straight in the pew, her gloved hands in her lap. At this late hour the lights had been dimmed, and the few lit candles on the altar cast a flickering red glow across the first few pews. She cast her gaze up at Jesus on his cross as the words of Father Oakley's sermon from yesterday's funeral washed over her. He'd spoken of the glory of God and her beloved Andre being in a better place, but while the words were meant to comfort, they did not. God and his glory. Where was He when that drunk driver got behind the wheel?

Techniques and Devices Used: Light and shadow

Resulting Effects: Hinting at backstory, reinforcing emotion, tension and conflict

COUNTRY ROAD

SIGHTS
A gravel or sunbaked road, wide open country, barbed wire fencing, leaning white mileage posts nearly lost in the weeds, grass growing on the road's shoulder and ditches, crops growing in pastures (whiskery barley, yellow canola flowers, tall stalks of timothy hay, harvested round hay bales sitting in crop stubble), grazing cattle, scruffy brush and stunted trees dotting fallow land, scatters of broken glass along the roadside, shredded rubber tires or plastic light casings from past accidents, cigarette butts and beer cans, clumps of dandelions and foxtail, birds (hawks, eagles, falcons) flying overhead, roadkill, buzzards gathering at the side of the road, hardy wildflowers, old rotting shacks and barn structures forgotten in fields, crows or ravens sitting on fence posts, streaks of cloud, bright sun and blue sky, a plane flying overhead, the occasional passing car, a tractor throwing up a plume of dust in its wake

SOUNDS
Wind feathering through the wild grass and crops, crickets and grasshoppers whirring, the cry of a predator bird, the rustle of a mouse or lizard skittering through a clump of weeds, the scuff of gravel under one's boots, the rumble of an approaching truck, rain pattering onto the pavement, thunder grumbling, the trickle and burble of water running along a ditch after a storm, the distant clank of a tractor

SMELLS
Hot pavement and road tar, dry grass, dust, the rotten decay of roadkill, flowering weeds or nearby crops, cow manure, clean air

TASTES
Chewing on a stalk of sweet grass while walking, water from a water bottle, dry mouth, dust

TEXTURES AND SENSATIONS
The smooth bounce of a pebble in the palm, gravel poking through thin-soled shoes, the gentle slap of grass against one's legs as one cuts across a field or walks in the ditch, seed heads of a ripe crop tickling one's hands, the prickle of sunburn on the neck, the pinprick of a spiny burr as one pulls it off one's pant leg, heat rising off the asphalt in waves, dust in the throat that makes one cough, sweat dampening one's clothes and hair, dust coating one's feet or shoes, gnats flying around one's face, heat from the sun beating down on one's head, a breeze blowing the hair off one's neck or brow, patting a horse's warm flank, the tickle of a horse's whiskery chin as it eats grass from one's palm, the weight of a backpack or jacket slung over one's shoulder on the walk home

POSSIBLE SOURCES OF CONFLICT
A breakdown or flat tire
Hitting an animal with one's car when it crosses the road
Getting lost in a desolate place

Becoming dehydrated

Creepy-looking adults who offer one a ride

Being caught out in the open during bad weather

A careless cigarette starting a grass fire

Coming across an animal who was hit by a car yet is still alive

A breakdown far from people with no cell phone or cell service

Coming across a wild animal while walking

Cutting across a field only to discover it has a bull protecting it

PEOPLE COMMONLY FOUND HERE

Farmers, locals, lost tourists looking for a shortcut

RELATED SETTINGS THAT MAY TIE IN WITH THIS ONE

Rural Volume: Barn (148), farm (160), farmer's market (162), meadow (224), pasture (176), ranch (180)

Urban Volume: Old pick-up truck (268)

SETTING NOTES AND TIPS

If your setting is located in a real place, research the types of crops and animals that might naturally be found in the area. As well, consider the growing season. The stubble of green spring growth will lend a different view to the scene than bright fall foliage. Sensory details will also differ based on climate and location.

SETTING DESCRIPTION EXAMPLE

Gravel crackled under the tires as we coasted along Old Red Mill road. Two nights in a row, people claimed to have seen lights in the dark sky and heard an odd whine that had no business being out among the wooden rail fences and cow pastures. Our headlights bathed the narrow road in light—and hit on two flashes in the ditch. Mary and I screamed and Jim hit the brakes, startling the mother deer and her spotted fawn into running across the road. The three of us busted up laughing. It was us who had no business being out here so late, chasing a silly rumor.

Techniques and Devices Used: Light and shadow, multisensory descriptions

Resulting Effects: Hinting at backstory, reinforcing emotion

COUNTY FAIR

SIGHTS
A giant parking lot, grassy fields, big canvas tents that hold agricultural sights (a livestock show, sheep shearing competitions, petting zoo, 4H events and demonstrations), amusement rides (a Ferris wheel, a carousel, giant slippery slides), carnival games (ring toss, duck fishing, shooting at targets), food trailers and carts selling both common and uncommon county fair foods (corn dogs, pretzels, deep-fried butter, chocolate covered bacon, potato spiral sticks, mini doughnuts, candy apples, cotton candy, deep-fried candy bars, scorpion pizza), colorful balloons, performers (clowns, jugglers, contortionists, folk musicians, fire breathers, sword swallowers), farmer's market stalls (selling local fruit, berries and produce, pierogies, honey, jams and jellies, hot sauce, baked goods, handmade jewelry, clothing and art pieces), face painting, kids' games, tractor or hayrides, colorful lights and flags, people in costumes, balloons drifting up into the air by accident, spinning rides and flashing lights, trash and cigarette butts stomped flat on the ground, sticky-faced children toting around stuffed animals or other prizes, hay bales to sit on

SOUNDS
Folk music, carnival music, people (yelling, shouting, laughing, calling to one another), animals making noises in their stalls (snuffling, shuffling in the straw, pawing at the ground, braying, squealing, neighing, lowing), auctioneers or announcers using microphones, the hum of the machinery used to run the carnival rides and food trailers, over-tired toddlers crying, game vendors calling out to guests, the whoosh of a plume of fire from a fire breathing act, the crowd gasping, children calling for their parents, the grind and rumble of tractors starting up, balloons popping

SMELLS
Deep fryers and grilling meat, popcorn, dust, hot dogs, animal manure, sweat, body odor, beer, cigarette or pipe smoke, motor oil, hot machinery, fresh straw, horsehide

TASTES
Oily and sweet batter, sugar-dusted doughnuts, water, beer, sweet snow cones or ice cream, fried chicken, potato chips, buttery popcorn, cheese, spices, barbeque sauce, hamburgers, hot dogs, oniony pierogies in sour cream

TEXTURES AND SENSATIONS
The rough fur of a farm animal, a hay bale scratching the backs of one's legs, greasy butter on fingertips, being tossed around on a wild midway ride, a soft stuffed animal prize, the smooth metal pole of a carousel horse, the whiskery tickle of a goat or llama eating food from one's palm, pillow-soft cotton candy fluff, sticky snow cone syrup running down one's arm, legs stretched wide to span a pony or horse's back, seasickness from too many rides and too much greasy food, the welcome shade of a tent

POSSIBLE SOURCES OF CONFLICT

A stage act going awry

Children getting lost or being abducted

Drug dealers working the crowds

Pickpockets on the prowl

Being bitten by an animal in the petting zoo

An animal getting loose and wreaking havoc

A ride breaking down with one still on it

Spending too much money trying to win a prize

Being ditched by one's friends while one is on a ride

Losing one's money on a ride or having it stolen

Discovering that one's animal is sick right before it goes up for auction

Falling off a ride and being injured

Food poisoning

Feeling watched in the crowd

A creepy carnival attendant who keeps turning up nearby

Being tasked with babysitting siblings when one wants to be off with one's friends

Witnessing an animal being abused

PEOPLE COMMONLY FOUND HERE

Artisans in the area, drug dealers or thieves, employees of the event, farmers and ranchers, local news crews, musicians, organizers, people living in the area, police, teens, tourists

RELATED SETTINGS THAT MAY TIE IN WITH THIS ONE

Rural Volume: Country road (156), farmer's market (162), pasture (176), rodeo (182)

Urban Volume: Parking lot (102), public restroom (112)

SETTING NOTES AND TIPS

Note that county fairs can vary according to country or region. Some may contain more agricultural events such as animal or farm equipment auctions and antique car shows, while others may have little more than a row of stalls displaying local goods from the area. Some fairs are themed, such as the Scottish highland games or medieval fairs. At these events, the games, costumes, and décor will match the fair's theme.

SETTING DESCRIPTION EXAMPLE

The sun dropped quickly out here in Marcus' field, and the families drifted back to their parked cars in hopes of getting their sugar-stuffed kids into bed. An older group took their place—couples holding hands and groups of teenagers giving off the subtle scents of pot and beer. The thrum of music changed to something deeper, and the sideshow tents opened, inviting the crowds in to see less mainstream acts of the strange and bizarre.

Techniques and Devices Used: Multisensory descriptions, weather

Resulting Effects: Establishing mood, foreshadowing

FARM

SIGHTS

A ranch-style house with a wide covered deck or screened porch, cows or goats grazing in a fenced pasture, a field of knee-high timothy hay or other crop (canola flowers, fescue grass, corn, barley, wheat), a barn and grain silos, a chicken coop, chickens wandering the yard and pecking at bugs in the dirt, a small greenhouse and garden full of neatly tended rows of vegetable crops (ferny carrots, green onion spears, leafy cabbages and turnips, white-flowering potato plants, tomato, pea and bean vines), a scarecrow rising up over a field of new corn, fruit trees, a water barrel to catch rainfall, bright yellow sunflowers nodding along a barbed wire fence, a variety of penned and free-ranging animals (horses, cows, goats, pigs, sheep, chickens, turkeys, geese, dogs, cats), tractors parked in a row with other farm machinery (a cultivator, backhoe, seeder, plow, combine harvester, bailing machine, auger), banged-up barrels of diesel fuel, dust trails following a tractor as it digs into the soil, rocking chairs on the porch, a tire swing hanging from a giant oak tree, farm workers in overalls and flannel shirts, round hay bales under a tarp, a pitchfork leaning against the shed (filled with shovels, axes, rakes, rope, horse tack, wheelbarrows), piles of brush waiting to be burned, a fire pit with lawn chairs around it, fences, derelict buildings with sagging roofs that lean off-kilter, broken-down trucks and farm equipment, weeds and tall grass around the buildings, trees surrounding the farm's yard, a family dog chasing a mouse under the shed, woods (with coyotes, bears, deer, wolves, moose, elk, foxes, rabbits, mice, birds), irrigation sprinklers, a porch swing in need of fresh paint

SOUNDS

Chickens clucking and scratching at the ground, roosters calling out to the sunrise, horses snorting or whinnying, cows lowing, buildings creaking in the wind, hooves stamping in the barn, horsetails swishing, pigs rooting for fodder in a trough, the wind sliding through crops and trees, fruit thumping to the ground, leaves rustling, mice skittering in the barn walls, birds fluttering as they roost, howls of nocturnal coyotes and wolves, the yip of a fox, the *whump* of a hay bale being tossed down from the hayloft, owls hooting, the screech of a bird of prey, the grind of a motor turning over, a plow breaking through roots and throwing up rocks, the crackle of a campfire, the roar of a chainsaw, an axe chopping wood, flies and bees buzzing, the whine of a mosquito, workers calling to one another over loud machinery, wind chimes ringing in the breeze, a summer storm filling the air with thunder

SMELLS

Manure, green growth from crops, ripening fruit (apples, strawberries, pears, peaches), pine needles, fresh hay, musty barns, dust, dirt, mildew, sun-warmed earth, the musk of animal flesh, gasoline and diesel fuel, motor oil and engine grease, exhaust from tractors, fertilizer, the floral scents of wildflowers (daisies, fireweed, Indian paintbrush, bluebells, etc.)

TASTES

Chewing on sweet grass, a wad of bitter chewing tobacco, cigarette or pipe smoke, tasting a carrot pulled right from the ground, a drink of cold water after a long day, potatoes roasted in foil in a campfire's coals, hot dogs and marshmallows charred over flame, fresh fruit or berries pulled from a tree or bush, iced tea, mint, fresh bread, vegetables, grit from blowing dust

TEXTURES AND SENSATIONS
Crumbling soil, the splash of cold water on the neck, sweat-stiff clothes that chafe, grit under the fingernails, the stiff bristles of barley or wheat heads, a heavy load of firewood in one's arms, the jarring sensation of an axe biting into a chopping block, the scratch of brambles, smooth wooden rails around a horse corral, calloused hands, stinging blisters, rope burns, chapped lips, the heat of sunburn on the neck and face, a cold glass of lemonade at lunch time, a wooden bucket that grows heavier as one collects fruit, the prick of thorns from a thistle or rosebush, the soothing motion of a rocking chair or porch swing, sore muscles at the end of a long day

POSSIBLE SOURCES OF CONFLICT
Equipment breakdowns at harvest time
Injuries from farm equipment
A horse breaking a leg in a gopher hole
Wild animals tearing holes in the fences, getting into the barn, or attacking animals or people
Poachers and hunters using one's land
Disease or an insect infestation in the crops
Adult children wishing to leave for the city but having to stay and help run the farm
Poor weather that delays seeding or harvesting
A drought that lasts several years in a row
A death in the family that creates an extra workload burden

PEOPLE COMMONLY FOUND HERE
Family members, farmers, hired hands, neighbors, ranchers, veterinarians, visitors and inspectors

RELATED SETTINGS THAT MAY TIE IN WITH THIS ONE
Rural Volume: Barn (148), chicken coop (48), country road (156), farmer's market (162), orchard (174), pasture (176), root cellar (82), vegetable patch (96)
Urban Volume: Old pickup truck (268)

SETTING NOTES AND TIPS
Some farms are strictly crop producers, while others may also raise animals. Most crop farms grow different types of grains, which minimizes the risk if markets sour or there's a low yield. If the farm has horses, it likely will have at least one field of hay to provide feed for them.

SETTING DESCRIPTION EXAMPLE
I stood in the middle of a cornfield that was impossibly green and tall, and I listened. No cars rushed past on the freeway, no screech of tires, no wailing sirens to herald imminent pain and suffering. Only wind, blessed wind, ruffled through the shiny stalks, blowing away my loss and replacing it with the promise of food for the table and hope for the future.
Techniques and Devices Used: Contrast, multisensory descriptions
Resulting Effects: Establishing mood, hinting at backstory

FARMER'S MARKET

SIGHTS
Rows of tables and booths filled with local seasonal produce (bundles of carrots, beets and asparagus, bags of potatoes, crates of shiny zucchini, cucumbers and peppers, trays of tomatoes, corn in husks), bright tablecloths and cloth awnings, signs and price guides, baskets of fruit (apples, pears, peaches, plums, cherries, strawberries, blackberries, raspberries), piles of eggplants and pumpkins, braids of garlic, bundles of herbs, jars of honey and beeswax products, jams and jellies, flowers and plants, craft tables with handmade items (knitted scarves, dolls, notecards, jewelry, soap, clothing), bins and coolers piled around tables, hanging scales, food vendors (selling hot cider, fresh fruit smoothies, cured meats, homemade bread, cookies and pies), entertainers (jugglers, magicians, dancers, buskers), people carrying plastic bags full of goods, picnic tables and benches, a band setting up on a platform, a petting zoo, arts and crafts activities for the kids, a tractor or old truck for kids to climb on

SOUNDS
Live local bands playing music, announcements being made over a microphone, the hum of many people socializing, children laughing, wind fluttering through leafy plants and flapping tablecloths, the sizzle of meat, boiling water, the hiss of steam, the rattle of plastic bags, the crunch as one bites into a fresh apple, vendors calling out to customers walking by, children asking their parents for sweets, animal noises from the petting zoo, cash drawers sliding open, people haggling over prices, the metal rattle of scales being used

SMELLS
Fresh herbs, flowers (roses, lavender), beeswax, citrus fruits, ripening berries, peaches and apples, pungent tomato vines, smoky cured meats, natural essential oils and fragrances from handmade soaps and creams, dirt clinging to root vegetables, car exhaust from the nearby parking lot, cooking oil, sugar and spices

TASTES
Sweet honey, tart apples, juicy peaches, spicy sausages and other meats, the crumbly sweetness of a fresh cherry or blueberry pie, apple juice or cider, crackers with jam, berries, hearty bread spread with freshly churned butter, homemade cookies, brownies, health bars, salads, fresh goat cheese

TEXTURES AND SENSATIONS
Peach juice sliding down one's arm, chewy bread, the smoothness of a tomato skin, the weight of a pumpkin in one's arms, a slippery plastic bag, heavy produce bags digging into one's palms, squeezing a plum or nectarine to judge ripeness, velvety flower petals, cold glass jars of fresh honey, lumpy potatoes, a steamy cup of hot chocolate or cider, the uneven boards of an old picnic table, sitting on a scratchy hay bale to eat a snack, the rough fur of an animal in the petting zoo

POSSIBLE SOURCES OF CONFLICT
A vendor caught selling commercial produce that he claimed to be local
Unsanitary preparations that cause an outbreak of food poisoning

A customer having an allergic reaction to a food or product

A drunk driver crashing into the crowd

Pickpockets

Feuds between vendors selling similar products

Vendors undercutting one another on price

A farmer selling out of a product that a customer specifically came to buy

Poor weather resulting in a low turnout

Too many vendors and not enough spaces

A bad economy resulting in fewer people being able to pay more for fresh food

PEOPLE COMMONLY FOUND HERE

Customers, entertainers, farmers, people interested in natural foods and sustainable living

RELATED SETTINGS THAT MAY TIE IN WITH THIS ONE

Barn (148), country road (156), farm (160), orchard (174), pasture (176)

SETTING NOTES AND TIPS

Farmer's markets are often held outside and are usually seasonal. Typically a rural event, they also can take place in a town's common area, such as a street or park, on the weekends. Since a market is both functional and recreational, it can nurture a feeling of community and well being in the neighborhood, and the presence of music and performers makes the event festive.

Larger cities may have a permanent indoor space for markets, but rather than all products coming from local farms, some are brought in from distant locations, especially in seasons when local produce is not available. These markets usually also have tables dedicated to artisans selling different types of handmade items (jewelry, pottery, paintings, dishware) or specialty items (kitchen gadgetry, teas, organic coffee and chocolate, health bars and powders).

SETTING DESCRIPTION EXAMPLE

I pulled at my shirt, unsticking it from my skin with a sweaty *shloop*. The afternoon sun slanted under the awning of my booth from the worst angle, baking every square inch of my space. Couldn't believe I was here when I could be down at the pond, where a body had a chance of staying cool. At the very least, I should have a chair to rest in, but Aunt Vera wouldn't allow it. *Can't sell honey whilst resting on your laurels*. I rolled my eyes and slumped against the table. The jars clacked together but what did I care? No one was buying anyway.

Techniques and Devices Used: Light and shadow, weather

Resulting Effects: Reinforcing emotion

GRAVEYARD

SIGHTS
Wrought iron fences and gates, a paved driveway winding between the graves, a chapel, sun-blanched stone angels, carved headstones (marble, concrete, or granite in hues of white, black and gray), a mausoleum, cordoned-off family burial plots, well-tended lawns, decorative flower beds, benches, real and artificial flowers left on graves, dried flowers and wreaths, black-clad mourners standing around a grave, backhoe equipment (usually hidden from viewers and only brought out during non-visiting hours), stone carvings of religious figures or symbols, established trees with moss hanging from their branches, framed portraits or meaningful trinkets left on the headstones, a hearse followed by a line of cars, funerals in process (a priest holding a Bible, a casket, groups of mourners, fresh flowers, graveyard workers hovering nearby), plaques with prayers written on them, a memorial wall for urns, birds, squirrels, chipmunks, decorative rock and stone, candles, signs of neglect in older cemeteries (leaves or twigs on graves, patchy or overgrown grass, dead trees and greenery, crumbling or cracked headstones, vandalized masonry, discolored headstones, broken gates, cracked cement pathways with weeds poking through)

SOUNDS
Mourners crying or sniffing, people speaking in low voices, whispered prayers, the rustle of dead flowers being removed, the snip of shears, a broom rustling as a maintenance worker sweeps an area clean, lawn mowers, cars and hearses rolling to a stop at the curb, graves being dug (after hours), the motorized hum of a casket being lowered into the ground, a fistful of dirt clattering against the coffin, extreme verbalized grief (wailing, moaning, inconsolable sobbing), a priest conducting the funeral or offering words of comfort, gates that creak open or closed, the wind whistling through grass and trees, birds and small animals that squeak and chirp, the slow click of shoes along a path, distant church bells, the tick of dead leaves tumbling along stone pathways, a visitor at a grave speaking quietly to a deceased loved one

SMELLS
Fresh-cut grass, hot stone, newly turned earth, floral scents from flowers left on graves, perfume or aftershave, smells associated with the seasons (crisp air in the winter, rain and rot in early spring or late fall, the smell of new plant growth in the spring and summer)

TASTES
Some settings have no specific tastes associated with them beyond what the character might bring into the scene (chewing gum, mints, lipstick, cigarettes, etc.). For scenes like these, where specific tastes are sparse, it would be best to stick to descriptors from the other four senses.

TEXTURES AND SENSATIONS
A cold headstone, the thud of one's shoes against the walkway, heels sinking into the grass, the numbness of grief, a rusty wrought-iron fencepost, chalky dust from a stone marker, dead flowers crinkling in the hand, tears on one's cheeks, gripping a loved one's hand, the prickle of cut grass as one kneels or sits, silky fresh flowers, dry dirt in one's fist, prickling eyes, tears clogging one's throat, a runny nose, a sweaty tissue in one's hand, a damp handkerchief

POSSIBLE SOURCES OF CONFLICT

Graves that are vandalized

Feuding family members visiting a grave at the same time

Theft of objects left near graves (flowers, meaningful tokens and keepsakes, letters)

Aggressive paparazzi at a high-profile funeral

Feeling watched in a graveyard

Being an empath and having to attend a graveside funeral where emotions run high

Paranormal events

A flood or groundwater situation that causes coffins to surface

A groundskeeper with morbid fetishes

Grave robbers

An equipment malfunction as a casket is being lowered into a grave

Mourning relatives that create shrines around the gravesite or are there all the time, unable to let go

Someone at a funeral who reacts strangely to grief (laughing during the proceedings, for example)

A mourner showing up who reminds everyone of something best forgotten (an indiscretion with a hooker, an affair, an arrest, etc.)

PEOPLE COMMONLY FOUND HERE

A graveyard custodian, clergy members, close family or friends, mourners, vandals, visitors or tourists to the graveyard (if it's an historical site)

RELATED SETTINGS THAT MAY TIE IN WITH THIS ONE

Rural Volume: Church (154), mausoleum (172), wake (98)

Urban Volume: Funeral home (68)

SETTING NOTES AND TIPS

Different cultures and customs will often affect a gravesite. If it is important to the story, consider the ethnic background of the mourners and the departed, and decide if there are any special customs or beliefs surrounding death that might influence the look of the site, steer religious proceedings, or dictate the actions of those present.

SETTING DESCRIPTION EXAMPLE

As the moon rose, the graveyard of my ancestors transformed. The translucent light breathed life into the worn, faceless statues of praying children and winged angels. It smoothed away fissures and softened broken edges. In the moonlight, the crooked headstones stood proud, keeping to their duty even as time wore away the messages they bore. I walked through the tangled weeds until I reached the back gate and an empty plot. This space, beneath the bower of an old oak, was my own. How odd to stand here in the dewy grass, knowing someday I would never leave it again.

Techniques and Devices Used: Contrast, light and shadow, personification

Resulting Effects: Establishing mood, reinforcing emotion

HUNTING CABIN

SIGHTS
Long grasses and wildflowers growing against the walls, a fire pit, an outhouse, a wood pile and a cutting stump surrounded by wood chips, a covered well, animal tracks in the mud near the creek, indigenous animals nosing around the property (bears, deer, moose, coyotes, grouse, squirrels, foxes), thickets and trees reclaiming the land, a small structure made of mud-chinked logs, a half-rotten step leading to a warped doorframe, a drooping roof covered in dead leaves and twigs, abandoned bird nests under the eaves, a creaky front door that needs a shoulder push to open it, a dented oil or kerosene lantern hanging off a rusty hook, a wood-burning stove or fireplace filled with ash and blackened wood chunks, a dust-enshrouded cooking stove, a wood plank floor, an old gun rack near the door, rough plywood shelves, a sleeping loft, a rickety wooden bench, dirty windows, mouse droppings scattered across the floor, dust, chew marks at the bottom of the door, a hole in the floor or gap in the chinking that allows small animals in, tin cups and a dented kettle covered in cobwebs, dead flies and curled up wasps on the windowsills, a mouse shooting across the floorboards and out an exit crack

SOUNDS
Leaves rattling in the wind, whistling drafts getting through cracks and coming down the chimney, an animal crawling through the dead leaves beneath the cabin, creaky floorboards, the wind shaking ill-fitting windows and doors, a large animal prowling outside and snuffling for food, birds, mosquitoes, the cry of a bird of prey, wolves or coyotes yipping or howling in the night, an owl hooting, the thump of boots across the creaking floorboards, dead leaves scuttling across the porch, tree branches scraping at the sides and roof of the cabin, the crackle of a wood fire, an armload of gathered wood clattering onto the hearth, the warped door scraping over the floorboards, soup bubbling on the stove, a creaky bed, a squeaky hinge on the door of a pot-bellied stove

SMELLS
Damp wood, a wood fire, soot and ash, rot, mouse droppings, musty earth, coffee

TASTES
Meat cooked over an open fire, dried meat and fruit, foraged nuts and berries, traveling food (trail mix, granola bars, crackers, peanuts), water from a canteen or nearby creek

TEXTURES AND SENSATIONS
The scrape of briars and branches against the arms, the slight give of a rotten step, a spiderweb tickling one's face, gritty dust, rough log walls, uneven floorboards, the jar of an axe biting into wood, using one's shoulder to force open a warped door, a fire's warmth, a frigid outhouse on a winter night, freezing cold well water, sitting off-balance on a wobbly or lopsided stool, rotten wood crumbling beneath one's fingers, the sharp lines of a name or date carved into the wall, cold drafts blowing through the cabin, a mosquito's sting

POSSIBLE SOURCES OF CONFLICT
Squatters using the space without permission
Teenagers using it as a party spot and causing damage
Animals getting inside and destroying the cabin
Mice or other rodents creating burrows and nests under or inside the building
A storm or snowfall that damages the roof between visits
Falling asleep with the fire burning and the cabin catching fire
Hearing a large animal prowling outside
Finding a journal that is filled with violent, disturbing images
Hearing footsteps just outside the door
Being close to hypothermic but having nothing to start a fire with
Getting caught using the hunting cabin as a clandestine place to meet
Finding human bones among the burned bits of wood in the stove or hearth
Finding something hidden under a floorboard
Leaving a cache of items behind that disappears before one's next visit
Needing the cabin in an emergency but being unable to get inside (the door is padlocked, windows are barred, etc.)

PEOPLE COMMONLY FOUND HERE
Campers, hikers, hunters, squatters

RELATED SETTINGS THAT MAY TIE IN WITH THIS ONE
Forest (212), hiking trail (216), lake (220), mountains (228), outhouse (78), river (236)

SETTING NOTES AND TIPS
Because of a hunting cabin's isolation, it is often left vacant; if it isn't properly cared for and sealed up after each visit, it will quickly fall into disrepair. It can also be used for a variety of unintended purposes: a party shack for teens, a secret rendezvous point for lovers, a temporary home for vagrants, or a serial killer's lair. One cabin can mean different things to different people within the same story; varying the cabin's purposes is one way to add unexpected layers to a setting.

SETTING DESCRIPTION EXAMPLE
A sliver of moon glinted through the grimy glass, shedding just enough light on the broken bench and crude table for me to avoid stumbling over them. I dropped my load of scavenged wood by the stone fireplace. My hands shook, exhaustion settling into my bones after dragging myself out of the ice-clogged river. I grabbed the tin of matches kept on the hearth but my hand shook so badly I didn't know if I'd be able to strike one. My lighter, along with all my other supplies, was at the bottom of the river with the snowmobile. I gritted my teeth and focused on gripping the end of a wooden match. It was either get the fire lit or freeze to death.
　　Techniques and Devices Used: Light and shadow, weather
　　Resulting Effects: Hinting at backstory, tension and conflict

LANDFILL

SIGHTS
Mounds of trash (bags, broken furniture, concrete pieces, wire, patio bricks, broken toys and dolls, empty cans and bottles, used diapers, old clothing, cardboard boxes and product packaging, hoses, broken plastic kiddie pools and playground equipment, yard clippings, car parts), garbage trucks dumping their loads in piles, front-end loaders pushing trash into pits, roads winding around the hills of trash, drainage pipes emptying into ditches, collection ponds, white methane collection pipes rising out of the ground, compactors driving across trash to compress it, vehicles kicking up dust, swarms of scavenging seagulls that take flight when a vehicle comes close, cranes and other heavy equipment, tarps covering sections of the landfill, grassy areas, drive-on scales, enclosed paying wickets, a sorting station (for chemical waste, rubber tires, electronics and heavy metal products, batteries, florescent bulbs, aluminum, propane tanks, and other harmful items), a designated dump-and-go site for residential loads

SOUNDS
Back-up monitors beeping, chugging diesel engines, heavy machinery grumbling to life, glass popping and breaking under the spiked metal wheels of a compactor or bulldozer, the tumble of heavy trash dropping into a metal sorting container, leveling blades scraping against the ground, workers yelling over the noise, the squeal of metal on metal, plastic crunching as it is crushed, the cry of a flock of birds, small animals scampering through the trash to scavenge, dump trucks rumbling, a truck's gate clanking and clanging as it drops its load, water trickling downhill

SMELLS
Rotting food, rust, dust and dirt, hot plastic in the sun, rancid meat, moldering produce and leaves, exhaust, gasoline and chemicals

TASTES
Some settings have no specific tastes associated with them beyond what the character might bring into the scene (chewing gum, coffee, cigarettes, etc.). For scenes like these, where specific tastes are sparse, it would be best to stick to descriptors from the other four senses.

TEXTURES AND SENSATIONS
The vibration of a heavy duty vehicle as one drives it, thick gloves, heavy work boots, uneven ground underfoot, windblown trash scraping one's pant legs, lifting a heavy sack or box out of one's car and onto a sorting platform, a rumbling sensation coming up through the ground when a piece of heavy equipment passes by, the ground shifting under one's feet as garbage moves, accidentally cutting oneself, stirred-up dirt or dust swirling into one's face, the hot sun beating down, the chafe of a heavy hardhat on one's brow

POSSIBLE SOURCES OF CONFLICT
Fires or injuries caused by exploding aerosol cans
A compactor or bulldozer getting too close to the edge of a hill and tumbling over it

Chemicals leeching into groundwater

Slipping while walking and tumbling down a trash slope

Discovering a dead body in a pile of waste

Being run over by a piece of equipment

Disease that spreads from the improper handling of waste

Breathing in toxic gases

Stigma over working at a landfill

Feeling unfulfilled, wishing one could be doing something more or different

Finding something that should not be there (a pile of medical waste, a truckload of lead-based paint cans, etc.)

Learning about improper waste disposal practices at the landfill but not wanting to blow the whistle and lose one's job

PEOPLE COMMONLY FOUND HERE

Contractors getting rid of industrial waste, employees of the landfill site (administration, equipment operators, inspectors, management, safety personnel), people dropping off small household loads

SETTING NOTES AND TIPS

Landfills are usually sided by large hills to hide the garbage collection process from the public. Many have sorting facilities and drop-off areas for recycling and the collection of other items that don't belong in the landfill. But because people do not always recycle, a lot of the waste in a dumpsite consists of items that don't belong there.

Municipal trash is brought into a processing facility or specific drop-off area, while residential drop-offs (single vehicles bringing in a load of household items) are sent to another area. Trash is piled into pits and compacted to allow for more trash to be placed on top of it.

SETTING DESCRIPTION EXAMPLE

Jake moved slowly up the hill. He jabbed with his stick, digging after a shine he'd glimpsed underneath, and pulled loose a length of bent copper wire. He stashed it in the sack over his shoulder and kept looking, careful with his feet. The ground looked solid enough, but you never knew what was underneath; a broken concrete block or flimsy papers could give way as soon as you stepped. It never ceased to amaze, what the landfill kept hid. A distant rumble vibrated through the worn-out soles of his shoes. Jake slipped down the incline and disappeared around the nearest hill as the garbage truck thundered into view.

    Techniques and Devices Used: Symbolism

    Resulting Effects: Characterization

LIGHTHOUSE

SIGHTS
A cylindrical domed structure standing on a high point of land near a large body of water, a rotating light at the top that flashes as it comes around, bushes and plants near the base of the lighthouse, benches for guests who don't want to climb to the top, garbage cans, a flagpole, bushes and greenery, butterflies, a door leading inside, latticed metal steps spiraling up the inside of the lighthouse, a hand railing attached to the wall, small landings every certain number of steps, small windows set into the brick walls, sightseers gathering on the landings to catch their breath on the way up, natural light coming through a trapdoor near the top of the staircase, the stairs opening onto the main gallery balcony, a narrow balcony with a chest-high railing going around the top of the lighthouse, small round windows at the top, sights from the balcony (water, sandy beaches, boats, bridges, cars, grassy hills or meadows, houses and hotels, construction cranes, trees, cloud shadows moving across the land), a narrow ladder leading up to the watch room, watch room supplies (a first aid kit, a fire extinguisher, storage bins, a folding chair, a lunch bag, a phone), chipping paint, rust spots, a plaque dedicated to lighthouse keepers or local mariners, a gift shop and museum (if the lighthouse is part of an historical site)

SOUNDS
Heavy breathing as one climbs, echoes within the lighthouse, shoes clanking against metal steps, sightseers talking, a tour guide's voice, boat engines down below, sea birds squawking, traffic thundering over a nearby bridge, insects buzzing, a whistling wind, fog signals, mechanical sounds from the rotating light, cameras clicking as visitors take pictures of the view

SMELLS
Musty and damp air, stuffy air inside, salt water, the mingling scent of a group of people (deodorant, hairspray, sweat, perfume)

TASTES
Some settings have no specific tastes associated with them beyond what the character might bring into the scene (chewing gum, mints, lipstick, cigarettes, etc.). For scenes like these, where specific tastes are sparse, it would be best to stick to descriptors from the other four senses.

TEXTURES AND SENSATIONS
Stuffy and warm air inside the lighthouse, moving air at the bottom and top of the staircase, a burning in the calves from climbing the stairs, dizziness as one moves higher up the staircase, brushing against the brick wall for comfort, the firm metal railing in one's grip, solid stairs beneath one's feet, fresh air drifting through an open porthole window on a landing, sweat dampening one's hair and clothing, a steady wind blowing when one emerges onto the balcony, leaning on the railing while looking out at the ocean landscape, the tug and snap of the wind catching the ends of a scarf, holding tight to the hand of one's young child who is a notorious climber and risk-taker

POSSIBLE SOURCES OF CONFLICT

Falling off or being pushed over the balcony

Tumbling down the stairs

Braving the stairs despite an existing health issue (heart disease, high blood pressure, pregnancy)

A fear of heights

A tourist who loses a camera or phone over the side

Witnessing a crime from the high vantage point at the top of a lighthouse

A broken light that puts seagoing vessels at risk

A wedding proposal performed on the balcony in front of tourists that ends with a "no"

A strong hurricane bearing down on a lighthouse that hasn't been well maintained

Rusty steps that feel a bit loose as one ascends

A large tour group monopolizing the lighthouse

People who dilly-dally as they take pictures, refusing to acknowledge closing hours

A prankster throwing items from the balcony

Being hit by lightning

Being chased and seeking refuge in a lighthouse and having nowhere to go but up

A visitor who uses the upper balcony to commit suicide

PEOPLE COMMONLY FOUND HERE

Groundskeepers and lighthouse attendants, locals, school groups, sightseers, tour guides

RELATED SETTINGS THAT MAY TIE IN WITH THIS ONE

Rural Volume: Beach (202), ocean (230)

Urban Volume: Fishing boat (260), marina (264), yacht (286)

SETTING NOTES AND TIPS

There's a good reason why people continue to be fascinated with lighthouses; so many of them exist, and each is a little different from the others. The outside markings on a tower are unique to each house in a given area; this is so sailors can recognize where they are in the daytime, when the light is turned off. Lighthouses are almost exclusively mechanized now, making lighthouse keepers no longer necessary. Still, their historical importance cannot be denied, which is why many of the structures have been taken over by government or nonprofit organizations who are responsible for their upkeep and maintenance.

SETTING DESCRIPTION EXAMPLE

Josie's breath came in stabbing gasps as she hurried up the cast iron steps of the lighthouse. It had gone dark thirty years ago, and she both blessed and cursed the solid blackness inside. She kept a sweaty grip on the handrail and scraped along the wall, the fabric of her blouse catching in the grout between the bricks. At the landing, she paused long enough to peer out the south-facing window. There was just a half-moon tonight, but in the cloudless sky, it shone strong and lit up the man on her trail as if it were a lighthouse beacon. Josie slammed back against the wall, stifling a sob.

Techniques and Devices Used: Light and shadow, multisensory descriptions

Resulting Effects: Foreshadowing, tension and conflict

MAUSOLEUM

SIGHTS

Outside: An angular structure made of concrete or stone (that can be humble or grand in size and style), columns, a door (made of stone, wrought iron gating, or wood), a small window to let in light, grass and trees, nearby gravestones, flowers and wreaths, a surname etched into the stone over the doorway, discolored stones (from mildew, bird excrement, water stains), climbing ivy, moss growing in cracks in the stone, statuary, religious symbols carved into the external surface (crosses, angels, praying hands), iron fences, piles of leaves gathering in corners, people gathering around a neighboring grave in remembrance, picnickers on a hill overlooking the graveyard to enjoy the beauty of an old graveyard and commemorate the passing of a loved one, artists with sketchbooks, maintenance carts carrying lawn waste and tools

Inside: independent or stacked crypts, urns containing cremated remains, sarcophagi standing in the center of the room or set into niches in the wall, flowers, busts on pedestals, statues, plaques, benches for guests to sit on, religious artifacts, personal items (shields, family crests, knickknacks, portraits, books of remembrance), beetles, spiderwebs, rats and other small animals, dirt and blown leaf curls, decomposed flowers poking out of a vase or urn, burned-out candles and wax drippings, light shining through the window, flashlight beams, flickering candlelight, wall mosaics, Latin words and sayings carved into the walls, dust

SOUNDS

Rusty locks snapping open, heavy stone doors or squeaking iron gates scraping open, noisy footsteps, whispers and murmurs that sound loud in such a small space, prayers being chanted, voices that echo and carry, branches creaking, the wind blowing and stirring debris on the ground, bird and insect noises, water dripping, bugs scuttling away from sudden light, matches being struck, sniffling and crying, maintenance vehicles driving by outside

SMELLS

Mildew, rust, mold, burning candles, the sulfur of matches, damp stone, dust, stale air, fresh flowers, standing water, old flowers

TASTES

Some settings have no specific tastes associated with them beyond what the character might bring into the scene (chewing gum, mints, lipstick, cigarettes, etc.). For scenes like these, where specific tastes are sparse, it would be best to stick to descriptors from the other four senses.

TEXTURES AND SENSATIONS

Damp walls, dusty surfaces, stray spiderwebs brushing one's skin, air that is clammy and cold, hard stone benches around the crypt, the groove of etched epitaphs under one's fingertips, rough stone, scabby mold growing on statues or stonework, soft handkerchiefs and tissues, hands being tightly held, the warmth of a candle flame, prickly flower bouquets being set on a crypt, dead leaves being crushed under one's feet

POSSIBLE SOURCES OF CONFLICT

Getting locked in

Losing one's light source

Discovering that the loved one's body is missing

Reluctantly having to enter a to hide from a pursuer

Finding a box or a book with a family mystery or secret inside

Discovering that the mausoleum is haunted

Discovering a secret panel or trapdoor that leads somewhere else

Wanting to loot a mausoleum but finding that it's been safeguarded in some way

Entering a family mausoleum to discover it has been vandalized or desecrated (graffiti everywhere, items stolen, statues and carvings defaced, evidence of a Satanic ritual, etc.)

PEOPLE COMMONLY FOUND HERE

Clergy, family members and friends of the dead, groundskeepers, historians, maintenance people, mourners, visitors or artists interested in the site's history or the haunted beauty of such places

RELATED SETTINGS THAT MAY TIE IN WITH THIS ONE

Rural Volume: Graveyard (164), secret passage (84), wake (98)

Urban Volume: Funeral home (68)

SETTING NOTES AND TIPS

There are different types of mausoleums. Cemetery-owned structures have many slots available for purchase; they contain a spacious visiting area inside, along with the usual things you would find. Family mausoleums are also large and are meant to accommodate many bodies. Vestibule mausoleums are smaller, with a small entryway where guests can gather to mourn their dead. Individual mausoleums are compact and only hold one person's remains. These structures are locked and no one goes inside.

While current-day burials follow strict rules to protect the bodies of the deceased, older burials lacked these guidelines—a detail to remember when writing period-specific stories. Guests visiting one of these mausoleums when a person was being laid to rest may also have had to deal with the more unpleasant sights and smells of death.

SETTING DESCRIPTION EXAMPLE

The pale stone of the mausoleum shone sickly in the dark. Moonlight flickered on and off between the clouds, flashing over the marble angels that guarded the tomb. Between them, the recessed door stood in shadow. I didn't want to go in, but if I wanted to unravel my family's dark history and discover the truth behind the governor's accusations of treason, I must.

Techniques and Devices Used: Light and shadow

Resulting Effects: Establishing mood, foreshadowing

ORCHARD

SIGHTS
Trees set out in orderly rows, grass that grows tall or is controlled by mowing, flowering trees in spring, wildflowers, beehives close by to aid in pollination, blossoms drifting in the breeze and blanketing the ground, branches covered in tiny buds, trees thick with green leaves in spring and summer, the ground littered with detritus (leaves, twigs, fallen fruit, branches), autumn leaves in the fall, trees laden with nuts (almonds, cashews, pecans, walnuts) or fruit (apples, oranges, figs, pears, peaches, cherries), fallen fruit dotting the ground, bare branches in winter, snow, sprinkler and irrigation systems, tractors and lawn mowers, wheelbarrows and pruning tools, bushels and baskets, ladders leaning against tree trunks, customers picking their own fruit, children from a school group running around, a vegetable patch that yields other produce crops (tomatoes, carrots, pumpkins, squash, beans, onions, herbs), a produce stand, a country store, distant farmhouses, a pond, scarecrows and hay bales, hayrides, bees, flies, ants, mosquitoes, birds, squirrels, voles and mice, rabbits, snakes, dogs, fences to keep out deer, sun filtering through the leaves overhead, shifting shade as sun glimmers through the leaves

SOUNDS
Rustling leaves, trees creaking in the wind, branches (rubbing together, tearing loose in a storm, being propped up by wedged poles to support the weight of fruit), heavy fruit thudding to the ground, the steady drip of rain, insects buzzing, the grass swishing against one's legs, leaves and twigs crunching underfoot, the methodical splash of sprinklers, the rumble of a tractor engine, a wheelbarrow's squeak as it's pushed between the trees, people talking and calling to each other, children laughing, birds chirping, dogs barking, nuts being cracked open, the rattle of nuts in a basket

SMELLS
Dirt and mulch, grass, fresh fruit, vegetables and herbs, rain and water, orchard flower blossoms, sweet clover, wood and wood rot, tractor exhaust, hay, rotting fruit, damp earth, pesticides, fertilizer

TASTES
Fruits and vegetables that have been picked, harvested nuts, homegrown honey, sweat on one's lip

TEXTURES AND SENSATIONS
Rough tree bark, soft earth underfoot, knobby tree roots and rocks that make the ground uneven, smooth leaves and soft blossoms, the intermittent heat of the sun as it filters through the canopy overhead, shoes and pant legs damp with dew, fat raindrops plopping onto the skin and hair, insects lighting on one's skin, sweat trickling, the slick and squishy feel of stepping on fallen fruit, twigs snapping under one's feet, wildflowers and tall grasses nodding against one's shins, being splashed by a sprinkler, a bumpy tractor or trailer ride out to the orchard, the slight give of a ladder under one's weight, dirt-dusted vegetables, smooth fruits, the heft of a basket full of fruit, the flat wooden handle of a basket pressing into one's forearm, a scratchy straw hat, the sting of a mosquito or bee, walking along the smooth ruts made by a tractor

POSSIBLE SOURCES OF CONFLICT
Falling off a ladder or out of a tree
A life-threatening allergy to bee stings
Hay fever that ruins the experience
Being morally opposed to the orchard's practices (use of pesticides or other chemicals, inclusion of genetically-modified products, employing illegal immigrants or children as pickers)
A drought that hurts the yield and causes a struggling orchard to flounder
A pest or disease that threatens the crop
Buying an orchard and having no idea how to run it
Losing fruit contracts to other orchards
Bankruptcy or financial difficulties that threatens one's ability to keep the orchard
Governmental interference (a river that is rerouted or a lake that is dammed and adversely affects irrigation of the orchard, an interstate being built nearby, etc.)
Having no desire to take part in the family's orchard business but feeling pressured to do so

PEOPLE COMMONLY FOUND HERE
Customers, families, farm hands, farmers, paid pickers, school groups

RELATED SETTINGS THAT MAY TIE IN WITH THIS ONE
Rural Volume: Barn (148), country road (156), farm (160), farmer's market (162), pond (232), vegetable patch (96)
Urban Volume: Old pick-up truck (268)

SETTING NOTES AND TIPS
An orchard is defined as an intentional planting of trees for food production. This includes trees grown for fruit, nuts, and syrup. Orchards can be extensive, like those connected to a commercial farm, or small, consisting of a handful of trees kept by a family for its own personal use and for harvesting produce to sell locally. The kind of produce that is grown in an orchard depends largely upon the climate and location, so this will need to be taken into account.

SETTING DESCRIPTION EXAMPLE
The oak's branches groaned in the breeze like a growling dog, and the rotting log at my feet proved that the old tree wasn't above parting with its limbs if doing so would gain it another year of life. Ants and beetles paraded over its faded bark, trying to gain purchase, but even in its twilight, the tree was as ornery as ever.
Techniques and Devices Used: Personification, simile
Resulting Effects: Establishing mood, passage of time

PASTURE

SIGHTS
A paddock of mixed grasses and clover, grazing animals (sheep, cows, horses), clumps of animal manure, flies, rocks, fence posts and barbed wire, rutted tracks from farm tractors and vehicles cutting through the pasture, dust plumes following trucks as they rush past on an adjacent gravel road, wildflowers adding spots of color, a stand of scraggly trees, a ravine or slough where water builds up when it rains, a farmhouse or farm buildings in the distance, tractors and farm equipment working the nearby fields, a creek framed by cattails cutting across the pasture, gophers popping out of holes, ant mounds rising out of the ground, birds flying overhead, coyotes on the prowl for food, rabbits and mice running for cover

SOUNDS
Breezes *shushing* through the grass, animals vocalizing (lowing, snorting, neighing), grass being ripped up and chewed, hooves pawing at the dirt, horses galloping across the pasture, tails swishing, flies buzzing, weather noises (thunder, gusts of wind, rain falling to the ground), the squelching sound of walking over ground that has recently been soaked by rain, mice scampering through the grass, the hoot of owls, hawks and eagles crying overhead as they scout for food, the rumble of a tractor, cars passing on a nearby road

SMELLS
Sun-warmed earth, dust, ozone after a storm, rain, blooming flowers, animal hide, manure

TASTES
Some settings have no specific tastes associated with them beyond what the character might bring into the scene (chewing gum, mints, lipstick, cigarettes, etc.). For scenes like these, where specific tastes are sparse, it would be best to stick to descriptors from the other four senses.

TEXTURES AND SENSATIONS
The slide of grass against the legs, spongy ground underfoot, scratchy grass catching on clothes, a breeze fluttering one's clothes and skin, the slow gait of a horse, a horse stumbling as it steps in a hole, an animal's warm flank, the sun's warmth on one's head, a fly buzzing around one's head, a mosquito's sting, rocks warmed by the sun, picking a flower and having the dirt-clumped roots come with it, burrs sticking to one's socks, the rumble of an all-terrain vehicle as one races across the pasture, the ground's trembling as a herd of animals runs away

POSSIBLE SOURCES OF CONFLICT
A broken fence that allows predators to come in or animals to escape
An animal that gets caught in a fence
Thieves taking the grazing livestock
People shooting at animals for fun
Stray bullets from poachers hunting too close to the farm
Stepping on a ground hornet's nest

Being thrown from a horse
Crossing through a pasture that's patrolled by a territorial bull
A cow stampede that results in an injury
Heading out to collect the herd and finding an animal missing
Drought and overgrazing that causes the soil to break down

PEOPLE COMMONLY FOUND HERE
Family members, farmers, ranchers

RELATED SETTINGS THAT MAY TIE IN WITH THIS ONE
Barn (148), country road (156), farm (160), ranch (180)

SETTING NOTES AND TIPS
Pastures are typically quiet, tranquil places where nothing much happens, so it might seem like a less-than-ideal setting. But sometimes it is this very contrast that makes a scene come to life: a placid ride turned deadly when a horse throws its rider, a farmer clearing his pasture and discovering a mass grave, a scream or gunshot that silences the soothing twitter of birds and chirping of insects. Contrast can be a powerful tool; use it effectively to turn a peaceful setting into a tumultuous one.

SETTING DESCRIPTION EXAMPLE
Slowly, I walked Granddaddy's pasture. The once-green grasses straggled brown and ragged—too short for even the wind to rustle. Through my sandal soles, I could feel how knobby and hard the ground had become. I shaded my eyes from the sun's glare and pictured how it used to look, golden with hip-high wheat that rippled in the breeze like an ocean wave. Like a pasture of sunlight. But that was before the summer of '09. Nothing I could do would save it now.

    Techniques and Devices Used: Simile
    Resulting Effects: Hinting at backstory, passage of time

QUARRY

SIGHTS
A vast space cleared of trees and vegetation, a perimeter of trees or shrubs to screen the quarry from view (in urban areas), a giant pit that has been dug into the ground, straight sides or graduated sides that look like steps rising upward, striated walls of different colored rock (red, pink, white, yellow, gray, black), dirt roads leading to different parts of the quarry, piles of rubble, stone slabs, huge mounds of sand and gravel, tractors, bulldozers, excavators, dump trucks, cranes, pick-up trucks, empty wooden pallets, a series of conveyor belts carrying materials from one place to another, scaffolding, pooling water, dust clouds, plumes of dust billowing up after an explosion, an administrative trailer, a parking area for personal vehicles, construction cones and roped-off areas, cannon-like machines spraying water to control dust, water-spraying trucks, generators, pumps to remove pooling water, portable toilets, boot prints and tire tracks in the dirt, stones or sand shivering down a large pile, workers in safety gear (neon vests, heavy boots, construction hats, goggles, hearing protectors, respirators), managers with clipboards, workers shouting to each other over the noise, hoses and wires crisscrossing the quarry

SOUNDS
The rumble of heavy machinery, the beeping noise as a truck backs up, muted underground explosions, the repeated banging of a rock hammer or post driver, rocks being ground in a crusher, big trucks shifting gears, the hydraulic raising and lowering of a dump truck bed, chains clinking and clanking, chunks of stone tumbling out of an excavator and onto a pile of rock, metal jaws scraping over rock, a rattling conveyor belt, the *tap-tap-tap* of a rock breaker, stones tumbling out of a dump truck's bed, a siren or other signal to inform people of an imminent explosion, the whisper of small stones or sand tumbling down a pile, ringing ears from loud machinery, vehicle doors squeaking or creaking open, heavy boots thudding into the dirt

SMELLS
Dust, rock, exhaust, diesel fuel

TASTES
Gritty sand in the teeth, dry air, water, coffee

TEXTURES AND SENSATIONS
Rock dust settling over the skin and hair, the jarring vibration of a jackhammer or drill, sand in one's clothing, sweat causing one's goggles or glasses to slide down one's nose, heavy slabs of stone, rough rock surfaces, pebbles being crushed beneath one's boots, the bouncy seat of a dump truck, sore calves from walking through loose sand in heavy boots, opening the door of an air-conditioned cab and being blasted with heat, the rolling sensation of being carried along by a caterpillar's treads, mist from a water sprayer cooling the skin, splashing through puddles, the muted shock wave under one's feet from an underground explosive blast, sand in the eyes, overheated skin from all the safety clothing one must wear, dry mouth and lips, a nagging cough caused by dust in the throat

POSSIBLE SOURCES OF CONFLICT

Slipping and falling on loose shale

Having a stone or rock dropped on one's head

Injuries from a heavy equipment malfunction

Injuries from explosives

Having explosives or other dangerous equipment go missing

Teenagers and college students sneaking onto the site at night to party

A high or hungover heavy equipment operator

Environmental protestors

Stolen or sabotaged equipment

A mudslide during the spring thaw and runoff

Working under an irresponsible quarry manager who cuts corners

Accidentally destroying archaeological or historical artifacts

Deteriorating health due to conditions at the site

PEOPLE COMMONLY FOUND HERE

Administration and a quarry manager, customers, engineers, environmental inspectors, heavy equipment operators, office personnel, quarry workers, safety inspectors, truck drivers, visitors from the head office

RELATED SETTINGS THAT MAY TIE IN WITH THIS ONE

Rural Volume: Abandoned mine (142), canyon (204)

Urban Volume: Old pick-up truck (268)

SETTING NOTES AND TIPS

Quarries are essentially construction sites and so are usually closed to visitors. But when a quarry shuts down, efforts at restoration are often made to turn the eyesore into a place of beauty. Some are turned into golf courses or scenic parks with lush vegetation and lakes. Rock climbers take advantage of the striated walls while swimmers, fishers, divers, and cliff jumpers take to the water. While these restored quarries are meant for use by the public, other abandoned quarries aren't safe. However, this doesn't stop people from visiting them to party or hang out.

SETTING DESCRIPTION EXAMPLE

The rough surface of the cliff wall plucked at Justin's jeans where his legs dangled over the edge. It was too dark to see anything, but he knew that the quarry pit was forty feet down and littered with bulldozers and dump trucks, post drivers, rock crushers, and all the other heavy equipment that got Dad so jazzed. Justin twisted the beer can, catching the moon's glimmer and letting it run along the edge. Then he dropped it from his hand, heard it crash into the rock ledges and bounce all the way down to the pit.

Techniques and Devices Used: Light and shadow, multisensory descriptions

Resulting Effects: Establishing mood, foreshadowing

RANCH

SIGHTS
Wide open pastures with tracks worn into them, long dirt roads, winding creeks or rivers, dusty ground, dust puffing under hooves and boots, wildflowers, trees and bushes, brambles and thickets, rows of fences, grazing livestock (cows, sheep, horses, goats), deer and rabbits, prairie dogs and gophers, a large barn, farming implements (pitchforks, shovels, grapples, brands, coils of rope), water and food troughs, piles of manure, mice scurrying into corners in the barn, feed buckets and pails, gas barrels, a tractor, old tires, rusted chains, water hoses, a cattle shed for shelter, cattle runs and horse corrals, salt licks, stacked hay bales, a shotgun leaning against a wall, cats lounging in the sun, a shed holding tack (saddles, reins, harnesses, stirrups, blankets, bridles and bits, curry combs), horse trailers, broken-down trucks and farm equipment, ATVs, a rain barrel, dust devils and tumbleweeds twisting across the prairie, a chicken coop, stray chickens and roosters pecking at the bits of grass poking through the dusty earth in the yard, a doghouse or kennel, a vegetable garden, a milking shed, a wood shed, an axe lodged in a splitting stump, free-ranging dogs, a sprawling farmhouse, a porch with rocking chairs, ranch décor (wagon wheels, cattle skulls, horseshoes), flies, spiders and cobwebs

SOUNDS
The wind blowing, horses whinnying, squeaking gates, the clop of horses' hooves, a dinner bell or other signal, music from a radio, talking and laughter, workers calling or talking to the animals, the creak of harnesses and tack, the scratch of rope being coiled or knotted, horses pawing at the ground, dogs yipping or baying, doors opening and closing, cowboy boots scuffing the ground, the slurp of mud sucking at boots, the cluck of hens, cows lowing, hay crunching underfoot, the backfire of an old tractor, a truck firing up, wheels squeaking, safety chains clanking, tailgates slamming shut, heavy hay bales being dragged to the edge of a loft, the tick of boot heels over planks, horses snorting at one another, cats meowing, horse hooves clanging against a metal horse trailer ramp, the rumble of hooves from a herd of running horses, hay being pitched out of a loft, bird chatter, insects buzzing, a shotgun blast, grain pouring into a metal feed bucket or wooden trough, cowbells, animals kicking a stall door or loading pen gate, milk whizzing into a pail, the crack of wood being split, the squeak of a rocking chair on the porch

SMELLS
Manure, dust and dirt, dry grass, horse hide, sweat, alfalfa and timothy hay, dirty straw, food cooking, campfire smoke, cigarette smoke, chewing tobacco, domestic animals, leather, horse blankets, saddle oil, rusty metal, rain, pine trees, wet earth

TASTES
Dust in the mouth, spit, water, cigarettes, chewing tobacco, coffee, tea, beer, hearty foods (biscuits, stews, steak and eggs, baked beans, ham steaks, meat loaf), fresh garden vegetables, fresh-picked berries, beef jerky, pickled and canned goods

TEXTURES AND SENSATIONS

The soft fuzz of a horse's nuzzling lips, hard-packed earth beneath one's feet, a rough-cut fence railing, balancing on the top rail of a fence, a cowboy hat on the brow, using a sweaty bandana to wipe one's forehead, rough nylon rope, a horse's warm flank, heavy work boots that are clogged with muck or mud, a finely woven horse blanket, the dusty feel of just-picked vegetables, water pouring over the back of one's neck, a horse's rough mane flicking over one's hands, back pain, headaches, sunstroke, exhaustion, the rocking motion of riding in a saddle, leather reins held between one's fingers, squeezing milk from a cow's teats in steady motions, the cool air against the skin as night settles in, spitting sunflower seeds, the bump of an animal trying to get one's attention, knee-high grasses catching on one's jeans, a dry mouth and throat, the poke of brambles through one's clothing, a shotgun's recoil, the handle of a milk pail or feed bucket biting into one's hand, a bouncing ride in an old pick-up truck over ruts and holes in a pasture

POSSIBLE SOURCES OF CONFLICT

Drought that makes it difficult to water the animals
Escalating prices in feed
Financial difficulties for the ranch owner
Cruel employees
Being kicked by a horse
Losing land (due to a lawsuit, government interference, etc.)
A salmonella outbreak that is traced back to the meat from one's ranch

PEOPLE COMMONLY FOUND HERE

Breeders, cowboys and cowgirls, customers purchasing animals or freshly butchered meat, family members, farriers, guests and visitors, paid workers, ranchers, veterinarians

RELATED SETTINGS THAT MAY TIE IN WITH THIS ONE

Rural Volume: Barn (148), country road (156), farm (160), meadow (224), pasture (176), rodeo (182), tool shed (88), vegetable patch (96)

Urban Volume: Old pick-up truck (268)

SETTING NOTES AND TIPS

Ranches and farms are subtly different in that farms are used primarily to grow food, while the purpose of a ranch is to raise livestock. The livestock may be raised for butchering, breeding, food production (such as raising cows to produce milk), or selling. Since both settings are rural and similar in purpose, there will be some overlap between the two.

SETTING DESCRIPTION EXAMPLE

Mandy stifled a yawn and rested her chin against the smooth top rail of the corral. Sundancer stood in the middle of the dusty yard with Logan, who took careful steps toward the horse with a training bridle in his hand. Shadow cloaked most of the area; the sun was only beginning to crest the eastern field. Early morning was the best time to break a horse, since even the orneriest beast was more reasonable after a night of rest. She squinted in the pink-streaked darkness, determined to learn her brother's methods.

Techniques and Devices Used: Light and shadow
Resulting Effects: Characterization

RODEO

SIGHTS
A dirt arena surrounded by bleachers or stadium seating, metal fencing separating the audience from the arena, people riding bucking broncos and bulls, barrel racers maneuvering around a series of barrels, riders chasing down and lassoing a calf or steer, steer wrestling, a water truck spraying the dirt in the arena, flying flags, dust clouds being kicked up, participants in traditional dress (ten-gallon hats, boots, button-down shirts, belt buckles, bandanas, jeans and chaps) with numbers pinned to their shirts, branded or tagged livestock, numbered chutes and stalls, livestock in pens, rodeo clowns distracting the bulls and jumping into empty barrels, digital timers on display, ads posted around the perimeter of the arena, hay bales, a parking lot full of pick-up trucks and horse trailers, portable toilets, a dance floor, livestock shows, an exhibition area with booths and vendors, mechanical bulls, a halftime show where young kids dressed in western duds come out for lasso competitions or to rope a calf

SOUNDS
Country music playing, an announcer's voice coming over a loudspeaker, people hooting and hollering, applause, air horns and cowbells, gates clanging open and slamming shut, the thundering of horse hooves, calves bleating, horses neighing, cows snorting, lassoes whipping through the air, horns blowing to signal the end of a timed event, jingling tack, buzzing flies, the flick of a horse's tail, cowboy boots clanging on metal bleachers, clowns yelling at the animals to draw their attention, food hawkers selling refreshments

SMELLS
Dust, horses, hay, leather, sweat, animal dung, rodeo food

TASTES
Dust, beer, soda, water, popcorn, cotton candy, turkey legs, ribs, sausage, nachos, tacos, fries, pie, barbeque sandwiches, burgers, chili, pizza, corn dogs, funnel cake, doughnuts, ice cream, cinnamon rolls, deep-fried foods (chicken and shrimp, bacon, cheesecake, pickles)

TEXTURES AND SENSATIONS
Dust in the throat, sweat trickling down the back, sunburn, sweaty hair plastered to one's head, an itchy ten-gallon hat, a damp handkerchief, sitting on a metal bleacher with no back support, sticky hands from eating messy food, a hard metal railing under one's forearms, the jolt and jar of a bucking bull or bronco, riding on a horse that's running flat-out, the rhythmic motion of swinging and throwing a lasso, hitting the ground with a thud and rolling to avoid a bull's hooves, riding a horse while weaving around barrels, a rough rope in one's hands, sun-warmed leather, a horse's mane flicking over one's fingers, flies buzzing around one's head, heavy leather gloves encasing one's hands

POSSIBLE SOURCES OF CONFLICT
Being trampled by a bull or horse
Getting hung up in a stirrup while a horse runs away

Being gored by a steer

Falling on one's head and being knocked out

Getting kicked in the head

Going up against an impressive competitor in one's event

One's horse coming up lame

Faulty equipment or sabotage (reins and ropes weakened to snap, a burr placed under a saddle, etc.)

Disagreeing with a judge's decision

Performing poorly

Pressure being exerted from managers or sponsors

Being distracted by fans or groupies

Being pressured by a bookie about one's debt

Eating too much greasy rodeo food and feeling sick

Drinking too much and using poor judgment

Losing one's child in the crowd

Animals getting loose

Handlers being cruel to their animal charges

PEOPLE COMMONLY FOUND HERE

Announcers, cowboys and cowgirls, event timers, judges, reporters, rodeo clowns, vendors, viewers

RELATED SETTINGS THAT MAY TIE IN WITH THIS ONE

Rural Volume: Barn (148), country road (156), farm (160), ranch (180)

Urban Volume: Old pick-up truck (268), sporting event stands (240)

SETTING NOTES AND TIPS

Rodeos can be huge, nationally televised affairs held in enormous arenas or they can be modest events in small towns. Hometown venues will likely include some competitions and a few concessions, while larger events will have much more to offer: livestock fairs, vendor exhibits, shopping, dancing, pageants, chuck wagon and barrel races, and an enormous variety of food. The standard events, the rules, and the prizes will also vary depending on where in the world the rodeo is being held.

SETTING DESCRIPTION EXAMPLE

Gina sat forward in the saddle and tried to slow her breathing while she waited for the calf to be released. Her horse stood still as stone, like he couldn't hear the announcer's voice booming over the loudspeaker or smell the musk of the animal in the chute next to them. Ransom's muscles beneath Gina's legs felt more like iron than flesh, and his ears stood at attention. Her grip on the reins loosened and her nerves calmed just a bit. Then the calf took off.

Techniques and Devices Used: Multisensory descriptions, simile

Resulting Effects: Establishing mood, tension and conflict

SALVAGE YARD

SIGHTS
Tall chain link fencing topped with barbed wire to deter theft, an attendant at the entrance, dusty earth, tiered racks of scavenged tires and rims, rows of broken-down vehicles with dirty windows and raised hoods, wires and hoses bleeding out of the engines, vehicles (cars, trucks, buses, taxis, motor homes) with numbers spray painted on their sides, grounds that are littered with debris (loose screws, sparkplugs, pieces of broken plastic and metal), doors missing handles, dented doors that won't close, shattered windshields, cars stripped of their interior parts (seats, steering wheels, dashboards, etc.), rusted paint and peeling roofs, people and attendants with toolboxes scavenging parts (transmissions, converters, windshields, bumpers, engine hoses, light casings, mirrors), burned and smashed-up cars that are beyond salvage and are stacked for scrap, a yard that is divided according to the vehicles (by make and model, domestic and export, etc.), wheelbarrows for transporting parts, rusted forklifts, roads that weave through mounds of scrap, rusted barrels for collecting trash and glass, tow trucks, mounds of rubber tires to be recycled, machinery (a crusher, a bailing press, shears, conveyer belts, hauling trucks, flatbed trailers, cranes, a movable car magnet), a business office located in a small trailer, chained-up guard dogs, security personnel, floodlights, smoke from heavy equipment and incinerators, sunlight gleaming off metal and glass, wind blowing up dust devils

SOUNDS
Hammering, metal squealing, metal scraping metal, swearing and grunting as a person attempts to work a particularly difficult part loose, various sounds as an engine tries to turn over, hoods creaking as they're opened, tools dropping into a toolbox, rumbling and revving motors from heavy equipment, the beep of a truck backing up, the whine of a hydraulic lift or winch, glass and plastic crunching underfoot, a voice coming through a loudspeaker, wind whistling through open doors and missing windshields, the clink of a dog's chain, barking, music playing on a vehicle's radio, people talking on cell phones, mice and small creatures scrambling through the junk

SMELLS
Motor oil, grease, gas, dirt, exhaust fumes, rusted metal, the mustiness of rotten foam and fabric in a car's interior, rubber

TASTES
The acrid taste of smoke from polluted air, dust

TEXTURES AND SENSATIONS
Rusted metal, slick grease, bashing one's knuckles as one works in a tight space, cutting oneself on a sharp edge, a hot metal hood burning the skin as one leans across it, grease on one's fingers, the slight bounce or give of an old car seat, one's wheelbarrow jolting over ruts in the yard, thick work gloves that decrease one's dexterity, a heavy toolbox, applying pressure to loosen a bolt or screw, dusty surfaces, sliding under a car to reach the undercarriage, glass crackling underfoot, muscles flexing and straining as one works to get at the part one needs

POSSIBLE SOURCES OF CONFLICT
Theft of rare vehicle parts

Accidental fires or harmful fluid leaks

Vandalism (windshields being smashed, door panels dented)

Propped-up or stacked cars shifting and crashing to the ground

Owners using the site as a criminal business front

Being unable to find the part that one needs and lacking the money to buy a new one

Being cut by rusty metal and not having an up-to-date tetanus vaccination

Discovering signs of a crime or a dead body in a car's trunk

Being attacked by a guard dog while prowling through the yard at night

Owners who use the secluded yard for illegal activities

Kids using the salvage yard as a drinking spot

Visiting late at night for kicks and witnessing a crime (a murder, body disposal, a drug deal)

Spotting a wrecked vehicle just like one's own and feeling superstitious about it

PEOPLE COMMONLY FOUND HERE
Car enthusiasts, mechanics, vehicle owners on a shoestring budget, yard employees

RELATED SETTINGS THAT MAY TIE IN WITH THIS ONE
Urban Volume: Mechanic's shop (86)

SETTING NOTES AND TIPS
Salvage yards are very common in industrial areas and have a strong focus on vehicles for part salvage. Vehicle owners and rebuilders can come in themselves and pay for parts by weight or piece; they can also call in a request, and for a fee, have an employee retrieve the part. Salvage yards should not be confused with scrap yards; while the two are similar in that their contents can be browsed and purchased, the latter contains mostly metal objects, from small pieces of corrugated metal and aluminum, to larger items like bikes, vehicles, airplanes, and demolished building materials.

SETTING DESCRIPTION EXAMPLE
Connor led me into the auto graveyard. We were alone, silent, as the howling wind crawled through missing doors and slid over peeling roofs. My footsteps dragged. I wanted to see it, and I didn't. We passed dozens of vehicles hoisted up on stacked tire rims, their hoods saluting the harsh sun, motors missing and their hose guts hanging from the carriages. Ahead, bright blue paint gleamed, and my stomach dropped. It was our Camry, the driver's side crushed so badly that firefighters had used the Jaws of Life to chew through the frame. Cold sweat drew away the sun's heat and Connor and I exchanged a painful look. How quick it had happened—one moment we were tunelessly singing to the radio with Josie, and the next, we were staring up at the hospital ceiling as a doctor delivered the news about our sister.

    Techniques and Devices Used: Personification, symbolism

    Resulting Effects: Establishing mood, hinting at backstory

SLAUGHTERHOUSE

SIGHTS
Animals being herded off trucks and into a large warehouse-style building, tattooed or ear-tagged livestock, crates of poultry, handlers herding animals with flags and shakers, boards set up to guide animals into a certain area, groups of animals being moved between chutes and yards, animal runs and holding pens, water troughs, conveyor belts, hydraulic equipment and coils, chains and hoists, workers wearing protective gear (hats and hairnets, face guards, earphones, surgical masks, gloves, plastic frocks, aprons), hoses for spraying off blood and filth, chambers or troughs holding animals being anesthetized, carcasses hung up by a hind foot, carcasses that continue to kick or twitch after the animals have been killed, animals bleeding out into a trough or onto the floor, scalding tanks for softening of hair, singeing machines to kill pathogens and remove any hair, machines for removal of skin, refrigerators and chillers, lines of workers doing different jobs, workers removing entrails and slicing the carcasses into parts, big saws for cutting the carcasses in half, meat moving down a conveyor belt, conveyor belts carrying away innards and other body parts, garbage receptacles, blood spatter

SOUNDS
Cows mooing and lowing, pigs oinking and snuffling, turkeys gobbling, chickens squawking, shakers used to drive the animals forward, animals walking on concrete flooring or wood shavings, wings flapping on poultry, heavy animals banging into boards and walls, the hum and clank of machinery, water spraying and splashing, handlers calling to or yelling at animals, animals slurping water, rumbling conveyor belts, rattling chains, workers calling out to each other over the noise, dripping blood and water, saws cutting through bone, knives slicing through meat or sliding into sheaths, muffled noises through one's earplugs, rubber boots squeaking on the floor, workers talking, the sprayer from a hose washing everything down a grate

SMELLS
Livestock, warm blood, feces and urine, animal fat, disinfectant, one's own breath trapped inside a facemask

TASTES
Some settings have no specific tastes associated with them beyond what the character might bring into the scene (chewing gum, mints, cigarettes, etc.). For scenes like these where specific tastes are sparse, it would be best to stick to descriptors from the other four senses.

TEXTURES AND SENSATIONS
A hairnet irritating one's neck, a hardhat perched on top of one's head, heavy rubber boots, plastic coveralls or aprons, gloves making one's hands and fingers feel thick, being jostled by the animals one is trying to corral, bumping into a metal wall, having one's foot stepped on by a pig or cow, tickly poultry feathers, stepping in feces, bristly pig's skin, soft cow hide, being swatted by a cow's tail, pushing or trying to move the dead weight of a carcass, heat from the singeing machine, a blast of cold from the chiller, a knife slicing through skin, the heft of a saw,

a saw cutting through bone, clingy strings of fat and skin, slimy innards, blood splattering one's clothing and shoes, soft cuts of meat, splashing water

POSSIBLE SOURCES OF CONFLICT

Workers not using the correct safety equipment

Animal cruelty

Faulty equipment

Mistakes made due to the tediousness of doing the same job all day long

Widespread sickness in the livestock that results in a shipment of infected meat

Frequent audits by nit-picking inspectors

A heavy-handed shift supervisor

Bad press and animal rights groups picketing

Circumstances that lead people to eat less meat (moral decisions, wanting to eat healthier, a financial depression that renders people too poor to afford meat)

Layoffs and union issues

Hating one's job but being unable to leave it

Becoming queasy at the sight of blood

PEOPLE COMMONLY FOUND HERE

Administrative staff, inspectors, maintenance and custodial staff, managers (acquisitions, public relations, sales, plant overseer), plant workers, truck drivers

RELATED SETTINGS THAT MAY TIE IN WITH THIS ONE

Country road (156), farm (160), ranch (180)

SETTING NOTES AND TIPS

It would be nice to think that all animals are treated with respect and care up to the moment of their deaths, and thanks to cultural awareness and governmental regulations, many slaughterhouses are held to higher standards for the humane treatment of the animals in their facilities. Unfortunately, other slaughterhouses don't follow such regulations. In these butcheries, the standards of cleanliness are lower, workers are treated less fairly, the equipment is less maintained, procedures are outdated, and the animals are often cruelly treated. If you're looking for an emotionally charged setting or one that is meant to evoke a deeply negative emotion, a slaughterhouse could be the way to go.

SETTING DESCRIPTION EXAMPLE

It was my first day on the job and though I'd been at it a good four hours, I still felt like I could hurl any minute. Warm blood flowed along the trough at my feet. Pig after pig passed in front of me dangling upside down by back hooves, like macabre laundry hung on a line. Blood crisscrossed my apron and splattered the floor. The guy next to me kept hosing it down, which just made it watery and easier to spread. I glanced at the clock. Ten minutes 'til lunch. I dragged a gloved hand over my lips and tried not to think about food.

Techniques and Devices Used: Simile

Resulting Effects: Reinforcing emotion

SUMMER CAMP

SIGHTS
Wood cabins in a forested area, bunk beds, curtained windows, sleeping bags and pillows, window air conditioning units, ceiling fans, knapsacks and suitcases on the floor or shoved under the bottom bunk, clothes on the floor, cobwebs in the corners and the ceiling rafters, **a bathroom cabin** with shower amenities and graffiti in the toilet stalls, muddy footprints across the bathroom floor, **a cafeteria or auditorium building**, lines of kids waiting for meals outside the cafeteria, segmented food trays, a stage with a piano in the corner and flags off to the side, a covered outdoor pavilion, volleyball nets, basketball hoops, horseshoe pits, picnic tables, a tug-of-war pit, archery targets, **a barn** with horses, stray cats wandering around, **a pond** with a dock, canoes turned upside down on the sandy beach area, lily pads floating in the water, a lifeguard stand, a shed holding outdoor supplies (fishing poles, orange life vests, oars, sticks for s'mores, bows and arrows, sports balls, maintenance equipment), pine needles and cones covering the ground, mosquitoes, flies, snakes, lizards, frogs, birds, squirrels, spiders, **a large fire pit** containing charred pieces of wood, log segments and stumps to sit on, flashlight beams bouncing across the campground at night, wet towels flung over a clothesline, a craft area with bins of supplies, wet crafts set out to dry, buildings with signs to help campers navigate

SOUNDS
Kids (laughing, chatting, yelling, singing), counselors shouting, kids splashing in the pond, the slap of oars against the water, a lifeguard's whistle, hands smacking at mosquitoes, wind blowing in the trees, birds chirping, squirrels chattering, insects buzzing, the hollow sound of a volleyball being smacked, horseshoes clanging, the clack of fishing line being reeled in, the thwack of archery bows, flip-flops slapping against cement, whispers and giggles in cabins after bedtime, doors creaking or slamming, extreme noise from the cafeteria during meals, feet rustling through pine needles and underbrush, a crackling campfire, a guitar being strummed, rain thrumming on a cabin roof, flies buzzing against the window, applause during the end-of-camp show, dripping faucets, wet towels snapping, the thump of pillows in a pillow fight, the whine of a rickety air conditioning unit starting up, whirring ceiling fans, creaking plastic mattress covers, the scratch of a pen on paper, a page turning as a camper reads in bed with a flashlight

SMELLS
Campfire smoke, chocolate, bug repellant, sunscreen, sweaty bodies, hamburgers and hot dogs being grilled, mildew, bleach, the musty smell of the cabins, rain, the metal smell of horseshoes, dirt, glue, markers, paper that has gotten wet, the rotten egg smell of well water, wet wood, soap, lotion, horses

TASTES
Sweet-and-salty s'mores, the acrid taste of smoke, charred hamburgers and hot dogs, potato chips, nuts, berries, trail mix, fresh fruit, homemade ice cream, watery lemonade, pond water, sweat, sunscreen smeared onto one's lips

TEXTURES AND SENSATIONS

Showering with little water pressure or with cold water, a heavy sleeping bag, a slab of a pillow, cool air from ceiling fans or air conditioning units, the slap of a pillow in a fight, wooden rungs as one climbs into bed, swimming in a cool lake, water dripping from a wet suit, prickly sunburn, mosquitoes and horsefly bites, the light touch of a fly landing on one's skin, the itch of poison ivy, prickly brambles and thorns, soft grass underfoot, warm sand, hot sun, a rough log, heat from the campfire, heavy horseshoes, the tug of a fish on a fishing line, the rough planks of a picnic table, a horse nuzzling one's palm, the leathery feel of a saddle horn in one's grip

POSSIBLE SOURCES OF CONFLICT

Falling into a patch of poison ivy
Homesickness and worry about what's happening while one is away
Sunburn and heatstroke
Body issues that make one feel self-conscious
Being the victim of a prank or being body shamed
Not bonding with any other campers and being lonely
Inattentive or mean counselors
Being injured (being hit by an oar on the backstroke, getting kicked by a horse, nearly drowning)
Getting lost in the woods
Love triangles and gossip (with older campers)
Unhealthy competition and rivalries

PEOPLE COMMONLY FOUND HERE

Camp personnel, campers, counselors, lifeguards, parents picking up and dropping off their kids

RELATED SETTINGS THAT MAY TIE IN WITH THIS ONE

Barn (148), campsite (152), cave (206), country road (156), forest (212), hiking trail (216), lake (220), meadow (224), pond (232)

SETTING NOTES AND TIPS

Summer camps are often all-encompassing and provide a variety of activities, like the ones listed in this entry. But they can also be very specific, focusing on a particular hobby, sport, or area of interest. Robotics, mathematics, foreign languages, fashion, drama, lacrosse, computers, music—the options are virtually endless. It shouldn't be difficult to zero in on the camp that is perfect for your character—or one that he's forced to attend, thereby creating a scenario that is full of conflict and tension.

SETTING DESCRIPTION EXAMPLE

The clearing in the woods held a circle of ten cabins. Rose bushes stood by each door, their silky blossoms attended by bumblebees. A soft breeze blew in from the surrounding woods, fluttering the curtains at each window and raising the hair on my arms. It looked as perfect as it had the first day of camp last year. I wondered if my cabin-mates had thought so, too, on the day they'd arrived. I wished even one of them was alive to ask.

    Techniques and Devices Used: Contrast, multisensory descriptions
    Resulting Effects: Establishing mood, hinting at backstory

TAXIDERMIST

SIGHTS
A glass door entry, mounted animal heads, skins with heads attached stretched out on the walls, butterfly species and beetles pinned under glass, birds mounted as if in flight, life-sized animals in natural poses, antler displays, a cash register, animal skin and antler products for sale under glass (wallets, knives, bottle openers), a radio, a fan, chairs, plastic wrap and bags for protecting products from the weather as they are transported home in a truck bed, a door leading to a workroom and processing area, a metal prep table with high sides or a trough to catch fluids, clamps, boxes of rubber gloves, magnifiers and movable overhead lighting, implements on a tray (wire brushes, scalpels, tweezers), bowls for gathering flesh and bones for disposal, trash cans, a hose for cleaning the area, a sink, a fleshing beam to place skins on while they're being prepared, drums of tanning solutions, an open area for mounting, urethane foam animal forms in different sizes and poses, stands, mounting supplies (cutting tools, sandpaper, epoxy, wire, monofilament, buckets of paste, needles and pins), drawers filled with glass and plastic eyes, jars of salt, oils and chemicals for hide preparation, greenery supplies (silk or plastic grass and leaves, natural and dried rushes, rocks, pine cones, branches) for creating lifelike displays, glass cases and terrariums for smaller pieces (birds, lizards, snakes), a blow dryer for fluffing feathers and fur, sketches and drawings pinned to a corkboard, animal reference books, posters and pictures of animals in motion used for inspiration

SOUNDS
The wet snick of a blade slicing skin from muscle, power tools, a blow dryer fluffing fur, droplets of tanning fluid falling from a hide, sandpaper scraping foam to smooth the shape and create the perfect fit, pages being flipped in a reference book, a pencil scratching on paper as one sketches, the wet slide of a paste brush against a foam form when prepping it for hide placement, a wire brush combing through fur to shake off dirt and debris, the clink of a scalpel being set down, pins dropping to the floor, a radio playing in the background, a chair rolling over the floor, water rushing into a sink, a sprayer hosing down the processing area

SMELLS
Blood, animal hide, tanning chemicals, soaps and salts, cleaning chemicals and sprays, paste, plastic, wood

TASTES
Some settings have no specific tastes associated with them beyond what the character might bring into the scene (chewing gum, mints, cigarettes, etc.). For scenes like these, where specific tastes are sparse, it would be best to stick to descriptors from the other four senses.

TEXTURES AND SENSATIONS
Greasy feathers, smooth hides, fighting with fur tangles, manipulating limbs to position them for cutting, pinching a scalpel, congealed blobs of fat and innards sticking to one's fingers, rubbery flesh, the poke of a broken bone through the animal's skin, the powdery feel of latex gloves, cold

flesh against one's fingers, water running over one's hands, soft fur, sticky paste, granular salts, pulling and adjusting the skin to fit it over a foam form, wiring a tail into place, applying pressure to stretch the skin as needed while sewing an invisible seam

POSSIBLE SOURCES OF CONFLICT
A taxidermist with ethical concerns, feeling conflict over what he does for a living
Refusing to take on jobs where an animal was killed for sport
Botching a job and having to tell the customer
Botching a job and trying to hide it (sewing up holes poked into the hide)
A taxidermist with a private collection of human trophies
Struggling with the stigma of being a taxidermist

PEOPLE COMMONLY FOUND HERE
Animal collectors, bereaved animal owners, hunters, taxidermists

SETTING NOTES AND TIPS
Taxidermies may be small businesses dedicated to preserving local wildlife or commercial operations that deal in local and exotic animals. Taxidermists see a variety of clients—hunters looking to preserve trophies, pet lovers struggling to release an animal companion, and people who find dead animals and want to preserve the beauty of their forms.

Taxidermists are both male and female and tend to view their profession as artistic. Most are very passionate about recreating the breath of life through their work. Note that some do have ethical boundaries that prevent them from taking certain jobs, such as preserving an animal that is endangered or was shot out of sport. This might be a detail to weave into your story, both to add realism and to break the cliché that taxidermists are creepy people with a creepy interest.

SETTING DESCRIPTION EXAMPLE
As I walked into the showroom, I wished again that Mrs. Turner could have made this trip herself. A man-sized bear loomed over me with gleaming claws. The deer heads on the walls glared at me as if they suspected I'd been the one to shoot them. But the wild animals were nothing compared to the pets—all counter-height so they were hard to avoid: a pair of terriers with their heads cocked to the side, cats in various poses of mischief, a Pekingese curled up on a doggy bed, a ferret peering around a rock. They looked so alive, until the light hit their eyes, which were as lifeless and empty as marbles. A sour taste rose in my mouth. If my eccentric neighbor wanted to memorialize her beloved Checkers for all eternity, no doubt they could do it here.

> **Techniques and Devices Used:** Simile
> **Resulting Effects:** Characterization, hinting at backstory

WEDDING RECEPTION

SIGHTS

Round tables covered in tablecloths strewn with confetti, floral centerpieces, china place settings arranged with place cards, champagne glasses, balloons and streamers, banners, twinkling strings of lights, artificial plants decorating the room, a dance floor and a band or DJ, a separate table for the wedding couple and bridal party, waiters moving through the crowd with trays of appetizers and drinks, a bar with a bartender, a small table holding a wedding cake, attendants in matching dresses or tuxes, dressed-up guests, pictures of the wedding couple on display, a guest book, a table piled with gifts and envelopes, a black-clad photographer's flashing camera, guests dancing, high heels on the floor where a guest has kicked them off, jackets hanging on the backs of chairs, clutches and cell phones sitting on tables, attendants holding microphones and toasting the happy couple, a running slide show of photos

SOUNDS

Loud music for dancing, quieter music during breaks where people chat and laugh, kids running, heels on a tile or hardwood floor, the rustle of suit jackets being removed, the DJ announcing members of the bridal party, applause and whistles as the wedding couple appear, chairs scraping the floor, silverware scraping dinner plates, ice tinkling in glasses, forks tapping against glasses to encourage couples to share a kiss, guests speaking in raised voices to hear each other over the noise, hooting and hollering from the dance floor, a Master of Ceremonies calling people up to do speeches and toast the couple

SMELLS

Burning candles, wispy candle smoke, flowers, hairspray, perfume and cologne, food, the musty smell of an old reception hall or lodge

TASTES

Tears, mints, appetizers, reception fare (either buffet style or kitchen-served), wedding cake, champagne, water, alcoholic beverages, soda, punch

TEXTURES AND SENSATIONS

A sharp-cornered envelope with a check inside, a greasy appetizer, the boxy weight of a wedding present, stiff linen tablecloths, a cloth napkin lying over one's lap, kicking off shoes under the table and wiggling one's toes, the stiff or starchy feel of new clothes, a tie pulling at one's neck, a too-tight dress, silky taffeta or silk, sweating as one dances in dress clothes, new shoes pinching one's toes, papery tissues, a twisted neck or back as one sits sideways to see a slideshow or watch the couple dance, eyes that prickle with tears, warmth from many burning candles, a cold drink sweating in one's hand, the thud of bass notes in one's chest, being bumped and jostled on the dance floor, cold metal silverware, struggling to balance too many things at once (a clutch, a cell phone, a plate and drink, a napkin, etc.)

POSSIBLE SOURCES OF CONFLICT

Bridezillas making unreasonable demands

Drunken guests

Drama between family members

Putting oneself in financial strain to pay for an extravagant wedding and reception

Wedding crashers or an ex-partner showing up to cause trouble

Running out of food or drink

A guest getting food poisoning or reacting to an allergy

Spilling wine or something dark on the bride's dress

Inappropriate displays of affection

Nieces and nephews stealing unattended drinks and getting drunk

Caterers showing up with the wrong food

The cake toppling over

Delivery people running late

The wedding couple's car breaking down on the way to the reception

The wedding couple getting into a fight

Inequality between how the bride's family is treated and how the groom's family is treated

In-laws controlling the event and vetoing decisions previously made by the wedding couple

PEOPLE COMMONLY FOUND HERE

A band or DJ, a flower girl, a ring bearer, attendants, caterers, family members, guests, photographers, servers and wait staff, the wedding couple

RELATED SETTINGS THAT MAY TIE IN WITH THIS ONE

Rural: Backyard (36), beach (202), church (154), mansion (72), tropical island (240)

Urban: Ballroom (194), black-tie event (196), community center (48)

SETTING NOTES AND TIPS

Wedding receptions are highly personalized; every detail is carefully chosen, so a reception can be a strong reflection of the people involved. Not only this, but a wedding can also provide clues about the culture of the wedding couple. Traditions vary among different nations, races, and religions. Choosing details carefully will provide not only a sense of authority to your reception scene but will also afford you the opportunity to reveal important information about the culture or heritage that will play a part in the story.

SETTING DESCRIPTION EXAMPLE

Flower bouquets christened each table and dainty yellow bows tied with white baby's breath decorated the backs of the chairs. Twelve potted arrangements bordered the dance floor, as bright as the floral dresses of the wedding party. Over in the band's corner, the grand piano was in danger of collapsing under the weight of roses on its lid. I wrinkled my nose as the mix of floral scents assailed my sinuses. Sara's poet mom had gone overboard with her life-and-renewal theme. Instead of birdseed baggies, maybe she should've passed out samples of allergy medication.

Techniques and Devices Used: Multisensory descriptions, symbolism

Resulting Effects: Characterization, establishing mood, tension and conflict

WINERY

SIGHTS

Fields of green leafy vines tethered to wire and posts, brown earth that's hard-packed into a track between rows, workers with wide-brimmed hats (spraying, watering, inspecting, trimming, harvesting), a tree-lined road through the fields leading to the winery's main building, **a well-tended garden area** (with water features, topiary and flowering plants, statues and iron gates, stonework walkways), décor that suits the region, fresh-mown grass, mirror-bright windows, a patio area outside the winery's restaurant or bistro, the winery's name and logo embossed on a sign near the entrance, doors leading inside to **a reception area** (artwork and décor that features oak barrels, corks, glassware and wine bottles, a black chalkboard announcing house brands and wine tasting times, floor-to-ceiling wine racks), **a sampling area** (a glossy wooden bar with wine bottles, glasses, an ice bucket and water decanter), guests swirling wine as an employee describes the ingredients and distilling process, **the wine cellar or vault** (long rows of stacked and labeled casks of aging wine barrels, cement flooring and walls, lights spaced out along the roof, temperature controls), **a processing area** for the crushing and pressing of grapes (stainless steel vats, tanks for fermenting and cold stabilization, a bottling line), **a gift store** (wine purchases, artisan products, items with the winery's logo), **a restaurant** (glass cases and towers displaying wines, white linens, tapas and entrees artfully arranged, tables overlooking the vineyard)

SOUNDS

Wind chimes, footsteps on stone walkways, the breeze sliding through the vines and trees, bird song, tractors and equipment near the fields, bees buzzing, cars pulling up, music or nature sounds wafting out of restaurant speakers, gardeners mowing or raking as they attend to the greenery, sprinklers running, shoes echoing on marble or stone floors, the clink of glasses, wine bottles being set on the bar, the glug and whistle of wine pouring through an aerator, the bustle of a busy kitchen staff behind closed restaurant doors, the tumble of voices, soft music, the rap of knuckles against an oak barrel, echoing voices and footsteps in the wine cellar

SMELLS

The honeyed scent of blossoming flowers in the spring, clean air, newly cut grass, ripening fruit, sun-warmed soil, pungent red or sweet white wine, oak, spices, fruit notes, sharp cheeses from a tasting platter, oiled wood and cleaning supplies, fresh-cut flowers, fermentation in the processing room, cooking smells from a restaurant's kitchen

TASTES

Wine on the tongue (fruity, tart, woodsy or spicy), sharp cheeses, savory crackers or breads, the sweetness of chocolate, swirling water in one's mouth to rinse the flavor of wine as one prepares for a new tasting

TEXTURES AND SENSATIONS

The weight of a bottle, a bumpy embossed label, a delicate stem pinched between fingers (white wine) or the cool bowl of the glass cupped in one's palm (red wine), crumbly cheese and crackers, smooth linen, the wet tartness of wine crossing the lips, the shifting weight of wine as one swirls it in a glass, light-headedness as alcohol takes effect

POSSIBLE SOURCES OF CONFLICT

Loud, drunk patrons who disturb the enjoyment of others
An entitled patron who refuses to pay a bill at the restaurant because he didn't like the food
Patrons who are too drunk to drive home but insist on doing so
An earthquake that causes bottles to fall and shatter
Calling a cab to get home and it never showing up
A competitor tampering with one's wine while it's in the barrel
Animals that tear up the vineyards (like feral hogs)
A patron with a sensitive food allergy who gets sick from one of the wine ingredients
Dangerous weather (tornadoes, frost, etc.) that ruins the yield
Alcohol fueling arguments between couples
A corporate wine tasting that leads to bad judgment and office romances
A snooty sommelier who looks down on people for their taste in wine

PEOPLE COMMONLY FOUND HERE

A hostess or host, bus and taxi drivers, cellar assistants, delivery personnel, employees (managers, event coordinators, farmers, gardeners, patrons, tasters, technicians, vineyard and other support staff), waiters, winemakers, winery owners

RELATED SETTINGS THAT MAY TIE IN WITH THIS ONE

Wine cellar (100)

SETTING NOTES AND TIPS

Wineries vary depending on the location, size, and products produced. Some wineries create wine from fruit other than grapes or experiment with blends. Others may not have an actual vineyard and instead buy grapes from local producers (a common practice for urban wineries).

The look and feel of a winery will have a lot to do with the region and the branding chosen by the wine producer (traditional, edgy and fun, etc.), so take this into consideration; think about how you can incorporate symbolism into your winery's logo and location to show, rather than tell, readers about the business and characters running it.

SETTING DESCRIPTION EXAMPLE

Josh snipped a bunch of grapes from the vine and placed them into his bucket. The other workers complained about the heat, biting insects, and the lack of wind, but Josh took no notice. The only thing he kept track of was where to place his cutters on the vine. Besides, he'd rather be out in the vineyard in August than in an empty house with too many memories.

Techniques and Devices Used: Contrast, weather
Resulting Effects: Hinting at backstory

Nature and Landforms

ARCTIC TUNDRA

SIGHTS
A flat landscape, blowing snow, ice sheets, glaciers, snow banks, streaking or low-hanging clouds, far-off snow-capped mountain ranges, caribou, wolves, musk oxen, hares, polar bears, foxes, snow geese, animal tracks in the snow, snow drifts, hardy tufts of grass peeking out of the snow, rock formations, igloos, sleds and sled dogs, snowmobiles, natives dressed in furs and leathers, hunters with jackets ringed in animal fur, snowmobile tracks, old fire pits and campsites, simple prefabricated tents and those made of skins, animal scat half-frozen in the ice, fogging breath, smoke from fires rising into the sky, a bright and possibly warmth-less sun (depending on the time of year), ice crust, icicles, frozen and barren patches of dirt, scattered and sparse trees, migrating birds, sunlight glaring off the snow and ice, isolated shelters and buildings, wind blowing at the snow and wearing it down into sleek curves and peaks

SOUNDS
Wind that howls and tears, a flapping tent, the crackle and hiss of a fire, a kettle whistling, the crinkle of cold fabric (a parka, a tent, bedding), snow crunching beneath one's boot, the steady whispering of runners in the snow, panting or howling dogs, the rev of an engine, a bear's roar, the pattering gait of huskies pulling a sled, yips and barks, the creak of a harness and its buckles, birds cawing as they scavenge or hunt, sneezing, sniffling, coughing, snow crystals rattling against one's coat, the crack of a snow axe cutting into ice, wind scratching through tufts of dry grass, the crackling sound as one steps through a crust of snow, melting snow falling into the fire with a sizzle, howling wolves

SMELLS
Sweat, the clean ozone-like smell of fresh snow, warming leather, dogs and animals, fresh kills and found carrion, the wind carrying the scent of briny water, wood smoke, tea, coffee, roasted or raw meat, dead grass, blood

TASTES
Raw meat, hardtack, biscuits, jerky, tea, coffee, cooked meat, trail mix, dried fruit or other nutritious foods brought for the journey, melted snow, salty sweat on the lips, gamy wild meat, fish, blubber, suet

TEXTURES AND SENSATIONS
The wind slicing at exposed skin, chapped skin and bleeding lips, cracked knuckles, numbness in the fingers and toes, sunburn on the face, windburned cheeks and foreheads, pain in the ears from the constant wind, rendered fat placed on the skin to protect it from the elements, a dry mouth, shaking from spent strength, breaths sawing at one's throat, pain in the chest from breathing cold air, the pinging darts of windblown snow hitting the skin, headaches, snow blindness, disorientation, dizziness, muscles that spasm and tremble, cold snow against one's hands, frozen boot laces, tired muscles being forced to slog through deep drifts, snow in one's boots or gloves, sweating from exertion, the painful tingle of warmth returning to frozen

extremities, a fire's heat pressing against one's face, brushing away ice crystals that have formed on one's facial hair, clumsiness due to numb digits

POSSIBLE SOURCES OF CONFLICT

Frostbite, hypothermia, and freezing to death
Running out of fuel for one's heat source
Losing one's supplies
Being attacked by wolves or other animals
Falling through the ice or snow into a canyon far below the ground's surface
Sustaining a serious injury that requires medical attention
Falling ill far from civilization
Being unable to find food
Losing a glove or hood
Running across hostile locals
Getting lost
Being partnered with a mentally unstable person (a guide, a work partner, etc.)
Getting caught in extreme weather without shelter
Being stalked by an animal
Worrying over local lore and superstitions
Drifting snow that creates a whiteout, causing one to lose one's sense of direction
Needing to find safety before an impending storm hits

PEOPLE COMMONLY FOUND HERE

Environmentalists, extreme sports enthusiasts (adventurers, dogsledders, mountain climbers), geologists and ecologists, homesteaders, native people, photographers, scientists

SETTING NOTES AND TIPS

Most of the Arctic tundra is frozen year round. In the southern regions, there is a brief summer season when the snow melts, inciting a burst of plant and animal life. Bogs and ponds form, insects swarm them, and migrating birds come to feed on the bugs. In some of these areas, the sun is up twenty-four hours of the day, and locals migrate to their favorite hunting and fishing spots, intent on catching and storing enough food for winter. As with any setting, thorough research is imperative to make sure that the climate and animal and plant life are correct for the region you have chosen.

SETTING DESCRIPTION EXAMPLE

I pulled the tent flap back and shielded my eyes. The sun lit up the ice crystals, transforming the ground into snow-crusted treasure. I smiled and took a deep breath of the cold, invigorating air, glad to have such beauty accompany me on the hike to the polar bear observation station.

    Techniques and Devices Used: Simile, weather
    Resulting Effects: Establishing mood, reinforcing emotion

BADLANDS

SIGHTS
Tall and unusual red and yellow rock formations resulting from wind and water erosion, cracked clay beds where water once flowed, sandy trails through bumpy terrain created by animals, sandstone or limestone rock walls, rock arches, flat-topped buttes and fins, small fossils on slabs of stone, deep fissures and dry ravines, thin rock spires (hoodoos) that rise like unsteady obelisks, a jagged ridgeline separating the sky from the earth, animal skulls and skeletons picked clean by scavengers and bleached by the sun, wide canyons, stunted yet hardy trees and bushes (juniper, green ash, sagebrush, buckbrush), prickly flowering plants (coneflower, thistle, milkweed), clumps of spiny cacti and wild grass (cordgrass, buffalo grass, foxtail, blue grama), jackrabbits resting in the shade of a boulder or beneath a bush, rock wrens burrowing into holes in the tall rock walls, reptiles scampering from rock to bush (scorpions, snakes, lizards), an open blue sky streaked with clouds, hikers wearing day packs, geologists roping off areas for digging, bighorn sheep

SOUNDS
The wind whistling across stone and through canyons, shale crunching underfoot, a mouse or lizard skittering through dead grass, the cry of a predator bird circling overhead, unsteady ground giving way and causing rocks to shift and tumble into the canyon below

SMELLS
Clean air, the tang of sandstone or limestone, dry grass, dust, pungent juniper needles, animal scat, sweat

TASTES
Hiking food for the trail (granola bars, raisins, nuts, dried fruit, sandwiches, beef jerky, water or electrolyte-replenishing drinks)

TEXTURES AND SENSATIONS
Wind-shaped sandstone that's smooth to the touch, straw-like grasses scraping one's calves, a mosquito's sting, the throbbing heat of sunburn on one's unprotected face or neck, chalky dust on one's hands, sweat dripping from one's brow, a shale sliver caught in a hiking boot, loose sand or shale shifting under one's feet, being scratched by a prickly leaf or spiny bush, wind twisting through a ravine or canyon and pressing against one's clothing and face, placing one's feet carefully on an uneven path

POSSIBLE SOURCES OF CONFLICT
A trip or fall that results in an injury
Getting turned around or lost
Exposure to the elements
Running out of water
Being left behind by one's tour group

Being bitten by a venomous snake or spider
Coming across a dangerous indigenous animal, like a cougar
Falling rock or crumbling ledges that give way
Sharing in the discovery of a rare fossil and fighting over who saw it first and who should have it

PEOPLE COMMONLY FOUND HERE
Archeologists, hikers, school groups learning about the area, tour groups and tourists

RELATED SETTINGS THAT MAY TIE IN WITH THIS ONE
Canyon (204)

SETTING NOTES AND TIPS
Badlands form naturally, but they can also be caused by man-made interference, especially through excessive mining or agricultural pursuits. Pollutants destroy water supplies in the area, killing vegetation, which fast tracks the erosion process. This makes this setting an interesting choice for dystopian stories.

SETTING DESCRIPTION EXAMPLE
There was no point denying it: I was lost. I pressed my back against the rock wall and tucked my freezing hands under my arms to warm them. The cold starlight and nail-sliver moon turned the hoodoos around me into stiff finger bones, and the quiet here was the sort reserved for graveyards. My breath fogged. It would be a cold night, but with no fuel to build a fire and no flashlight, the smartest thing was to wait for sunrise. Risking the weather was better than trying to find the trail in the dark and stepping on a rattler's nest.

    Techniques and Devices Used: Light and shadow, metaphor
    Resulting Effects: Establishing mood, foreshadowing

BEACH

SIGHTS
Colorful beach towels laid on the sand, giant umbrellas, beach chairs and sunbathers, children wearing florescent-bright water wings, teens playing volleyball or football, families unpacking food coolers and blowing up water toys and loungers, a boardwalk lined with food and drink vendors, people fishing off nearby reefs or from the pier, sunbathers with red bellies or burned shoulders, floppy hats and sunglasses, bottles of tanning lotion and sunblock sticking out of beach bags, flip-flops abandoned in the sand, a white lifeguard tower with flags flying, streamers of seaweed rolling in the surf, cigarette butts and bottle caps peppering the golden sand, smoke rising from portable barbeques, picnic baskets brimming with food, brightly colored buckets and pails, half-formed sandcastles, vendors trolling the crowds (selling jewelry, hats, sunscreen, beach toys), skittering crabs and sand flies, inner tubes and floating loungers rocking in the current, kids tossing striped beach balls in the shallows, frothy water (blue, green, sea-green, or brown with silt, depending on the location and time of year), waves rolling inland to dissolve into foam on the beach, an uneven shoreline (strewn with rocky bits, shells, and chunks of seaweed), the glow of sun on the horizon, cruise ships and sailboats out in the distance, planes flying overhead with advertising banners, chunks of driftwood tangled together with trash and fishing line, wavy sand dunes, cattails nodding softly in the wind, starfish or jellyfish washed ashore, seagulls darting overhead, tide pools cutting wet paths through the sand

SOUNDS
The crash of waves and fizz of foam as it sweeps ashore and spreads across the sand, wind gusts causing beach umbrellas to twist and flap, seagulls crying as they dive for food, children laughing, people talking on their beach towel islands, snatches of conversation carried on the wind, dogs barking, music, children shrieking as a wave hits or crying as exhaustion sets in, Jet Skis or powerboats thundering past, highway traffic from nearby streets, music from radios or the boardwalk businesses, the slide of sea grass as a breeze ruffles through it, planes flying overhead, kite streamers rattling in the wind, the hiss of air pumps as vacationers inflate floating toys

SMELLS
Coconut-scented sunscreen and tanning lotion, briny sea air, smoky hot dogs and burgers on the grill, wet towels, seaweed, spilled beer, cigarette smoke (if smoking is allowed), spicy taco chips, grease from food cooked by vendors, bug spray

TASTES
Salty air and water, a lip rimmed in sweat, cold bottled water, chargrilled hot dogs and burgers, soda, a bitter taste of lotion smeared too close to one's mouth, cold ice cream treats and popsicles, salty chips, crunching down on gritty sand that has blown into one's sandwich

TEXTURES AND SENSATIONS
Hot sand burning one's feet, the chafe of sand caught inside one's swimsuit, bug bites, sweat trickling down one's forehead and nose, the prickling heat of sunburn on the back of the neck,

the kiss of warmth as one lies in the sun to dry, the shock of cold water as the first wave hits, water pouring off one's head and down the back, sand on one's blanket, gritty sand sticking to one's body, oily lotion or sunscreen, the clamminess of a wet towel, an icy drink, a cooling breeze, getting sand or sunscreen in one's eye, ridged seashells, prickly seaweed, water splashing one's bare legs, the sudden pull of undertow, pain at slipping or stepping on a sharp rock, the shock of something bumping one's leg underwater, wet hair tangling in the wind or sticking to one's neck

POSSIBLE SOURCES OF CONFLICT
Stepping on glass
Rowdy beachgoers or loud sunbathing neighbors
Fussy children who won't stop crying
Someone stealing one's possessions
Wind that knocks over umbrellas and kicks up sand
A painful sunburn
Dangerous or inconvenient ocean life (jellyfish, stingrays, sharks, sea lice)
Rough waters that make swimming dangerous
Being carried away by a rip current
Aggressive vendors who can't take no for an answer

PEOPLE COMMONLY FOUND HERE
Families, fishermen, food vendors, life guards, locals on their days off, police, surfers and boating enthusiasts, swimmers, teenagers, tour excursion operators, vacationers

RELATED SETTINGS THAT MAY TIE IN WITH THIS ONE
Rural Volume: Beach party (150), lighthouse (170), tropical island (240)
Urban Volume: Cruise ship (258), marina (264), yacht (286)

SETTING NOTES AND TIPS
Beaches can be vastly different depending on where they're located. Sand might be white, black, or even red. Some beaches are well maintained, while others are riddled with cigarette butts, food wrappers, seaweed, and dead fish. Public beaches might be crowded and tiny, while private beaches can be hidden and expansive. The setting's fine details will affect the character's mood and offer different sensory descriptions to play with, so it's important to choose wisely.

SETTING DESCRIPTION EXAMPLE
Wet sand massaged my tired feet as I admired the moon, as round and china-bright as one of Gram's dinner plates. The sky here was so clear and wide, with no buildings or smog to hide the velvety blackness. The surf crashed, a soothing melody, as the wind pressed and pulled at my hair and clothes, trying to steal the tucked-in edges of my shawl. I closed my eyes and drew in the briny air, bookmarking this moment before I had to return to the hotel, and the suitcases needing to be packed, and what awaited me at home.
Techniques and Devices Used: Multisensory descriptions, simile
Resulting Effects: Establishing mood, foreshadowing

CANYON

SIGHTS
A massive winding ravine with a river or dry bed at the bottom, towering layered rock walls in varying shades of color (gray, brown, black, orange, white), scrub brush, wild grasses growing in tufts, stunted trees, shade and shadow where the walls block sunlight, deadwood, birds of prey, lizards, ants, spiders, hearty animals, insects, rocks or deadfall sticking up out of the river, rapids and drops, goat trails, shale and dust, small dirt slides as water erosion chews at the banks and escarpments, animal bones, horse trails, animal scat, tall spires that are smooth and wind-worn, cacti, ledges and plateaus, undisturbed rock slides from long ago, birds nesting in holes bored into the rock, small caves, sand, snakes

SOUNDS
The wind whistling over stone, water rushing downstream over rocks, rocks falling, footsteps on a gravelly path, horses' hooves clopping along the trail, voices bouncing off high canyon walls, a spooked mouse or lizard running through a patch of dead grass, the shriek of a predator bird echoing off the canyon walls, the rattle of a snake's tail, the amplified sound of a jet engine as a plane flies overhead

SMELLS
The tang of limestone, dust, dry air, a campfire, the musk of an animal, perfume from the rare wildflower or blooming cactus, sweat and body odor

TASTES
Food or drinks brought in for a trail ride or excursion (water in a canteen, nuts, seeds, jerky, dried fruit, energy bars, hard fortified biscuits)

TEXTURES AND SENSATIONS
The grit of dirt and sweat on the skin, a dry and forceful wind blowing one's clothing and hair, uneven ground and shale under one's boots, muscle strain as one climbs a slope or wall, cold river water on the skin, smooth stone worn down by the wind, sweaty or dirty clothes that chafe, bug bites, a sandstorm that peppers one with dirt and sand, warm horseflesh, a leather saddle horn or reins, the sway of a burro as it moves downhill, the ache of one's legs as they span a horse's wide back, the sun's heat beating down on one's body, a pack that grows heavier as the day goes on, eyes tearing up and drying out, blown sand and dust creating a crusty rim at the corners of one's eyes

POSSIBLE SOURCES OF CONFLICT
Getting lost or becoming injured during an excursion or trail ride
Running out of survival supplies
A lame horse or burro
Exposure to the elements (causing heatstroke or dehydration)
A sudden rockfall that blocks one's exit

Aggressive animals

Discovering that one's tour group has moved on while one was going to the bathroom or taking photos on an escarpment

PEOPLE COMMONLY FOUND HERE

Hikers, ranchers, sightseers

RELATED SETTINGS THAT MAY TIE IN WITH THIS ONE

Badlands (200), campsite (152), cave (206), desert (210), river (236)

SETTING NOTES AND TIPS

Canyons are found all over the world and have features that are indigenous to each location and climate. Some are very large, with many splits and crevasses, making them difficult to navigate and almost impossible to explore completely, while others follow a water source or form naturally between mountains, providing natural landmarks for explorers. Think about the reasons for using this setting, and which type of canyon has features that will naturally supply conflict and provide challenges for the characters in your story.

SETTING DESCRIPTION EXAMPLE

Flies stormed Ricky and me, drawn in by the sourness of fear sweat. Buzzards appeared overhead, no doubt wanting to feast on our horse that'd died in the fall. Ignoring the pain in my twisted ankle, I dragged myself over to my brother to check his thread-thin pulse. The shakes had set in, so at best he had a fever; at worst, his wound had turned septic. My shoulders sagged as my choices evaporated. I stoked our fire as high as I could with the sparse deadfall I'd scavenged and hoisted myself up, praying I could be back with help before night fell. Behind these boulders, he'd be shielded from the sun, but at night, the coyotes would be out. Hopefully, the smoke would mask Ricky's scent.

> **Techniques and Devices Used:** Multisensory descriptions
>
> **Resulting Effects:** Establishing mood, foreshadowing, hinting at backstory

CAVE

SIGHTS
Bumpy stone walls with fingerlings of tree roots growing through, dirt and dead leaves tracked in by animals or blown in by the wind, twigs, animal scat, clumps of fur, chewed bones, tracks in the dirt, claw marks on stone made by bears or mountain lions, stalactites hanging from the ceiling, bats roosting up high, stalagmites protruding from the floor, water dripping from cracks in the ceiling or dripping from tree roots, puddles, passageways leading to other caves or to underground rivers, earthworms churning in the soil, spiderwebs, bright sunlight at the cave's entrance that diminishes as one moves away from it, hieroglyphs or cave paintings (if the site was inhabited by older civilizations), graffiti and trash (if it is used by transients or partiers of today), water dripping down the walls, lichen and moss, crumbling rock, bat guano, spongy mushrooms growing in cracks

SOUNDS
The wind whistling through breaches in the stone, trees swaying outside, shoes or paws shuffling over the floor, an animal skittering away, the flutter or squeak of an agitated bat, the dripping plunk of water, dead leaves and twigs crackling underfoot, crickets or frogs calling out from somewhere outside, a crackling campfire built near the cave's mouth, a flashlight clicking on, voices echoing, loose rocks being kicked in the darkness, growls, the rumble of breath as a cave-dwelling animal slumbers, wind rustling, dead leaves and grass at the entrance, the squeak and chatter of small animals

SMELLS
Cold or wet stone, animal scat, musky fur, decaying animals, rotting vegetation, stale air, stagnant water, wood smoke, char from food cooking, sweat or body odor

TASTES
Water, food cooked over a fire (trapped animals, fish, hot dogs), drinks made or brought (tea, coffee, water), nuts or berries foraged from the woods nearby

TEXTURES AND SENSATIONS
Bumpy or knobby stone walls, uneven crumbling rock, slipping on a patch of wet rock, jamming one's fingers into fissures for handholds, scraping one's side in a tight part of the cave, a fist of stone poking one's back, bumping one's head on a low ceiling in the darkness, dust on the hands, running a fingertip along a vein of quartz or other ore (gold, silver, turquoise), walls that are wet and slimy with condensation, the shocking cold of the cave's passage opening up and stumbling into a freestanding pool or grotto, water dripping from cracks in the roof to slide down the back of one's neck, cold wind or snow finding its way into the cave, bones or twigs crunching underfoot, the stone's cold seeping into one's body at night, sleeping on a hard stone floor

POSSIBLE SOURCES OF CONFLICT
Poor drainage that causes the cave to fill with water during a storm
Animals that live in the home and don't want to share it

Startling bats inside and having them rush out in a flurry

Discovering poisonous scorpions or snakes within

Having to fend something off from entering the cave but having no weapons

Being pursued into a cave and discovering that there's no way out except through the entrance

Poor ventilation that causes the cave to fill with smoke

Spores from mushrooms growing within that cause hallucinations

Getting lost exploring side passages

Passages that narrow down to a point where one could easily get stuck

Hearing voices coming from another adjoining cave or passageway

An injury that festers or worsens, making mobility difficult

Having enemies camp outside to wait one out

Finding supplies in the cave that one needs but feeling conflicted over taking someone else's things

Discovering something disturbing in the cave (a human skeleton, satanic drawings, a chest filled with finger bones)

PEOPLE COMMONLY FOUND HERE
Cave divers or explorers, locals in the area who like to camp or party at the site, survivalists

RELATED SETTINGS THAT MAY TIE IN WITH THIS ONE
Beach (202), canyon (204), forest (212), hiking trail (216), hunting cabin (166), mountains (228)

SETTING NOTES AND TIPS
Caves come in all shapes and sizes, and while some may be warm (in volcanic areas), most are cool. Critters who may call the space home will vary depending on the climate, season, and location. Caves can be at ground level and bore into the ground, opening up under the earth. Some large ones may even have their own ecosystem if enough light and water are found inside. Caves can also lead to underground rivers or be found along the coastline where the crashing sea has worn holes into the limestone. And still others may be found at higher elevations, such as on the side of a mountain. With so many options in so many places, you have a lot of choices when it comes to combining the right elements for your cave explorers.

SETTING DESCRIPTION EXAMPLE
Ryma leaned closer, orange tongues of fire from his torch lapping at the drawings set down by his ancestors. Powerful henna strokes depicted warriors with stone spears and lynx fur mantles running the Great Hunt for Grandfather Bear. His throat grew thick. His father had stood here, his uncles, his grandfather. Had they looked upon this story and reflected on what it meant to become a man, to earn the right to a mantle, just as he was doing now?

Techniques and Devices Used: Light and shadow

Resulting Effects: Foreshadowing, hinting at backstory, reinforcing emotions

CREEK

SIGHTS
Trees and brush hemming a meandering flow of water, uneven ground, undergrowth (fallen trees covered in moss, bark fragments, dead leaves and pine cones tangled in the tall grass), forest trails made by animals visiting the water's edge, grassy banks edging the shallow water, rocks creating small islands in the stream, water slipping over wet stones, leaves and pine needle fragments drifting along the sun-dappled surface, rippling water, minnows and small fish flashing beneath the surface, a mottled bottom of green and brown (sand, rock, and algae), pebbles and gravel half-buried in the muddy creek bottom, the water coursing around reeds and grasses, leeches, frogs, turtles, snakes, tadpoles and skimmers, paw prints along the muddy bank, drifting leaves and air bubbles floating lazily downstream, exposed tree roots at the bank, partially submerged twigs in the water, animals (foxes, deer, rabbits, squirrels, raccoons) stopping to drink, birds taking a bath in the water, dragonflies swooping along the surface, lightweight litter gathered along the water's edge (drinking cups, bits of tinfoil, plastic baggies), picnickers enjoying a private lunch on a blanket, a child hunting frogs or toads along the edge, kids splashing and throwing water at one another on a hot afternoon

SOUNDS
Water trickling around rocks and over twigs, the whine of mosquitoes, humming dragonfly wings, birds splashing in the water or calling to each other from the trees, crickets and frogs chirping and croaking, the wind sliding through the leaves and tall grass, a thrown rock dropping with a plop, the frantic splashing of a fish caught on a hook, the creak of tall trees on a windy day, small animals rustling the underbrush, kids splashing and laughing, a shriek as someone reels in a fish, a louder rush of water downstream where the creek joins a river

SMELLS
Algae, grass and greenery, sun-warmed soil and rock, rotting bark and leaves, wet earth, sweat, rubber boots, a fishy smell, mud

TASTES
Clean water from a mountain-fed creek, picnic food (sandwiches or wraps, cheese, crackers, potato salad, fruit, chips), hiking fare (a nutty trail mix, beef jerky, dried fruit, protein or granola bars), berries or rosehips picked from a bush, nuts and greens scavenged in the woods

TEXTURES AND SENSATIONS
Scratchy grass and underbrush, the soft squish of mud as boots sink into the wet earth, rocks on the creek bottom poking into one's bare feet, mud oozing between the toes, the cold shock of water running over one's feet, water seeping into shoes or boots, the soft give of spongy moss and grass, the weight and tug of a caught fish on the end of a line, a slippery fish, a gentle current flowing around one's bare ankles, a mosquito's bite, warm rocks, a twig brushing one's leg as it drifts on the current, the tickle of minnows nibbling at one's toes, lying on the soft grass at the water's edge and staring up at the treetops and sky

POSSIBLE SOURCES OF CONFLICT
Coming across a dangerous animal during mating or calving season
Discovering that a creek is being poisoned
Rivals taking over one's favorite fishing spot
Discovering a dead body
Finding a dry creek bed when one is lost and desperately needs water
Drinking polluted water and getting sick
Learning that one's favorite creek has dried up
Enjoying a quiet lunch for two and realizing one is being watched
Discovering dead fish and salamanders along the banks
Running into a landowner who is upset with one trespassing on his property
Camping too close to a creek and being flooded out during a heavy rainstorm
Nesting birds that swoop and claw to drive one away
Looking up to discover one is sharing the creek with a potentially dangerous animal (a bear, a cougar, a moose, etc.)

PEOPLE COMMONLY FOUND HERE
Campers, fishermen, hikers, hunters, nature enthusiasts, property owners

RELATED SETTINGS THAT MAY TIE IN WITH THIS ONE
Campsite (152), canyon (204), country road (156), forest (212), hiking trail (216), hunting cabin (166), meadow (224), mountains (228), pond (232), river (236)

SETTING NOTES AND TIPS
Creeks are smaller than rivers, both in width and depth. Slow-moving and shallow, creeks can be found almost anywhere the climate allows but may seasonally dry up in hotter months. As the water flows slowly, creeks freeze solid in the winter, unlike a faster river where a channel in the middle usually remains open. Some creeks are silty and difficult to see through, while others (especially those close to mountains) may be like a clear looking glass all the way to the bottom.

SETTING DESCRIPTION EXAMPLE
I sat on the creek bank, letting the water dribble over my toes, massaging my soles against the pebbles underfoot. I listened to the water trickling along, to the insects droning and leaves rustling, and underneath it all, the rumble and crash of the river just over the ridge. I rolled my neck on my shoulders. Hard to believe that a five-minute walk would see peaceful Blue Creek turned to the rushing, crashing river that sliced through our property and divided my family in half.

Techniques and Devices Used: Contrast, weather
Resulting Effects: Hinting at backstory

DESERT

SIGHTS
A sand and rock landscape dotted with cacti (tall saguaros, barrel, prickly pear), acacia trees, mesquite bushes and desert broom, rolling foothills, tumbleweeds and dust devils, riverbeds and ravines with crackled dry beds, crumbling rock, sandstone, vast canyons, wind-worn rock formations, a bright flash of light as sun winks off a bottle or broken piece of glass, animal tracks (squirrels, antelope, foxes, whitetail deer, bighorn sheep, coyotes, jackrabbits, mice, bobcats), thick-stemmed yellow and green grass, vibrant desert blooms (of yellow, pink, and white) after a rainfall, flash flooding cascading from the mountains and carving riverbeds into the soil, snakes leaving sidewinding ripples through the sand, a velvety black night sky with glinting stars, a glowing moon, withered trees, wide open skies, the blue haze of the atmosphere and mountains or foothills in the distance, heat waves rising off stone, lizards sunning themselves on rocks or hiding beneath the spines of a bush, bright green aloe spears, billowing sand storms that cross the land in a curtain of brown, sun-bleached bones or skulls, hawks and buzzards circling in the sky, stunted bushes, thorny shrubs, wasps, animal burrows, tarantulas and scorpions, dying cacti riddled with bullet holes, a watering hole from an underground spring surrounded by green vegetation

SOUNDS
Wind (whistling, howling, piping, tearing, weaving, winding, gusting), birds cawing and squawking, wings flapping, the fluttering shift of feasting birds that jockey for space, screeching eagles, the sound of one's steps thumping on stone and displacing sand, a heavy silence, sand trickling down a hill, baying wild dogs, the night sounds of predator and prey, dry branches rubbing against each other in the wind, rocks shifting underfoot as one walks along a dry riverbed, small stones rumbling down a ravine and making a hollow *tock* sound when they collide with something, coyotes howling

SMELLS
Hot and dry air, dust, one's own sweat and body odor, dry baked earth, carrion, cacti fruit (when it's in season)

TASTES
Grit, dust, a dry mouth and tongue, warm canteen water, a copper taste in one's mouth, the bitter taste of insects one might be desperate enough to eat, stringy wild game (hares, rats, coyote), the tough saltiness of jerky, dry biscuits, an insatiable thirst or hunger, salty sweat coating one's lips

TEXTURES AND SENSATIONS
Clothes that chafe from sweat and dirt or stick to the skin, sweat dripping into one's eyes, a dry wind blowing over one's cracked lips, pebbles getting into one's boot, gritty sand sticking to the corners of one's eyes, dragging one's fatigued footsteps through the dirt, the blistering cold at night, pain from split lips, dehydration, numbness in the legs, heat and dizziness from sunstroke,

swiping a bandana at one's neck or face, muscles that seize and shake, skin that burns, clothes that feel stiff from dirt, painful blisters that rub and pop, sand in one's clothing, a prickly cactus, thorny bushes poking and scraping as one passes, running a hand along a dusty canyon wall to stay upright, tripping over pebbles on the trail, a tarantula scuttling over one's boot

POSSIBLE SOURCES OF CONFLICT

Running out of food or water
Being stalked by a desert predator
Becoming lost
Misjudging the time and fighting exposure at night
Sunstroke
Being bitten by a venomous animal (a snake, scorpion, spider, or lizard)
Falling and injuring oneself
A breakdown on a rarely traveled road
Discovering that one's road has led to a dead end
Being caught in a desert storm or dust storm without any shelter
Unpredictable flooding of riverbeds in the rainy season
Wandering away from the road and not being able to find one's way back
Having no knife or a way to make a fire
Needing help and finally running into people who turn out to be uncooperative or dangerous
Seeing a plane or helicopter and having no way to signal for help

PEOPLE COMMONLY FOUND HERE

Campers, hermits, hunters, indigenous peoples, locals, people who love the outdoors, survivalists, teens letting off steam in jeeps and quads, tour groups, tourists

RELATED SETTINGS THAT MAY TIE IN WITH THIS ONE

Badlands (200), canyon (204)

SETTING NOTES AND TIPS

Deserts are filled with life during certain seasons, but even in the heat of summer they can supply food, water, and shelter if one knows where to look. The biggest dangers are getting lost, or being bitten by a venomous snake or spider, some of which can kill a full-grown man within hours (if not minutes) without treatment.

SETTING DESCRIPTION EXAMPLE

I shivered on my bed of stones and turned my back to the fierce wind. Hours earlier I'd have given my soul for a cooling breeze. Now, teeth chattering worse than they did in the dead of winter, I longed for the sun's merciless kiss.

Techniques and Devices Used: Contrast, multisensory descriptions
Resulting Effects: Establishing mood, tension and conflict

FOREST

SIGHTS
Tall trees rising out of the earth to brush the sky, sun-dappled leaves creating flickering shadows on the ground, animal trails disappearing into the undergrowth, dead leaves and pine needles caught in clumps of moss, bark fraying off broken branches, fat tree burls, moss winding around trunks, wisps of old man's beard dripping off dead spruce branches, pine cones dotting the ground like spilled trinkets, wood beetles bumbling across rotten fallen logs, the flicker of a chipmunk's tail around a pile of stones, a ravine cutting through the earth, a river meandering through the trees, wind-damaged or fallen trees leaning drunkenly against one another, animal burrows hidden beneath the tree roots, light dancing across fern fronds and glittering off morning dew, dead logs becoming beds for moss and mushrooms, birch trees losing their bark in giant white curls, flat cedar branches, the raised edges of tree bark, piles of animal droppings on the trail, pine needles and other debris caught in old spiderwebs, thick brambles, bright berry bushes, acorns, insects, rabbits, birds, squirrels, mice, foxes, the wind shuddering through the branches, deer grazing along a path, wild mushrooms and toadstools, butterflies and moths fluttering close to wildflowers (bluebells, daisies, goldenrod)

SOUNDS
The wind rustling through leaves, the spongy crunch of layers of dead pine needles and twigs underfoot, birds calling and squirrels chattering, the hum of insects, a grassy rustle as a deer grabs a mouthful of greenery, animals rooting around in the underbrush, the scrabble of claws against tree bark as a squirrel races to the top, limbs crashing to the ground in a windstorm, rain pattering to the dirt floor, tall trees that creak and groan as they sway, the crack of a branch breaking in the distance, a screech or cry from a pursued animal, the occasional gunshot sending a flock of birds into the sky, animals panting or snorting, yips at night, the ticking tap of a woodpecker, storm water rushing through a ravine, the whine of a bee or fly

SMELLS
Pine, floral wildflower scents, an earthy smell of decomposing leaves, animal scat, rotting wood, fresh and clean air, dew, the wind carrying odors from nearby locations (wood smoke, the ocean, exhaust), wild mint and herbs, foul decay (bogs, stagnant pools of water, dead animals), the ripe stench of skunks or skunk weed, sweet cedar, the mustiness of moss

TASTES
Tart cranberries, sweet wild strawberries or saskatoon berries, mealy rosehips, woody nuts, pungent mushrooms, wild onions, seeds, edible leaves and bark, food and water brought in by hikers and campers (granola bars, beef jerky, nuts, apples, dried fruit, sandwiches)

TEXTURES AND SENSATIONS
The rough cracked ridges of tree bark, a falling leaf landing in one's hair, branches scraping the skin, piercing thorns or burrs, the give of spongy moss underfoot, uneven ground pitted with rocks and roots, sticky sap beads, underbrush that tangles and grabs, leaves slick with dew,

hanging moss sliding across a cheek, walking into a spiderweb, a cooling breeze, strong gale winds that lift debris and throw it around, muggy trapped heat, sweat trailing down one's back, dead moss that crumbles when one touches it, slipping on a patch of slimy mushrooms, the wind pushing back one's bangs, wet grass that slides against one's legs, moisture seeping into one's boots, pine needles scratching at the arms, a rock caught in one's shoe, clothes sticky with sweat, slimy lichen, washing one's hands in a creek and wetting a bandana before winding it back around one's forehead

POSSIBLE SOURCES OF CONFLICT
Stumbling upon a wild animal
Becoming turned around in the forest and losing one's sense of direction
Starting a campfire for warmth and having it jump to the trees and scrub
Being chased by a predator (animal or human)
Meeting a landowner who is mentally unstable
Strange noises at night that one cannot identify
Drinking contaminated water from a river or stream
Being plagued by midges or horse flies and having no way to protect oneself against their bites
Discovering illegal activity taking place in the woods (captives being held prisoner, a dump site for dead bodies, a meth lab)
A vehicle breakdown that leaves one stranded in an unpopulated area
Hiking in an area with no cell service and needing help

PEOPLE COMMONLY FOUND HERE
Campers, hermits, hikers, hunters, nature photographers, outdoor enthusiasts, poachers, runaways

RELATED SETTINGS THAT MAY TIE IN WITH THIS ONE
Abandoned mine (142), cave (206), creek (208), hiking trail (216), hunting cabin (166), lake (220), mountains (228), rainforest (234), river (236), summer camp (188), waterfall (242)

SETTING NOTES AND TIPS
Forest flora and fauna depends entirely on location and climate. A forest in Canada will differ from one in Switzerland or Germany. If your setting is tied to a real location (such as Montana, USA) then do your research for that area so you can populate your forest with plants and creatures commonly found there. Also, think about the time of year that your story takes place. A forest landscape will vary season to season and some animals may migrate or hibernate.

SETTING DESCRIPTION EXAMPLE
As the light faded, it left behind shadows and dark patches to surround me. Eyes glimmered from tree hollows. The wind wailed between distorted trunks, carrying the sickly stink of wood rot. I moved faster, ignoring the briars that caught at my jeans and the damp leaves that grimed my skin.
   Techniques and Devices Used: Light and shadow, multisensory descriptions
   Resulting Effects: Establishing mood, tension and conflict

GROTTO

SIGHTS
High arched ceilings of rock, shafts of light slipping in through cracks in the stone, rippling water that rises and falls with the tide (shoreline grottoes) or storms (inland grottoes), moss and lichen, smooth rock walls worn by wind and water, small waterfalls (running down the walls, stalagmites, ledges, and outcroppings), bat guano, bats clinging to high rock shelves, pockets of dark shadow, snails clinging to wet rocks at the shoreline, crabs hiding in crevices, water creatures (barnacles, fish, minnows) that are suited to low or no light, silt stirring underfoot and muddying the water, tunnel offshoots above and below the water line, dead leaves or debris that has worked its way underground, an out-of-place clump of hardy greenery growing in a patch of light, twisted roots dangling from the rock ceiling that drip water when it rains, rocks and sand stained by salt and algae (if the grotto is a coastal one), fish swimming in the water

SOUNDS
Surf crashing against the rocks, water droplets raining down onto the surface after a big wave rushes through, sea birds shrieking nearby, the scuttle of crab legs over stone, echoes, crumbles of rock being dislodged and falling as one walks around, water from a waterfall rushing through holes overhead, echoes against the stone, dripping water, water lapping at the edges during calmer weather, squeaks and flutters from bats

SMELLS
Mildew, wet stone, algae, salt brine (in coastal grottoes), greenery and wild grass (in inland grottoes)

TASTES
Salt water on the lips, fresh water, the tang of minerals in the air

TEXTURES AND SENSATIONS
Sharp rocks and barnacles cutting one's hands and feet, gritty sand between one's toes, slipping on a rock and scraping one's skin, cold water closing over one's head during a swim, water dripping from the roof and landing on one's skin, worn stones, a lizard or crab scuttling over one's fingers, a piece of driftwood that has been worn smooth, the surf or current surging against one's body

POSSIBLE SOURCES OF CONFLICT
Being trapped when the tide comes in
A storm that raises the water level and seals off one's exit
Panicking in the dark or at being in an enclosed place
Slipping and becoming injured
Exploring underwater caves and getting turned around
Getting separated from one's friends in an underwater cave system
Losing one's light in the water, or one's batteries going out
Finding something hidden on a high shelf that suggests a crime (a bloody knife, a collection of

wedding rings in a cloth bag, etc.)
Something bumping one's leg underwater
An injury that makes swimming out impossible

PEOPLE COMMONLY FOUND HERE
Adventure seekers, archeologists, cave divers, hikers and climbers, treasure-seekers

RELATED SETTINGS THAT MAY TIE IN WITH THIS ONE
Beach (202), cave (206), rainforest (234), tropical island (240), waterfall (242)

SETTING NOTES AND TIPS
Coastal grottoes and those inland caused by underground rivers and wells will have different looks, smells, and sounds because of the tides. Some grottoes may have a single pool and cave, while others may have miles of connected cave systems.

SETTING DESCRIPTION EXAMPLE
The tide gently pulled against me as I climbed out of the pool into the underground cave. Light slid through a tiny crack overhead, past the fuzz of dripping tree roots, spilling a shaft of light across the water. I sat on a flat rock, listening to the water lapping the walls, the cry of a gull somewhere far above, and the scuttle of crabs on rocks as they searched for food. It had been nerve-wracking, diving through the underwater hole in the reef without knowing where it went, but discovering this untouched place of beauty made it completely worthwhile.

    Techniques and Devices Used: Light and shadow, multisensory descriptions
    Resulting Effects: Reinforcing emotion

HIKING TRAIL

SIGHTS
A meandering dirt or stone path, plants and ferns on either side, mossy rocks, a trail passing between sheer rock faces, breathtaking views, tree roots crisscrossing the trail, branches hanging out into the path, overgrown sections where the trail seems to disappear, half-buried pebbles and stones, fallen leaves and twigs, wildflowers and berry bushes, broken spiderwebs, areas of shade and sunlight, signposts and trailheads showing hikers the right direction, footbridges or logs placed over streams and ravines, shallow creeks that must be crossed on foot, small puddles formed by rainwater, rivulets of rainwater trickling along the path, fallen tree trunks, decaying branches and leaves, rough steps that have been carved or built into steep slopes, distant waterfalls, stacked boulders, rough benches, hikers with walking sticks and backpacks, birds flying overhead, squirrels, rabbits, deer, dogs, gnats, flies, mosquitoes, ants, beetles, spiders, lizards, snakes, viewing points off the trail where hikers can take a break and check out a new vantage point

SOUNDS
Birds chirping, squirrels scrabbling around tree trunks, flies and mosquitoes buzzing, insects humming, lizards scampering over fallen leaves, shoes scraping over rocky paths, leaves crunching underfoot, pebbles bouncing along the path, the wind in the trees, branches creaking in the wind, leaves skittering over the hard path, dogs barking and panting, chuckling streams and trickling creeks, water splashing over rocks, stones tumbling down a steep slope, small animals moving in the underbrush, heavy breathing, the crackle of a food wrapper being opened, jingling bits of a hiker's equipment, bear bells, hikers chatting or calling out to each other

SMELLS
Dirt, rain, decaying wood and leaves, wildflowers, sweat, insect repellant, wet stones

TASTES
Fresh berries, hiking food (granola or energy bars, trail mix, nuts, fresh and dried fruit, candy, crackers, cheese, beef jerky), water

TEXTURES AND SENSATIONS
A bulky pack strapped to one's shoulders, heavy shoes, an uneven path under one's feet, prickly briars, burrs sticking to one's clothes, stones shifting on a natural stone stair, a rough walking stick in one's hand, sweat dampening one's skin, the sting of mosquitoes, gnats buzzing around one's face, rough tree bark, warm berries, being slapped by a tree branch, slick leaves underfoot, raindrops dripping from the trees onto one's head, fatigued and burning muscles, dry mouth, thirst, fuzzy moss, tripping over a tree root, placing one's feet carefully when climbing uphill or crossing a narrow bridge, cold creek water, walking barefoot across a stream, changes in air temperature when moving from sunny to shady spots, sitting and resting on a cold stone or rough log, the breeze in one's hair, heat exhaustion

POSSIBLE SOURCES OF CONFLICT

Being attacked by animals
Being stung by bees or bitten by a snake
Falling over a cliff or down an embankment when one gets too close to the edge
Unreliable cell phone service
Gravely injuring oneself and being unable to get back to one's vehicle without assistance
Running out of supplies (water and food especially)
Faulty hiking equipment (hiking poles that snap, a strap on one's shoe breaking, etc.)
Over-packing one's bag and struggling with the weight
Overestimating one's hiking ability
Pushing oneself too hard out of a need to prove oneself to others
Traveling with others who are well below or above one's hiking level
Heat stroke or dehydration
Suffering an asthma attack
Eating poisonous berries or mushrooms
Missing a trailhead sign and getting lost
The trail giving way and dumping one into a river
Encountering a dangerous animal (a grizzly bear, a cougar)

PEOPLE COMMONLY FOUND HERE

Campers, exercise enthusiasts, hikers, nature lovers, nature photographers, survivalists

RELATED SETTINGS THAT MAY TIE IN WITH THIS ONE

Badlands (200), campsite (152), canyon (204), cave (206), creek (208), forest (212), hot springs (218), hunting cabin (166), lake (220), marsh (222), meadow (224), moors (226), mountains (228), pond (232), river (236), waterfall (242)

SETTING NOTES AND TIPS

Near rural areas, hiking trails are quite common and will vary in difficulty level. The location will obviously play a large part in what can be seen, since a hike through the mountains will look very different than a trek across a plateau or lowland forest. The trail itself is also optional for experienced hikers and those with a sense of adventure who are apt to forge their own paths through new areas. Whether they get lost, encounter wildlife in ways they did not anticipate, or face challenges resulting from their off-the-path escapades—the possibilities are endless and are entirely up to you.

SETTING DESCRIPTION EXAMPLE

A rough wind raked my scalp and tossed leaves along the trail, turning it into an orange-red mess. Sunlight freckled my skin without warmth; the air smelled like dry leaves and cold tree bark and impending winter. I listened for the squirrels and their chatter, but they were already gone, chased into their holes by the bullying wind. If this foul weather kept up much longer, it would chase me off, too.

    Techniques and Devices Used: Multisensory descriptions, personification, weather
    Resulting Effects: Establishing mood, foreshadowing

HOT SPRINGS

SIGHTS
Lazy heat trails drifting up from the water, rock slabs and wet stone ledges around the pool, rising heat causing bubbles to ripple up through the water, hazy air, pink-faced visitors swimming and relaxing at the edge, clear water, a sandy or smooth rock bottom, towels sitting near the edge of the springs, discarded flip-flops, leafy branches and palm fronds curling out over the water, birds flitting through the trees, rocks and ledges poking up through the water in places, a crust of white or yellow minerals along the waterline, sunlight flickering over the water's surface, water bottles sitting near the edge

SOUNDS
The burble of water as it's heated and pushed to the surface, splashing, water dripping, contented sighs, laughter, people talking with friends, the slap of sandals on wet stone, water rushing over a small waterfall drop, water lapping at the stone edges of the pool, birdcalls, the whir of crickets and other insects, rain pattering against the surface in a cooling rainforest shower, the crunch of small stones underfoot, condensation dripping off overhanging bushes and trees, couples talking and laughing as they sit in the pool with their heads bent close

SMELLS
Sulfur, minerals, damp rock, rich mud, sweat, nearby flowers or greenery

TASTES
Sweat licked from one's lip, a sip from a water bottle, the tang of mineral-rich water in the pool (which might be bitter or unpleasant)

TEXTURES AND SENSATIONS
Uneven rocks under one's bare feet, silky hot water sliding over one's skin, steamy air warming one's face and neck, smooth rock ledges to sit or lean on, toes sinking into a muddy or gravelly bottom, wet hair dripping water onto one's shoulders, muscles releasing their tension, aches and pains that fade to nothing, breathing in thick and moist air, a feeling of euphoria, a sheen of sweat covering one's skin, stepping out of the hot pool into cold air and wrapping oneself in a fluffy towel, slipping wet feet back into flip-flops

POSSIBLE SOURCES OF CONFLICT
A hot springs location slated for destruction to make way for urban or corporate development
Disrespectful patrons leaving behind trash
An amorous couple with no regard for other visitors
Buzzed patrons who grow dizzy at the combination of alcohol and hot water
Entitled patrons who ignore the rules (bringing drinking glasses to the pool and accidentally knocking them in, causing breakage that result in the pool being shut down, etc.)
A loud group that disrupts the peaceful setting
Pollution contaminating the hot spring

A patron becoming overheated

Slipping on wet rocks as one leaves the pool

Bashing a knee on a rock or scraping a thigh

A couple that loudly complains about everything

Rowdy children splashing and yelling

Discovering a dead body in a deserted pool

PEOPLE COMMONLY FOUND HERE

Locals, naturalists desiring the healing benefits of hot spring mineral water, staff running the pools, tourists

RELATED SETTINGS THAT MAY TIE IN WITH THIS ONE

Canyon (204), grotto (214), hiking trail (216), mountains (228), rainforest (234), tropical island (240)

SETTING NOTES AND TIPS

Hot springs vary greatly in appearance due to location, commercialization, and mineral content. Water may be clear or cloudy and can be found in mountains, rainforests, and more arid locations. If a spring is turned into a tourist destination, the waters may even be diverted to create a large, modern-looking pool that can accommodate many patrons. Some pools have easy access, while others may be in remote locations, making them difficult to visit but worth the trip because of their privacy and beauty.

SETTING DESCRIPTION EXAMPLE

I lowered myself into the thermal waters, and with each inch, my worries and aches slipped away. There was only the moist air being drawn into my lungs, the press of warmth against my body, and the sounds of nature around me. Bathed in peace, I locked away all thoughts of the life I'd left this morning and resolved to enjoy this getaway as much as I possibly could.

    Techniques and Devices Used: Multisensory descriptions

    Resulting Effects: Establishing mood, reinforcing emotion

LAKE

SIGHTS
A rocky shoreline with colorful gravel in shades of gray and white, knobby driftwood at the water's edge, waves lapping the shore, spindly-legged skimmers skittering across the surface, minnows darting between rocks, ducks floating among the weeds, geese plucking grass along the shoreline or preening elegant wings, seagulls searching picnic areas for garbage left behind, dragonflies skimming the water's surface, mosquitoes and horseflies, blankets spread out for families or friends to lay on, a long dock, tied-up boats swaying with the current, a paved boat launch, children in swimsuits playing at the water's edge, older kids floating on inner tubes or inflatable floaters, fishermen dropping lines into the water, boats and Jet Skis racing back and forth in the deep water, canoes holding paddlers wearing bright life vests, fishing boats and rowboats dotting the water, turtles sunning themselves on driftwood, a floating dock packed with teenagers preparing to dive or sunning on the wooden planks, fish, duckweed, lake scum floating along the shoreline, bits of broken glass and frizzy spools of fishing line caught in the rocks, beer cans left behind in the grass, trees bowing over the lake and casting reflections in the water, sunshine glittering off the waves, houses with private docks, deer drinking at the water's edge, tiny flowers hidden in the grass, deadheads (thin tree stumps) sticking out of the water

SOUNDS
The roar of a boat motor, a speedboat thumping across another boat's wake, music from portable players, friends talking and laughing, the gentle lap of water hitting the shoreline, insects buzzing, wind whispering through the trees, water splashing, turtles plopping into the water, seagulls crying, the rev of an engine as a boat is maneuvered onto a trailer at the boat launch, an oar sliding through the water, the creak of trees on a quiet day, feet crunching along a gravel shoreline, plunking down a folding chair, the rustle of food wrappers, the hiss of a beer or pop can opening, crickets, frogs croaking, the crackle of a beach campfire

SMELLS
The peaty smell of algae, fresh air, food cooking on portable grills, grass, wet earth, water, gasoline fumes from boats, sunscreen, flowers, rotten vegetation along the shoreline, the char of a marshmallow on a stick

TASTES
Lake water, food cooked on a portable grill (burgers, hot dogs, chicken, steak), potato salad, chips, pop, coleslaw, takeout food (a bucket of chicken, pizzas), beer, sandwiches from home, water, pop, beer or coolers, juice boxes, marshmallows

TEXTURES AND SENSATIONS
Sharp gravel poking one's bare feet, water sliding around one's shins, the shivers, grass sticking to one's ankles, picking and plucking at a bathing suit that won't stay in place, water seeping through shoes or sandals, sand caught in one's shoes, gritty sand on one's skin, greasy sunscreen, the sun's warmth, water droplets falling from one's hair onto one's shoulders, jumping as

something brushes one's leg in the water or nips at a leg, hair blowing into one's face, hair that is tangled from a speedy boat ride, sunglasses sliding down one's nose, the shock of cold ice as one rummages through a cooler, a warm blanket, a scratchy towel, friction between wet skin and dry clothing just pulled on, the warped wooden boards of a fishing dock, sitting on the dock and swinging one's legs, dragging an oar through the water

POSSIBLE SOURCES OF CONFLICT

Obnoxious boaters making it dangerous for swimmers
Inattentive parents with toddlers near the water's edge
Forgetting the bug spray and being eaten alive by mosquitoes
Rowdy partygoers
Leg cramps while swimming
Feeling something alive in the water as it rubs against a leg
Being surprised by a freshwater snake
A truck and boat trailer getting stuck in the mud
Getting caught fishing without a license
A boat that springs a leak or capsizes
Not being able to swim but being too embarrassed to say anything

PEOPLE COMMONLY FOUND HERE

Campers, conservation officers, families, fish and wildlife officers, ice cream or food truck operators, sports fishermen, teenagers, vacationers

RELATED SETTINGS THAT MAY TIE IN WITH THIS ONE

Beach party (150), campsite (152), forest (212), hiking trail (216), meadow (224), mountains (228), pond (232), river (236)

SETTING NOTES AND TIPS

While many lakes are simple, peaceful places, others may be high-traffic areas that are connected to campgrounds and government-run parks. Many of these have a higher amount of tourism in the summer months, meaning there are more boats, vacationers, watercraft activities, and noises. Areas that are used to high volume tourism usually have amenities one might not normally find in a lake environment, such as floating gas stations, restaurants, and stores that accommodate owners of houseboats and other watercraft.

SETTING DESCRIPTION EXAMPLE

Moonlight flickered against the lake's surface as I shivered in the shallows, cold radiating up through my feet. Everyone else had already jumped in and was busy splashing and dunking, filling the air with happy shrieks. I wrapped my arms around my waist, thinking about all the things waiting in the deeper water—broken glass to cut my feet, rocks and slimy algae to slip on. What if a fish touched my leg in the dark? And alligators . . . I clambered back out of the water and went looking for my towel.

    Techniques and Devices Used: Contrast, multisensory descriptions
    Resulting Effects: Characterization

MARSH

SIGHTS
Standing water (fresh or salty), water that forms pools or snakes its way through grassy plains, muddy soil, half-submerged logs and dead snags, beaver dams and muskrat houses rising out of the water, grasses and reeds rippling in the wind, saw grass and sedges growing in clumps, papyrus heads nodding on thin stalks, low-growing shrubs, water lilies and bright green duckweed floating in the water, frogs and toads, turtles sunning themselves on rocks, snakes slipping through the grasses, alligators stealing through the water, salamanders, water birds (herons, egrets, ducks, cranes, geese, kingfishers) snapping at insects and fish, hawks and eagles riding the air currents far above, damselflies, glistening spiderwebs strung between grass stalks, water bugs dancing across the surface, dragonflies weaving through the reeds, mosquitoes biting and flying near anything that moves, grasshoppers flying short distances, beetles crawling along exposed deadfall, beavers and muskrats, mink and otters, foxes, fish, shrimp, snails, deer drinking at the water's edge, raccoons looking for crayfish, air boats racing along the water channels, rowboats and motorboats, people hunting for frogs or taking pictures on vacation, swampy air bubbles that rise to the surface and break, a flattened grassy area and a hidden clutch of eggs, mist rolling along the water

SOUNDS
Wind rustling the grasses, the plop of turtles sliding into the water, the splash of water suddenly disturbed by fish or birds, birds trilling, insects humming and buzzing, the flap of wings as birds take flight, the croaking of frogs, rain splashing into the water, thunder booming in the sky, the tapping of woodpeckers, grasses swishing as animals swim through them, grasses crackling as animals walk over them, the sucking sound of animals moving through mud, boat motors, the slap of boat oars, reeds and submerged driftwood scraping against a boat hull

SMELLS
Stagnant water, hydrogen sulfide, rotten eggs, decaying plant matter, wet grass, marsh gas, humid air, salty water, wood rot, mold and mildew, fish

TASTES
Some settings have no specific tastes associated with them beyond what the character might bring into the scene (chewing gum, mints, lipstick, cigarettes, etc.). For scenes like these, where specific tastes are sparse, it would be best to stick to descriptors from the other four senses.

TEXTURES AND SENSATIONS
Grasses catching at pant legs and sleeves, a boat sluicing fluidly through the water, boats jerking and slowing as they scrape over muddy places in the water, the sting of blisters from using oars, the sun beating down on one's head, the wind whipping water against the skin, the bite of mosquitoes and other insects, insects alighting on one's skin, mud oozing up between the toes, pruning fingers, wet clothes that chafe, the weighted feel of muddy shoes, raindrops, the jerk of a fishing line going taut

POSSIBLE SOURCES OF CONFLICT

Falling out of one's boat

Springing a leak

Alligators and snakes in the area

Running into locals who like their privacy and hate trespassers

Being abandoned on the marsh at night with no transportation or shelter

Getting blisters from walking in wet shoes

Getting caught in a downpour

Losing one's sense of direction

Losing possessions in the water (fishing gear, a change of clothes, wallet, phone, sleeping bag, etc.)

Getting lost with no idea how to get out

Portaging made difficult because of the danger of alligators

Stopping at a dry spot and coming across a nesting area for alligators

Running out of fresh water

One's boat overturning

Being bitten by something and not knowing what it was

Creatures in the brackish water bumping against the hull of one's boat

Running out of gas or experiencing an airboat malfunction

Exhaustion from walking through grassy areas that suck at one's boots with every step

PEOPLE COMMONLY FOUND HERE

Birdwatchers, ecologists, fishermen and women, locals in rowboats, people on a motorboat tour

RELATED SETTINGS THAT MAY TIE IN WITH THIS ONE

Creek (208), meadow (224), river (236), swamp (238)

SETTING NOTES AND TIPS

Marshes and swamps are similar in some ways, but they're distinctly different landforms—mostly due to the plant life that inhabits each. While both are wetlands, marshes contain herbaceous plants like grasses, sedges, and reeds. Swamps tend to be deeper than marshes and consist of lots of woody plants such as mangroves and cypress trees. Marshes can consist of salt water, fresh water, or a mixture of both; the kind of water will determine which plants and animals live there, so take that into consideration.

SETTING DESCRIPTION EXAMPLE

The tall grass shivered in the wind—brownish-green waves flickering over the water's surface. Clouds screened the sky, with light flashing against their gray bellies. Thunder drummed loudly, startling the geese into flight and telling me it was time to go.

Techniques and Devices Used: Weather

Resulting Effects: Foreshadowing

MEADOW

SIGHTS
Long grass seeded with wildflowers, ample sunlight, dry leaves trapped in the grass mounds, tall trees surrounding the meadow, butterflies and dragonflies flying here and there, ants moving through the grass, bees flitting between flowers, spiders building webs, leaping frogs near streams and brooks, nesting birds bursting out of the grass at a human's approach, deer grazing, foxes slinking low to the ground, rabbits and mice feeding, moles venturing out of their holes, a snake slithering around the grass stems or along a fallen log, grasses swaying from the movement of animals hiding in them, clouds drifting across the sky, shafts of golden sun lighting up the meadow in patches, a stream bubbling across the meadow, distant mountains or hills, shadows drifting over the meadow as clouds pass overhead, mossy rocks, broken branches around the perimeter, gopher holes, trees rocking in the wind, autumn leaves twirling and drifting to the ground

SOUNDS
The swish of grasses blowing in the wind, the drone of bees and other insects, birds singing and chirping, the flapping of bird wings, leaves rustling, water gurgling, muffled footsteps in the grass, animals running away, leaves rustling and clattering, wind shushing, small critters scampering through the grass, a cricket's song, water trickling over stones and roots from a nearby creek, the hum of bees and dragonflies, the whine of flies and mosquitoes, birds cawing and squawking, squirrels or chipmunks chittering, grass crunching underfoot

SMELLS
Grass, warm earth and sunlight, pollen, sweet flowers and berries, clean air, dew, creek water

TASTES
Chewing on a stalk of sweet grass, picnic food brought to the area (sandwiches, wine, cheese, bread, cold cuts, dried fruit, potato salad, chocolate and cookies, fried chicken, fruit, crackers, fruit salad), wild berries collected in season (strawberries, raspberries, blueberries, gooseberries, saskatoons), bottled water

TEXTURES AND SENSATIONS
Warm sun on the face, a breeze brushing one's hair and skin, a gusty wind pushing one off-balance, warm earth, soft grass, scratchy dead leaves or grass close to the ground, the sting of a bee or bite of an insect, grass sliding against one's legs, dead leaves and grass giving way underfoot, a change in temperature as clouds pass over the sun, hillocks and holes that make the ground uneven, a long flower stem tucked behind the ear, sweat sticking a shirt to one's back, leaves or pine needles that fall from the trees and stick in one's hair, rolling up one's pant legs and dangling one's feet into a shallow brook, unfurling a picnic blanket and laying out food, a loose shirt being pressed against one's body when the wind picks up, the tickle of an ant crawling across the back of the hand, lying back in a bed of grass to stare up at the sky, holding one's breath as a doe steps into view, the scratch of a pencil on paper as one sketches the landscape

POSSIBLE SOURCES OF CONFLICT

Being stung when one steps on an underground wasp nest
Being bitten by a snake in the grass
Falling asleep and getting sunburned
Encountering strangers when one is out alone on a hike
Not taking proper precautions and getting heatstroke
Stepping in a gopher hole and turning one's ankle
Getting caught in the rain or snow
Feeling watched from the tree line
Seasonal allergies that ruin one's outdoor trip
Coming across a poacher dressing his kill
Finding a grave marker but not knowing who was buried there
Finding a picnic laid out on a blanket with no one in sight
Having bear cubs enter the clearing and knowing the mother can't be far off
Crossing a patch of recently bloodstained grass

PEOPLE COMMONLY FOUND HERE

Campers, hikers, ornithologists, picnickers

RELATED SETTINGS THAT MAY TIE IN WITH THIS ONE

Campsite (152), country road (156), creek (208), forest (212), hiking trail (216), hunting cabin (166), lake (220), mountains (228), pond (232), river (236), summer camp (188)

SETTING NOTES AND TIPS

The meadow has many ecological cousins. A meadow that is mown for hay becomes a pasture. A steppe is a grassland that, due to its dry climate, has a smaller variety of plant life. Heaths are similar to meadows but are dominated by low shrubby bushes instead of grasses.

Meadows tend to be peaceful places full of gentle sounds and textures. But there are dangerous features, too: snakes and poisonous spiders, hidden gopher holes, stinging insects, and unfriendly weather. Any setting can be tumultuous; it's the author's job to add the troublesome elements.

SETTING DESCRIPTION EXAMPLE

I moved quickly through the meadow, knowing it would take most of the morning to cross. Weedy-looking flowers scraped my knees while briars caught at my socks. Sweat soon dampened my collar and ran down the small of my back. I slapped a mosquito. I couldn't wait to get back to the city.

Techniques and Devices Used: Multisensory descriptions
Resulting Effects: Characterization, establishing mood

MOORS

SIGHTS
Rolling hills with low-growing vegetation, low clouds, scrubby bushes growing in clumps, stunted trees, a carpet of purple or red flowers when the heather is in bloom, early morning mist, yellow gorse blossoms, boulders and rocks dotting the landscape, sedges growing near a pond or creek, animals grazing (sheep, cows, deer, ponies), a variety of birds (grouse, merlins, peregrines), worms wiggling back into the earth, voles and mice scuttling from bush to bush, rabbits hiding in the shrubs, foxes nosing about for dinner, bees bumbling from flower to flower, moths and butterflies fluttering, peat bogs, berry bushes, shallow streams crisscrossing the land, tiny ponds, hazy smoke and flashes of orange fire from controlled burns, shepherds herding animals, a winding dirt path

SOUNDS
The cry of hunting birds, birds chirping, wind whistling through the heather, gusting winds, bees buzzing, rumbling thunder, animals rustling in the vegetation, the crackle of a controlled burn, animals bursting from cover to escape a burn, a stream's gurgling, the lowing of cattle, sheep bleating, shepherds calling to their animals

SMELLS
The scent of heather, grass, dung from grazing animals, smoke, rain, the decomposing smell of peat, stagnant water, wet earth

TASTES
Some settings have no specific tastes associated with them beyond what the character might bring into the scene (chewing gum, mints, lipstick, cigarettes, etc.). For scenes like these, where specific tastes are sparse, it would be best to stick to descriptors from the other four senses.

TEXTURES AND SENSATIONS
Damp soil, stumbling over the rocky ground, the woody stems of heather, burrs pricking one's skin, the wind blowing into one's face, uneven ground under one's feet, cool boulders, rain dampening the hair and skin, scrubby bushes catching on one's skirt or pants, soft grass underfoot, the throat-tickling odor of distant smoke, the cool night air on one's skin

POSSIBLE SOURCES OF CONFLICT
Not being able to find wood to build a fire for a heat source
Falling into a stream and developing hypothermia
Tripping over the uneven ground and injuring oneself
Being bitten by snakes
Suffering from hunger
Not knowing edible berries from the poisonous ones
Getting caught in the rain or snow
Getting caught by a controlled burn and needing to outrun it or get past it

An enemy deliberately setting a fire

Being trapped in a smoke-filled area and growing light-headed

Stumbling into a hidden bog

Finding oneself lost without a landmark for guidance

Mist or smoke haze screening the landscape and hiding possible dangers

A constant drizzle that causes arthritis to flare and bones to ache

PEOPLE COMMONLY FOUND HERE

Hunters, locals, moor keepers, people on vacation, shepherds

RELATED SETTINGS THAT MAY TIE IN WITH THIS ONE

Ancient ruins (144), creek (208), meadow (224), river (236)

SETTING NOTES AND TIPS

Moors are found in highland areas with high rainfall. Their soil is peaty and acidic, providing a home to a limited variety of plants that have adapted to survive in nutrient-poor conditions. Due to their high elevation, moors tend to be cooler than low-lying places, and their high rate of precipitation results in elevated rain and snowfalls.

SETTING DESCRIPTION EXAMPLE

The campfire shivered, and I huddled closer to its light. Firelight sharpened every blade of grass, each clump of heather—but only within a tiny circle. Beyond that, ink-like darkness. I could hear the wind howling through scrub, but I couldn't see it shivering the branches. I heard the cry of a hunting bird but couldn't find it in the night. A breeze threatened my flame. It sputtered. I fed it a handful of twigs and burrowed deeper into my sleeping bag.

    Techniques and Devices Used: Contrast, light and shadow

    Resulting Effects: Establishing mood, reinforcing emotion, tension and conflict

MOUNTAINS

SIGHTS
Stones and boulders dotting the landscape, craggy cliffs, shale and scree underfoot, cracks and fissures in the rock, slate and pebbles covering the ground, rock slides, avalanche paths, tree trunks decorated with bits of moss, tree lines demarcating the edge of a forest or wooded area, low-hanging clouds that cover the mountain tops in mist, steep slopes, waterfalls pouring into ravines or running gently down a rock face, snow piled in shadowy spots, animal tracks and scat, hunting birds (hawks, eagles, ravens, falcons, owls), mice skittering through the brush, deer traveling in cautious groups, bashful foxes, bighorn sheep, mountain predators (wolves, bears, cougars), rabbits freezing at the sound of a human's approach, beetles scuttling across rock, spiders spinning webs between trees, mosquitoes, clouds of gnats, pine cones and pine needles littering the ground, twigs and detritus on the forest floor, downed trees, streams flowing downhill, wildflowers growing in grassy spots and along creeks, grasses silvered with frost, tufts of grass, wild onions, wild berry bushes (cranberry, saskatoons, raspberry, gooseberry), big nests in the tops of trees for predator birds, peaks in the distance, valleys far below, sheared-off or wind-worn rock faces, meandering trails, leaves drifting down from the trees, pollen motes in the air

SOUNDS
Wind whistling along the slopes and rustling the trees, animal howls, rustling leaves, frothing waterfalls, water trickling into snowmelt, scree shifting beneath one's feet, rockfalls, birds calling and hooting, animals pattering through the underbrush, branches snapping, the crunch of pine needles underfoot, labored breathing during a steep climb, pebbles shifting and sliding, a gently splashing creek, a stream roaring with snowmelt, the sharp cry of hunting birds, the whine of mosquitoes, heavy animals stepping on twigs, small rocks clattering down the mountainside

SMELLS
Pine needles, crisp air, clean water, earthy moss, rotting logs and trees, vegetation, cold or wet rock, wildflower blossoms, snow and ice, ozone and minerals

TASTES
Wild plants (berries, wild onions, tubers, nuts, seeds), tea made from edible leaves and barks, the gamy flavor of captured animals or birds, spring waters, traveling food (dehydrated food meals, ramen noodles cooked with a camp stove, sandwiches, trail mix, power bars, bags of beef jerky, mixed nuts and seeds for energy, dried and fresh fruit

TEXTURES AND SENSATIONS
Unyielding stone, sharp finger holds, grit drifting into one's face, spongy moss, prickly pine needles caught in one's boot, slippery shale, fingertips grasping at a rock face handhold, wedging one's boots into toeholds, rope burns, wet sleeves from plunging one's hands into a freshwater stream, sweat trickling down the neck and on the face, becoming overheated and having to strip off a layer of clothes, smooth metal carabiners, tightly woven rope, chapped skin and lips from the cold, a raw throat from the thin air, exposure to wind and weather (shivering, numbness, icy

fingers, frozen cheeks, disorientation, hunger, strength depletion), cuts and bruises from slips and falls, the sting and itch of insect bites

POSSIBLE SOURCES OF CONFLICT

Being stalked or attacked by an animal

Injuring oneself in a way that makes it impossible to ascend or descend a steep slope

Falling off a cliff

Being washed away by a raging river

Hypothermia

Running out of or losing one's supplies (in a fall, to a mountain stream, etc.)

Falling ill and having to put the climb on hold

Avalanches and rockslides

Sudden inclement weather

A fear of heights

Falling through the snow and ice into a crevasse

Rock climbing with ropes and pins that aren't secured properly

A camera strap breaking, resulting in the loss of expensive equipment

Forgetting one's sunglasses and going half-blind from the snow glare at high elevations

Having no guide or a guide who doesn't know the hazards of the area

Planning a climb but not having the right gear (snow cleats, an ice axe, rope, etc.)

PEOPLE COMMONLY FOUND HERE

Campers, climbers, hikers, hunters, professional photographers, rangers, rock skiers, survivalists

RELATED SETTINGS THAT MAY TIE IN WITH THIS ONE

Rural Volume: Abandoned mine (142), campsite (152), cave (206), creek (208), forest (212), hiking trail (216), hot springs (218), hunting cabin (166), lake (220), meadow (224), river (236), waterfall (242)

Urban Volume: Ski resort (238)

SETTING NOTES AND TIPS

As with most settings, there are different kinds of mountains: snowy Alps and green Catskills; dome mountains and those with sharp peaks; sprawling ranges vs. lone volcanoes. Know what kind of mountains you're dealing with and where they're located to write knowledgeably about your mountain setting.

SETTING DESCRIPTION EXAMPLE

Janet stumbled over something in the trail, barely catching her balance. She muttered under her breath and glanced upward. Stars glittered through the gaps in the trees, and somewhere, a crescent moon was shining. Just . . . not here. Her foot turned on a stone, and a wolf howled in the distance. She swore. Where was the campsite?

Techniques and Devices Used: Light and shadow

Resulting Effects: Establishing mood, tension and conflict

OCEAN

SIGHTS
A sandy floor, sand bars and descending slopes, gravel, shoal bottoms, sea grass, half-buried shells, sea cucumber and sponges, anemones, colorful sea glass, spiky dark sea urchins, bright and dark spots in the water as shafts of light filter down, caves and caverns, different kinds of coral (brain, staghorn, sea fan) waving in the current, limestone trenches, a colorful array of fish (tuna, cod, swordfish, clown fish, salmon, blowfish, sunfish, sailfish, marlin, grouper), octopi sliding among the rocks and across the floor, crabs, giant clams and conch shells, bobbing sea horses, plankton, eels, lobster, manta rays invisible against the ocean floor, sharks swimming past, prawns, algae-covered rocks, starfish partially hidden in the rocks, seaweed drifting on the current, sea snails and snakes, turtles feasting on thin patches of sea grass, huge whales, playful dolphins, quick barracuda, squid and jellyfish, air bubbles floating up from a scuba diver's gear, boat wake trails on the water's surface, the hulls of boats passing overhead, scum and oil slicks floating on the surface, fish carcasses and ruined exoskeletons of crabs and lobsters half-buried in the sand, shrimp and crab traps lying on the ground, shipwrecks scabbed in rust and algae, shipwreck debris (old netting, timbers, bottles, barnacles, rusted chains and anchors), modern trash (tires, garbage, bottles, and cans), dead spots on the coral reef

SOUNDS
Breaths magnified through a tube, one's pulse beating in one's ears, whale calls, the hiss of air from one's gear, the slight swish of kicking flippers and water being displaced, water lapping the hull of a boat

SMELLS
Canned air, rubber, sealant on the mask, sweat, sunscreen

TASTES
Some settings have no specific tastes associated with them beyond what the character might bring into the scene (chewing gum, mints, lipstick, cigarettes, etc.). For scenes like these, where specific tastes are sparse, it would be best to stick to descriptors from the other four senses.

TEXTURES AND SENSATIONS
Cold or warm water, dangling bikini strings tickling one's skin, a wet suit encapsulating the skin, wet neoprene, the feel of water against one's skin and suit, air bubbles bouncing off one's cheek, hair rising up from the scalp and waving in the water, fingers dipping into the sand and brushing against coral or rock, flippers knocking into solid objects (the sea bed, shipwrecks, other divers swimming too close, rocks), fish brushing against the hands or body, the pull of water currents, skimming one's hand over a hard turtle shell, the awkward feel of the mouthpiece in one's mouth, pulling oneself along the ocean floor by grabbing chunks of limestone, floating with the current or swimming against it, muscle exertion from fast swimming, mask straps rubbing at the back of the head and sides of the face, the weight of heavy gear pulling at one's shoulders, brushing away sand to see an object, fanning the water close to the sea floor to dislodge sand,

swimming backward to move away from danger (sharks, barracudas, an octopus or jellyfish), a claustrophobic sensation at the realization of all the water that is pressing down from above, picking up shells and starfish to examine them before setting them down again

POSSIBLE SOURCES OF CONFLICT

Panicking on a dive

Faulty equipment

A near-drowning

Becoming separated from one's group

Dangerous marine life (sharks, jellyfish, eels, rays, barracuda)

Being saddled with an inexperienced dive partner

Incurring an injury underwater

Running out of oxygen

Getting caught underwater (in a cave or shipwreck)

A mask that leaks

Limestone that shifts when one touches it and traps one's fin between the rocks

Treasure hunters salvaging a shipwreck who view one as a threat to their operation

Fast-moving underwater currents that pull one away from one's tour group

PEOPLE COMMONLY FOUND HERE

Marine biologists, scuba divers, snorkelers, underwater photographers and filmmakers

RELATED SETTINGS THAT MAY TIE IN WITH THIS ONE

Rural Volume: Beach (202), beach party (150), grotto (214), tropical island (240)

Urban Volume: Fishing boat (260), marina (264), yacht (286)

SETTING NOTES AND TIPS

An underwater setting offers both creativity and challenge. Novelist Peter Benchley (*Jaws* and *The Deep*) made it look easy, so it can be done. Sounds are muted underwater, and since there's not much to taste or smell from inside a scuba mask, the setting will depend largely on sight and touch. Still, the visuals are stark and unique, making this setting an interesting and intriguing option for a story.

SETTING DESCRIPTION EXAMPLE

My heartbeat roars in my ears like an oncoming train as I yank and twist at my foot, trying not to scrape my skin—the last thing I need is blood in the water. How did this happen? Only a minute ago I'd been leaning over the rocks to grab that shot of the jellyfish and now my foot is jammed. Gulping at oxygen, I jerk my head left and right, trying to spot another diver, praying someone will find me before something larger and more dangerous does.

Techniques and Devices Used: Simile

Resulting Effects: Reinforcing emotion, tension and conflict

POND

SIGHTS
A pool of standing water, lily pads and water lilies floating on the surface, reeds and long grasses standing out of the water, weeds and wildflowers (dandelions, daisies, wild strawberries, clover blooms, bluebells) growing along the edge, a muddy bank strewn with rocks and pebbles, algae fuzzing up rocks below the surface, broken branches half-in and half-out of the water, waterlogged sticks floating at the pond's edge, trees growing around the shore, leaves floating on the water's surface, minnows and tadpoles swimming in the shallows, frogs leaping into the water, a variety of water birds (herons, egrets, ducks, geese, swans), swirling water as air bubbles drift up, water striders skating over the surface, snakes slithering along the top of the water, alligators sunning on the bank, deer drinking, rabbits, squirrels, muskrats, otters playing, beetles trundling along a rotten log, dragonflies and butterflies flying here and there, grasshoppers shooting out of the grass, flies and bees, meandering lines of ants, mosquitoes, spiders, turtles sticking their heads out of the water, leeches, snails, trees and clouds reflected on the water's surface, an old row boat pulled up on the shore, a rickety dock, a bridge, tadpoles swimming in the shallows

SOUNDS
Water splashing, wings flapping as birds bathe and preen, birds trilling and frogs croaking, small animals in the underbrush, a doe lapping up water, squawking birds, the buzz and hum of insects, wind rustling the leaves of the nearby trees, the music of crickets and grasshoppers, flat rocks skipping across the pond's surface, the squelching noise of walking in the mud, a bird's flapping wings as it takes flight, the plop of frogs or turtles jumping into the pond, a rowboat's oars breaking the surface of the water, raindrops splashing into the pond, distant thunder, the creak of a bridge as someone walks over it, flip-flips crossing a small pier or dock

SMELLS
Stagnant water, grass, wildflowers, wild mint, sweet clover, pine and spruce trees, wet earth, decaying matter, water slime

TASTES
Seasonal berries (saskatoons, gooseberries, strawberries, gooseberries, wild raspberries, blackberries), dirt from a fresh-picked berry, rose hips, pond water, a lunch brought from home (peanut butter sandwiches, fruit, crackers, cheese, granola bars), pulling a stalk of grass free and chewing on the inner sweet center

TEXTURES AND SENSATIONS
Cold water slipping over the skin, mud squishing between the toes, warm sun, soft grass or moss against one's back, insects landing or crawling over one's skin, the bite of an insect, the slimy feel of a frog or tadpole, pulling up grass and ripping it apart, silky flower petals, tossing smooth or muddy rocks into the water, pulling a leech off one's skin, clothes that stick as one pulls them onto one's wet body after climbing out of the pond, a fluffy dandelion that breaks apart when it's blown, water seeping into one's shoes, woody flower stems, berry juice staining one's fingers and

lips, the warmth of a rock baking in the sun, sunburn, grit under the nails, rinsing one's hands in the water, walking barefoot along a grassy bank, slimy rocks at the bottom of a pond, water plants brushing one's feet and legs as one swims, kneeling on the bumpy logs of a homemade raft that's floating in the murky water

POSSIBLE SOURCES OF CONFLICT

Ingesting water-borne bacteria while swimming in the pond
Alligators and snakes
A bee-sting allergy
Finding a dead animal floating in the water
Eating poisonous berries
Not catching any fish
A younger sibling nearly drowning
Stepping in mud and soaking one's shoes
Falling into the water
Getting caught in bad weather
Having one's raft collapse or one's canoe fill with water
Not being a naturally outdoorsy person
Having a fear of bugs
Climbing out of the water to discover one is covered in leeches
Peer pressure to do something gross (drink the water, eat a tadpole)

PEOPLE COMMONLY FOUND HERE

Campers, kids fishing, picnickers, the landowner and his family

RELATED SETTINGS THAT MAY TIE IN WITH THIS ONE

Campsite (152), creek (208), country road (156), farm (160), lake (220), meadow (224), orchard (174), ranch (180), summer camp (188)

SETTING NOTES AND TIPS

A pond ecosystem supports an incredible amount of plant and animal life for characters to interact with. If more human counterparts are needed, there are also urban ponds that people would be more likely to frequent, such as one in a public park or a pond that is commonly used as the locals' swimming hole.

SETTING DESCRIPTION EXAMPLE

Flinn and I sit on the damp bank, our poles dripping lines into the motionless water. A bullfrog lifts his head near a patch of duckweed, eyeing us curiously before dropping back into the murk. We don't know for sure if this pond has fish, but we do know what isn't here: shouts and curses, the reek of stale beer, and dad's unpredictable temper.

Techniques and Devices Used: Contrast
Resulting Effects: Hinting at backstory

RAINFOREST

SIGHTS
A lush canopy of gleaming leaves, palm fronds and snatches of bright sun and sky, ropy vines snaking down tall trees or curling around trunks in suffocating loops, dense green undergrowth sprouting across a bed of rich soil and rotting vegetation, monkeys dropping half-eaten fruit on the ground, colorful birds, waterfalls and wet stone, a creek or stream feeding into a rippling lagoon pool, dead leaves knocked loose by the wind and swirling to the ground, hidden cliffs and rocky outcroppings, downed trees hidden by new growth, colorful small critters (lizards, frogs, toads, bats, beetles, and spiders), a swarm of army ants devouring rotten mangoes, a puma stalking prey in the shadows or sleeping on a high branch, gorillas and howler monkeys foraging and marking their territory, silent tigers drifting along animal paths, boars rooting in the dirt and scraping their tusks against trunks, snakes looping around branches and sliding over tree roots, stands of tall bamboo, banana bunches hanging from trees, breadfruit, fig trees, taro, brown plant pods dusting the ground, leeches lurking in black pools, twisting tree roots creating bumps in the path, cashew trees, a praying mantis clinging to a branch, iguanas hidden in the foliage, mosquitoes and gnats swarming and biting, giant termite nests attached to tree limbs, leaf cutter ants sawing through stems and leaves, spiky pineapple bushes with fruit ready to pick, wicked thorns waiting to catch flesh, shiny leaves of all sizes and shapes, rain dropping in a deluge, water pooling on leaves, meandering rivers and streams, game trails, hanging moss and air plants growing in spiky bursts, brief flashes of sunlight or sky, trees and other vegetation growing in cracks and on the sides of cliffs, indigenous tribes (out hunting, foraging, or fishing in hand-built canoes)

SOUNDS
Exotic birdcalls, wings fluttering, monkeys hooting and shrieking in the trees, animals moving through the undergrowth (paws scraping at the ground, slithering sounds, dead branches snapping), animal noises (growls, grunts, snorts, snuffles, hisses, roars), the chuckle of a small stream or creek, the roar of a waterfall, rain clattering through the canopy, one's own heavy breathing, a far-off cry quickly silenced, trees that creak in the wind, insects whirring and buzzing, the thump of an overripe piece of fruit dropping to the ground

SMELLS
Air that is thick with growth and rotting vegetation, body odor, natural plant smells (both sweet and acrid), animal musk and scat, the occasional floral scent, the over-sweet smell of rotting fruit, mud, swampy water, wood smoke

TASTES
Water, air that tastes thick on the tongue, edible leaves, roots, nuts, and fruits (mangoes, pineapple, papaya, bananas, figs, dragon fruit, lychee), prey caught and cooked over a fire (meat flavor that is gamy while also being stringy, chewy, or rubbery), one's own stale breath, fresh rain, sweat

TEXTURES AND SENSATIONS

Wet leaves sliding across the skin, sweat beading and leaving trails down one's back and front, swiping a bandana at one's sweat-damp face, rough vines, the ground sinking with each step, the stinging bite of an insect or snake, tension in a branch as one bends it back to pass by, the jolting catch of a machete into a hard stem, the rub of bamboo against one's chest as one tries to squeeze past a stand, sipping dew from a thick leaf, spongy moss, creek water running over one's boots, the rough burn of a vine against the palm when one uses it to climb, scratches from thorns and spiny leaves, a downpour that soaks one to the bone within seconds, sweat and grime chafing the skin, feet that pulse with painful blisters, grit under one's nails, plunging into a pool of water, a waterfall's spray against the skin, rotting wet leaves, the tickle of a spiderweb touching one's skin, leaves falling into one's hair

POSSIBLE SOURCES OF CONFLICT

Getting lost
Being hunted by a large animal, such as a leopard, lion, or puma
Accidentally entering a territorial animal's space
Snake or spider bites
Falling into an army ant's nest
Getting stuck in a monsoon
Dehydration and hunger
Losing one's weapon
Running across a hostile militant group
An open wound that has a high risk of infection in the humid environment

PEOPLE COMMONLY FOUND HERE

Big corporation surveyors and operational staff looking to develop, conservationists, farmers, guides, historians and anthropologists, humanitarian advocates for indigenous tribes, nature photographers, soldiers representing different political groups, tourists

RELATED SETTINGS THAT MAY TIE IN WITH THIS ONE

Creek (208), hot springs (218), mountains (228), river (236), tropical island (240), waterfall (242)

SETTING NOTES AND TIPS

Many towns and cities are carved into the rainforest, along with farms that raise crops. Because of the rapid growth that resists man's attempts to tame it, a rainforest can make an excellent setting for militant groups, lost villages, ancient folklore, and secrets people wish to keep hidden.

SETTING DESCRIPTION EXAMPLE

The faintest glimmer of the campfire's glow had just appeared when Melody screamed. Shadows flickered, and I caught sight of a torch. Strange voices threw unrecognizable words into the air. I surged forward, yelling for her, but the vegetation trapped me—a huge web of slapping leaves, tangling vines, and bamboo barriers.

    Techniques and Devices Used: Personification
    Resulting Effects: Tension and conflict

RIVER

SIGHTS
Eddies and whitecaps creating constant movement, leaf-dappled sunlight, water that is sparkling in some spots and murky in others, silt and mud along the river bottom, reeds growing near the bank, trees hanging out over the water, grasses on the banks that bend in the wind, a fast- or slow-moving current, boulders breaking the water's surface and causing white water and foam, litter (paper cups, soda cans, plastic bags, discarded clothing) caught at the river's edge, spiderwebs stretched between branches along the bank, fish jumping, smooth stones, algae-slick underwater rocks, banks dotted with wildflowers and weedy growth, organic debris floating on the current (flower petals, twigs, leaves, dead bugs, branches), cracked mud along the river's edge as the water level goes down and exposes more of the bank, murky polluted waters, a dam of branches and twigs created by beavers, deadwood gathering at a bend in the river, a fork in the river's path, rapids and waterfalls, deer and foxes coming to drink, otters playing in the river, birds (herons, loons, kingfishers, ducks, egrets) gliding across the surface to fish, annoying midges and mosquitoes, dragonflies whirling through the reeds, turtles resting on logs, alligators sunning themselves on the bank (in certain locations), canoes and motorboats, kids swinging from a rope out into the river, people fishing in the shallows or on the banks, teens jumping off pedestrian bridges into deep water or floating down the river on calm days in tubes and rubber boats

SOUNDS
Rough water frothing and crashing, gentle water trickling and chuckling, water splashing over rocks and thundering down a waterfall or set of rapids, birds calling, chattering squirrels, buzzing insects, animals scampering through nearby undergrowth, fish jumping, turtles plopping, alligators sliding into the water, branches and twigs dropping with a splash, a canoe or kayak hull sluicing through the water, oars slapping the river's surface, the whir of a fishing line being thrown, swimmers splashing and laughing, the slurp and splash of someone walking in waders, wings flapping as a bird takes flight, voices from picnickers, kids shrieking, distant urban noises (traffic, people calling to one another, doors slamming), a boat's motor

SMELLS
Algae, wet earth, a clean water or stagnant water smell (depending on the area and time of year), wildflowers, grass, rotting deadfall or leaves, fresh-caught fish

TASTES
River water accidentally swallowed, snacks (chips, pretzels, candy, granola bars), picnic foods (sandwiches, fruit, cookies, brownies), cold drinks from a cooler (bottled water, beer, soda), wild berries or rose hips found along the banks

TEXTURES AND SENSATIONS
Cold or warm river water, being splashed by a friend, leaves and twigs brushing against one's skin, slimy rocks underfoot, mud oozing between the toes, sitting on a sun-warmed rock, water from an oar dripping onto one's legs when one changes paddling sides, a hard plastic canoe seat,

an ache in the lower back from sitting on a backless seat, sunburn, wet skin being dried by the sun, the tug of a biting fish on the end of one's line, mosquito bites, the shock of cold river water when one's canoe tips over, the pull of a strong river current

POSSIBLE SOURCES OF CONFLICT
Someone drowning or experiencing a near-drowning
Hitting one's head on a rock
Ingesting contaminated water
Alligators, crocodiles, and snakes (in certain climates)
Being run over by a boat and knocked unconscious
Developing hypothermia from falling through the ice or being stuck in the water for a long time
Going over a waterfall or set of rapids and being injured
A fear of water
Stepping on unseen garbage at the river's bottom and cutting a foot
Capsizing a canoe in fast-moving water
Getting lost in the adjoining woods and missing one's boat rendezvous point
Canoeing with a partner who has no clue what she's doing
Hooking something troubling while fishing (a garbage bag with a body part inside, a shirt with bloodstains on it)

PEOPLE COMMONLY FOUND HERE
Canoers, fishermen, kayakers, locals out for a walk, people picnicking, swimmers

RELATED SETTINGS THAT MAY TIE IN WITH THIS ONE
Campsite (152), canyon (204), creek (208), forest (212), hiking trail (216), lake (220), marsh (222), meadow (224), mountains (228), rainforest (234), waterfall (242)

SETTING NOTES AND TIPS
Rivers and their smaller cousins (streams and creeks) are a great choice for a natural setting because the inherent activity associated with them will add a sense of motion and movement to the scene. But rivers don't have to be fast flowing and exciting to be meaningful; a stagnant, polluted river can set a completely different mood for your story. And while rivers often flow through forested areas, they also can be found cutting across a plain, meandering down a mountain, or rushing through canyons and gorges. Their versatility makes them a strong setting choice for a story.

SETTING DESCRIPTION EXAMPLE
I stumbled up the hill, my body baked as dry as the land I'd crossed. Flashes of liquid light winked through the trees ahead and my legs tremored. Cocking my head, I heard it at last: the gentle burble of salvation.

    Techniques and Devices Used: Metaphor, simile, symbolism
    Resulting Effects: Reinforcing emotion, tension and conflict

SWAMP

SIGHTS
Black-trunked trees with water dripping down the bark, rotting vegetation, scummy water, reeds, frogs resting on tree roots, slugs and bloated leeches, catfish darting in the depths, crawfish and shrimp crawling along the muddy swamp bottom, beetles trundling over downed branches, spiders spinning webs in the trees, snakes curled up on branches or sliding through the water, a turtle's slick shell parting the duckweed as it swims through the water, flies and mosquitoes buzzing, clouds of gnats hovering in the air, lizards scrambling around tree trunks, swooping bats, bears, algae floating on the surface, dead trees, alligators or crocodiles slipping through the water with only their eyes and bumpy snouts exposed, worms wiggling into the muddy soil, water birds (egrets, osprey, cranes) standing on long legs, owls flying at night, woodpeckers drilling holes, rippling water, curling mist, moss hanging from tree branches, deadfall, trees leaning crookedly over the water, muddy banks, slime-coated rocks, gas bubbles rising to the surface and breaking, shifting shadows, motorized boats sliding across the surface

SOUNDS
Dripping water, splashes, the slurp of mud, frogs croaking and flies buzzing, the snap of twigs, the screech of animals or birds hunting and being hunted, heavy silence, the burp of trapped air breaking the water's surface, turtles sliding into the water, birds flying out of the water, the *tap-tap-tap* of a woodpecker, the splash of something heavy falling into or entering the water, an alligator's hissing, a hand slapping a stinging insect, wet boots or shoes squelching over the ground, the hull of a boat or skiff sluicing through the water and scraping underwater debris, a lizard scrabbling over tree bark, bird wings flapping, bats squeaking overhead

SMELLS
Decay, rot, briny algae, sweat, methane gas bubbles

TASTES
Some settings have no specific tastes associated with them beyond what the character might bring into the scene (chewing gum, mints, lipstick, cigarettes, etc.). For scenes like these, where specific tastes are sparse, it would be best to stick to descriptors from the other four senses.

TEXTURES AND SENSATIONS
Sticky clothes from the hot and moist air, water seeping into one's boots, the chafe of wet clothing, algae and duckweed clinging to one's skin, dead leaf fragments and mud clumps sticking to one's wet skin, something in the water brushing one's leg (a fish, a floating branch, a snake), a pole of wood clasped tightly in one's grip, a gnat or mosquito bite, sweat dripping down the face and between the shoulder blades, the chill of cold water, a fluttery heartbeat at every sound and splash, mud sucking against one's boots, cuts and scrapes from climbing through the deadfall, slimy moss on rocks and trees, pulling leeches off one's skin, hanging moss brushing one's head

POSSIBLE SOURCES OF CONFLICT

Alligators, crocodiles, and snakes hidden under the murky water

Mosquitoes and stinging flies in large numbers, leading to irritation that results in rashness

Springing a leak in one's boat

Losing one's oar or pole

Running into a spiderweb or disturbing a snake

Falling into the mucky water

Getting lost in the swamp

Losing one's light source

Sustaining an injury (a cut, scrape, or puncture) that can easily get infected in such an environment

Losing one's boat (due to running out of gas, an airboat engine malfunction, hull damage, etc.)

Developing trench foot

Running out of food and water

Ground that looks solid but is not

Spotting a python close by

Needing to get to high ground to see where one is and finding none

Having to camp overnight in the swamp and not being able to make a fire

Running into locals who dislike strangers and who do as they please

PEOPLE COMMONLY FOUND HERE

Locals who live nearby and use the swamp to get from one place to another, people fishing or hunting, tourists on guided tours

RELATED SETTINGS THAT MAY TIE IN WITH THIS ONE

Marsh (222)

SETTING NOTES AND TIPS

Swamps may consist of fresh water or salt water and will have different types of flora and fauna depending on where they are located, so make sure your choices align with the type of swamp you want to use. This wetland is a place where few people typically go; as such, it is often shrouded in mystery.

SETTING DESCRIPTION EXAMPLE

Something splashed behind me, and I scrambled for the nearest tree. Slimy bark provided a challenge for my boots but I managed to swing up to a creaky lower branch. Breath quivering, I scanned the mist that clung to the water's surface. My pulse faltered as a faint trench carved through the almost solid mass. Something moved through the water, gently displacing the white curtain above it, heading straight for me.

    Techniques and Devices Used: Light and shadow, multisensory descriptions

    Resulting Effects: Tension and conflict

TROPICAL ISLAND

SIGHTS
Sandy white beaches, leaning palm trees, lush undergrowth, water in varying shades of blue and green, footprints in the wet sand, seashells and seaweed strewn along the beach, driftwood washed up on the shore, stray coconuts, docks and piers leading out into the ocean, neighboring islands that are hazy with distance, people laying out on plastic loungers, private huts and bungalows on the beach or set out over the water, large resorts taking up acreage, rental services (for bicycles, wave runners, umbrellas, catamarans, surfboards, snorkeling equipment), green mountains, waterfalls pouring over cliff edges or sheeting down a rock wall, active or dormant volcanoes, tropical rainforests that are dense with plant and animal life, ancient ruins and historical sites, tour groups (on boats, buses, mopeds, jeeps, bicycles, horseback and quads), plantations (cinnamon, vanilla, coffee, sugarcane, banana, cacao, pineapple, coconut), colorful parrots in the trees, tortoises and lizards sunning on the sand, snakes, insects, spiders, monkeys congregating in the treetops or dipping down to steal items tourists have left unattended, urban areas (featuring restaurants, bars, street vendors, festivals), adrenaline junkies engaged in thrill-seeking activities (zip lining, cliff diving, parasailing), fishing vessels anchored off the coast

SOUNDS
The soothing swish of the surf, waves crashing into rocks, the cries of seagulls, people talking and laughing, children playing, swimmers splashing, book pages turning, boat engines roaring by, music from a nearby resort, palm fronds scraping together in the wind, rain pattering on a hut roof or thudding to the sand, booming thunder, a beach umbrella flapping as it fights a high wind, the wind howling during a storm, the roar or trickle of a waterfall, tropical birds screeching, flies buzzing, insects humming and chirping, monkeys chattering, critters scurrying through the underbrush, a chuckling river, locals speaking rapidly in the native tongue, customers haggling with vendors, sneakers crunching through rainforest debris, live music being played on the street, jeeps and cars driving in town, a bicycle rattling over rough streets or dirt roads

SMELLS
Salt water, food from a nearby establishment, wood smoke, sunscreen and tanning oil, sweat, rain, the earthy smell of a rainforest, decaying vegetation, fresh fruit and unique blends of spices

TASTES
Salt water, sweat, tropical fruits (pineapple, mango, apricots, bananas, figs, melons, guavas), coconut, sugarcane, local restaurant fare, fresh seafood, cold bottled water, soda, tropical beverages, smoothies, local beers and wines, street foods (fried doughnuts, spiced nuts, kabobs, wraps and tacos, grilled pineapple)

TEXTURES AND SENSATIONS
Warm sun and hot air, sand sticking to the sunscreen on one's skin, wind tugging at one's hair, rough driftwood, a wet swimsuit, prickly sunburn, warm ocean water sliding over one's skin, hot sand underfoot, sinking into the sand with each step, seaweed brushing one's leg underwater,

stepping on a sharp seashell or rock, a warm and scratchy towel against one's skin, a bicycle shimmying over bumpy roads, a jeep bouncing over uneven ground, motion sickness from traveling over twisty roads, the humid air under a rainforest canopy, detritus being crushed underfoot, a lurch in the belly as one's helicopter rises into the air, an adrenaline rush as one prepares to zip line or cliff jump, a sudden drop in air pressure as a storm moves in

POSSIBLE SOURCES OF CONFLICT

Jellyfish and sharks
Being caught in a riptide
Being victimized or assaulted
Having one's luggage or purse stolen
Montezuma's Revenge
Difficulty communicating with the locals
Losing one's passport
Having a family tragedy back home and being unable to get there
Boating accidents

PEOPLE COMMONLY FOUND HERE

College students on spring break, couples, families, honeymooners, hotel employees, locals, timeshare sellers, tour guides, tourists, vendors

RELATED SETTINGS THAT MAY TIE IN WITH THIS ONE

Rural Volume: Ancient ruins (144), beach (202), beach party (150), hiking trail (216), mountains (228), ocean (230), rainforest (234), waterfall (242)

Urban Volume: Airplane (250), airport (252), cruise ship (258), golf course (206), yacht (286)

SETTING NOTES AND TIPS

Tropical islands cover a vast spectrum from private havens to touristy destinations. The former offers isolation, privacy, and solitude, while the latter includes more amenities, exciting excursions, and guided opportunities. Some tropical destinations are affected by hurricanes and monsoons during certain times of the year, so this is definitely something to be researched to keep you from running into trouble—or to put your character directly into trouble's path.

SETTING DESCRIPTION EXAMPLE

Jake slammed the screen door behind him but Trina's voice clawed through the open windows and pursued him down the beach. He jogged far enough to leave her anger behind, then slowed to a sluggish walk. *All you two need is a vacation*, his parents had said. Jake snorted. What they needed was a referee. Only two days into a weeklong getaway and they were at each other's throats. Something stung him and he slapped his arm. It was pretty sad when you'd rather brave invisible bugs than spend another second with your fiancée.

Techniques and Devices Used: Multisensory descriptions

Resulting Effects: Foreshadowing, tension and conflict

WATERFALL

SIGHTS
A frothy cascade of water falling into a plunge pool, rocky outcroppings, lichen and moss clinging to rocks and tree trunks, slippery rocks, lush grasses growing around the pool, plants and flowers with shiny leaves and foliage, water spraying as it hits the pool, rainbows shimmering at the edge of one's vision, ripples in the water, leaves and branches that are wet with water droplets, trees clinging to cliffs and hanging over the pool, insects flitting about (butterflies, flies, dragonflies, mosquitoes), birds flying, animals wandering close for a drink, fish scales flashing under the water, sunbaked rocks, soft beds of grass, tourists swimming or taking pictures, sand and shale at the bottom of the pool, multicolored pebbles at the shoreline, weeds and cattails, ferns growing in the shade, mossy boulders, blue-green water, gentle waves lapping the shoreline, sunlight glittering across the water, multi-tiered drops, mist in the early morning, ledges and crevices in the cliff walls, wet rock platforms, caves behind the fall of water, a wide open sky framed by a green canopy

SOUNDS
The roar of the water, droplets pattering against rock and leaves, people speaking with raised voices, laughter, birdcalls, insects buzzing around one's head, swimmers splashing in the pool, echoes in a cave behind the waterfall, music from someone's portable player, jeeps and cars driving by on gravel roads, jumpers on a high ledge whooping as they jump into a deeper area of the water hole, fish splashing as they quickly surface and then duck under again

SMELLS
Water-saturated air, rich earth, flowers perfuming the air, moss, slimy algae, suntan lotion or sunscreen, food odors from picnickers

TASTES
Some settings have no specific tastes associated with them beyond what the character might bring into the scene (chewing gum, mints, water, etc.). For scenes like these, where specific tastes are sparse, it would be best to stick to descriptors from the other four senses.

TEXTURES AND SENSATIONS
Mist on one's skin, the cool slide of water over the skin, a shock of cold water touching one's feet, water seeping into one's shoes, knobby pebbles or rocks pressing into the soles of one's feet, tall grass sliding across one's calves, a warm rock, rough stone handholds, wet or algae-covered rocks, the sting of an accidental scrape, the tattoo beat of water falling on one's head and shoulders when one is directly beneath the waterfall, water filling one's ears, hair slicking against one's scalp, cold water closing over one's head as one dips below the surface, air bubbles sliding against the skin, a fish tickling one's toes, the stomach tightening as one contemplates jumping from a ledge, wet shoes and socks, the sting of makeup or sunscreen getting into one's eyes, blurred vision from fine water droplets accumulating on one's glasses

POSSIBLE SOURCES OF CONFLICT

Going over a powerful fall (in a boat, slipping off a rock, being caught in a current)

Jumping from a waterfall ledge and landing on an unseen object in the water

Being bitten by fish

Slipping on a mossy rock and falling during a waterfall climb

Cutting oneself on a sharp outcropping

Noisy tourists ruining one's peace and quiet

Strangers invading one's private place

Poisonous water snakes or other hazards

The fall's noise drowning out an important sound (an injured person's yells for help, a lost child's cries, the growl of a wild animal)

Pollution that makes the spot dangerous to swim in

Drinking the water and getting sick

Being pressured to jump off a ledge when one is a poor swimmer

Swimsuit malfunctions

Skinny-dipping alone and having a busload of tourists show up

Needing to navigate a flow of water down a mountain to safety but being forced to take another route

PEOPLE COMMONLY FOUND HERE

Hikers, locals, picnickers, swimmers, tourists

RELATED SETTINGS THAT MAY TIE IN WITH THIS ONE

Ancient ruins (144), campsite (152), canyon (204), forest (212), hiking trail (216), lake (220), mountains (228), pond (232), rainforest (234), river (236), tropical island (240)

SETTING NOTES AND TIPS

Waterfalls occur in places all over the world that contain high-elevation landforms, so the setting will change depending upon whether the falls are found in mountains, glaciers, forests, or a rainforest. Some tumble into a vast pool of water, a wide river, or the ocean. Others trickle over rock walls and cliff faces to enter a shallow stream or slow-moving river. Some drops span a great distance, while others are relatively short. Waterfalls have distinctive looks and are classified by type—cataract, tiered, punchbowl, fan, plunge, horsetail, etc.—so it's important to know which kind you're dealing with in order to describe it accurately.

SETTING DESCRIPTION EXAMPLE

Moonlight glittered off a million water droplets in the fall, but near the bottom, mist concealed the pool from view. Somewhere under that silvery canopy, Josie was climbing out of the water, waiting for me to follow her maniacal lead. I couldn't hear anything over the noise of the falls but I could imagine her sitting at the pool's edge, streaming water, shivering in the night air and yelling at me to *Jump, already!* My fingertips tingled with adrenaline. Who was crazier—the daredevil who leaped blindly into a waterfall at night or the idiot who followed her?

Techniques and Devices Used: Light and shadow, weather

Resulting Effects: Characterization

APPENDIX A: SETTING EXERCISES

Flex your descriptive muscles with the following exercises. First, choose a location from the table of contents and list two sensory details for each of the five senses.

SIGHT

1) _____ 2) _____

SMELL

1) _____ 2) _____

SOUND

1) _____ 2) _____

TEXTURE

1) _____ 2) _____

TASTE

1) _____ 2) _____

Now, write a paragraph describing this setting through the eyes of a character who has never visited this location before. Weave in the quality of light, the time of day or the season (if it applies), and use at least 3 of the 5 senses above. Try to show us who the character is and what he or she feels.

_____
_____
_____
_____

Rewrite this passage, this time using foreshadowing to imply that something bad is about to happen. Concentrate on building a subtle mood of unease or hone in on a detail that does not fit in the setting, drawing attention to it. Try out some new sensory description choices if you like.

_____
_____
_____
_____
_____

Time to ramp up the tension. Rewrite this again to show your character interacting with the setting as he or she either flees, fights, or hides. Description should flow with the action of the scene, showing emotion and mood. Remember to try some shorter sentences to reflect urgency.

_____
_____
_____
_____
_____

A printable version of this checklist is available at www.writershelpingwriters.net/writing-tools.

APPENDIX B: SETTING PLANNER TOOL

Setting descriptions should be multi-faceted and do more than simply anchor readers. Plan ahead and weave in the five senses, the quality of light, weather and seasonal elements, the desired mood, and/or symbols that will remind the POV character of past events, a choice to be made, old fears, or hopes for the future.

SYMBOLISM (PEOPLE AND OBJECTS WHO REPRESENT A PAST EVENT, CHOICES, FEARS OR HOPES)				
MOOD AND EMOTIONS				
LIGHT QUALITY & TIME OF DAY OR NIGHT				
WEATHER ELEMENTS				
TEXTURES				
TASTES				
SMELLS				
SOUNDS				
SIGHTS				
LOCATION & SCENE				

A printable version of this checklist is available at www.writershelpingwriters.net/writing-tools.

THE URBAN SETTING THESAURUS: A WRITER'S GUIDE TO CITY SPACES

I f you have enjoyed this setting thesaurus book, we have good news for you: there is a second volume in this series. *The Urban Setting Thesaurus* has over 120 additional settings and more how-to help, including valuable lessons on using sensory description, as well as how the setting can help characterize the members of your cast, facilitate necessary backstory, and steer your character's actions and decisions through emotional triggers.

Add deeper authenticity to your writing by bringing fiction and the real world together through common urban settings. Here are the locations included in *The Urban Setting Thesaurus*:

Airplane
Airport
Alley
Ambulance
Amusement Park
Antiques Shop
Art gallery
Art studio
Bakery
Ballroom
Bank
Bar
Bazaar
Big City Street
Black-Tie Event
Boardroom
Bookstore
Bowling Alley
Car Accident
Car Wash
Carnival Funhouse
Casino
Casual Dining Restaurant
Cheap Motel

Circus
City Bus
Coffeehouse
Community Center
Condemned Apartment Building
Construction Site
Convenience Store
Courtroom
Cruise Ship
Deli
Diner
Elevator
Emergency Room
Empty Lot
Factory
Fast Food Restaurant
Fire Station
Fishing Boat
Fitness Center
Flower Shop
Funeral Home
Gas Station
Golf Course

Green Room
Grocery Store
Hair Salon
Hardware Store
Homeless Shelter
Hospital Room
Hotel Room
Ice Cream Parlor
Indoor Shooting Range
Jewelry Store
Juvenile Detention Center
Laundromat
Library
Limousine
Liquor Store
Marina
Mechanic's Shop
Military Base
Military Helicopter
Morgue
Movie Theater
Museum
Newsroom
Nightclub

Nursing Home
Office Cubicle
Old Pick-Up Truck
Outdoor Pool
Outdoor Skating Rink
Parade
Park
Parking Garage
Parking Lot
Pawn Shop
Penthouse Suite
Performing Arts Theater
Pet Store
Police Car
Police Station
Pool Hall
Prison Cell
Psychiatric Ward

Psychic's Shop
Pub
Public Restroom
Race Track (Horses)
Rec Center
Recording Studio
Refugee Camp
Rock Concert
Run-Down Apartment
Sewers
Shopping Mall
Skate Park
Ski Resort
Small Town Street
Spa
Sporting Event Stands
Submarine
Subway Train

Subway Tunnel
Tank
Tattoo Parlor
Taxi
Therapist's Office
Thrift Store
Train Station
Truck Stop
Underpass
Used Car Dealership
Vegas Stage Show
Vet Clinic
Waiting Room
Water Park
Yacht
Zoo

RECOMMENDED READING

As writing coaches, we come across many great books on all aspects of writing craft. If you are looking to boost your knowledge, we suggest starting with these.

Super Structure: The Key to Unleashing the Power of Story will teach you how to translate your story into a form that enables reader connection . . . and sells more books! (James Scott Bell)

Conquering Writer's Block and Summoning Inspiration will help you position yourself to live an inspired life and send the dreaded writer's block packing. Learn practical, actionable steps for nurturing creativity and using it to write your best book yet. (K.M. Weiland)

Writing the Heart of Your Story: The Secret to Crafting an Unforgettable Novel will teach you how to mine the heart of your plot, characters, themes, and so much more. If you want to write a book that targets the heart of readers, you need to know the heart of your story. (C. S. Lakin)

Writing Characters Who'll Keep Readers Captivated (Nail Your Novel 2) will teach you how to create people who will enthrall readers—and make you want to tell stories. (Roz Morris)

Writing Screenplays That Sell, New Twentieth Anniversary Edition teaches all writers to think deeply about their characters' motivations, story structure and the art of selling. (Michael Hauge)

PRAISE FOR...

THE EMOTION THESAURUS

"One of the challenges a fiction writer faces, especially when prolific, is coming up with fresh ways to describe emotions. This handy compendium fills that need. It is both a reference and a brainstorming tool, and one of the resources I'll be turning to most often as I write my own books."

~ James Scott Bell, International Thriller Writers Award Winner

THE POSITIVE AND NEGATIVE TRAIT THESAURUSES

"In these brilliantly conceived, superbly organized and astonishingly thorough volumes, Angela Ackerman and Becca Puglisi have created an invaluable resource for writers and storytellers. Whether you are searching for new and unique ways to add and define characters, or brainstorming methods for revealing those characters without resorting to clichés, it is hard to imagine two more powerful tools for adding depth and dimension to your screenplays, novels or plays."

~ Michael Hauge, Hollywood script consultant and author of *Writing Screenplays That Sell*

THE URBAN AND RURAL SETTING THESAURUSES

"The one thing I always appreciate about Ackerman and Puglisi's Thesauri series is how comprehensive they are. They never stop at just the obvious, and they always over-deliver. Their Setting Thesauri are no different, offering not just the obvious notes of the various settings they've covered, but going into easy-to-miss details like smells and tastes. They even offer to jumpstart the brainstorming with categories on potential sources of conflict."

~ K.M. Weiland, best-selling author of *Creating Character Arcs* and *Structuring Your Novel*

THE EMOTIONAL WOUND THESAURUS

"This is far more than a brilliant, thorough, insightful, and unique thesaurus. This is the best primer on story—and what REALLY hooks and holds readers—that I have ever read."

~ Lisa Cron, TEDx Speaker and best-selling author of *Wired For Story and Story Genius*

ADD WRITERS HELPING WRITERS® TO YOUR TOOLKIT!

Over a decade of articles are waiting to help you grow your writing skills, navigate publishing and marketing, and assist you on your career path. And if you'd like to stay informed about forthcoming books, discover unique writing resources, and access even more practical writing tips, sign up for our newsletter onsite (https://writershelpingwriters.net/subscribe-to-our-newsletter/).

Printed in Great Britain
by Amazon

46573489R00147